Cape Verde

WORLD BIBLIOGRAPHICAL SERIES

General Editors:
Robert G. Neville (Executive Editor)
John J. Horton

Robert A. Myers   Ian Wallace
Hans H. Wellisch   Ralph Lee Woodward, Jr.

John J. Horton is Deputy Librarian of the University of Bradford and currently Chairman of its Academic Board of Studies in Social Sciences. He has maintained a longstanding interest in the discipline of area studies and its associated bibliographical problems, with special reference to European Studies. In particular he has published in the field of Icelandic and of Yugoslav studies, including the two relevant volumes in the World Bibliographical Series.

Robert A. Myers is Associate Professor of Anthropology in the Division of Social Sciences and Director of Study Abroad Programs at Alfred University, Alfred, New York. He has studied post-colonial island nations of the Caribbean and has spent two years in Nigeria on a Fulbright Lectureship. His interests include international public health, historical anthropology and developing societies. In addition to *Amerindians of the Lesser Antilles: a bibliography* (1981), *A Resource Guide to Dominica, 1493–1986* (1987) and numerous articles, he has compiled the World Bibliographical Series volumes on *Dominica* (1987) and *Nigeria* (1989).

Ian Wallace is Professor of Modern Languages at Loughborough University of Technology. A graduate of Oxford in French and German, he also studied in Tübingen, Heidelberg and Lausanne before taking teaching posts at universities in the USA, Scotland and England. He specializes in East German affairs, especially literature and culture, on which he has published numerous articles and books. In 1979 he founded the journal *GDR Monitor*, which he continues to edit.

Hans H. Wellisch is Professor emeritus at the College of Library and Information Services, University of Maryland. He was President of the American Society of Indexers and was a member of the International Federation for Documentation. He is the author of numerous articles and several books on indexing and abstracting, and has published *The Conversion of Scripts* and *Indexing and Abstracting: an International Bibliography*. He also contributes frequently to *Journal of the American Society for Information Science, The Indexer* and other professional journals.

Ralph Lee Woodward, Jr. is Chairman of the Department of History at Tulane University, New Orleans, where he has been Professor of History since 1970. He is the author of *Central America, a Nation Divided*, 2nd ed. (1985), as well as several monographs and more than sixty scholarly articles on modern Latin America. He has also compiled volumes in the World Bibliographical Series on *Belize* (1980), *Nicaragua* (1983), and *El Salvador* (1988). Dr. Woodward edited the Central American section of the *Research Guide to Central America and the Caribbean* (1985) and is currently editor of the Central American history section of the *Handbook of Latin American Studies*.

VOLUME 123

Cape Verde

Caroline S. Shaw

Compiler

CLIO PRESS

OXFORD, ENGLAND · SANTA BARBARA, CALIFORNIA
DENVER, COLORADO

DT
671
C2I5
S33
1991

British Library Cataloguing in Publication Data

Shaw, Caroline 1963
Cape Verde – (World bibliographical series v. 123)
1. Cape Verde. Bibliographies
I. Title   II. Series
016.96658

ISBN 1–85109–119–X

Clio Press Ltd.,
55 St. Thomas' Street,
Oxford OX1 1JG, England.

ABC-CLIO,
130 Cremona Drive,
Santa Barbara,
CA 93117, USA.

Designed by Bernard Crossland.
Typeset by Columns Design and Production Services, Reading, England.
Printed and bound in Great Britain by
Billing and Sons Ltd., Worcester.

THE WORLD BIBLIOGRAPHICAL SERIES

This series, which is principally designed for the English speaker, will eventually cover every country in the world, each in a separate volume comprising annotated entries on works dealing with its history, geography, economy and politics; and with its people, their culture, customs, religion and social organization. Attention will also be paid to current living conditions – housing, education, newspapers, clothing, etc.– that are all too often ignored in standard bibliographies; and to those particular aspects relevant to individual countries. Each volume seeks to achieve, by use of careful selectivity and critical assessment of the literature, an expression of the country and an appreciation of its nature and national aspirations, to guide the reader towards an understanding of its importance. The keynote of the series is to provide, in a uniform format, an interpretation of each country that will express its culture, its place in the world, and the qualities and background that make it unique. The views expressed in individual volumes, however, are not necessarily those of the publisher.

VOLUMES IN THE SERIES

To Sally and Donald and Cathy, with all my love

Contents

Contents

Contents

Introduction

The Republic of Cape Verde is an archipelago of ten islands, (nine of which are inhabited), in the eastern central Atlantic lying approximately 300 miles off the coast of Senegal, West Africa. The islands fall into two groups: Sotavento (leeward) includes the islands of Brava, Fogo, Santiago and Maio; Barlavento (windward) includes Boa Vista, São Nicolau, Sal, São Vicente and Santo Antão.

The islands are volcanic in origin, and are a manifestation of the considerable tectonic activity which takes place along the mid-Atlantic ridge. The island of Fogo is an active volcano which last erupted in 1951. The archipelago as a whole has attracted considerable interest from geologists.

The topography of the archipelago demonstrates varying degrees of wind and marine erosion acting upon a volcanic landscape. The island of Santo Antão, for example, has a dramatic configuration of high peaks deeply incised by *ribeiras* – narrow fertile valleys. A coastline of dark beetling cliffs is fiercely pummelled by the sea. Contemporary accounts from the 18th and 19th centuries report that such paths and tracks which existed were so dangerous that deaths from falling rocks or slipping from the way were so common as to be considered 'natural' deaths.

Conversely, other islands are relatively flat, probably because they have been subjected to less recent volcanic activity and to greater erosive forces. These islands are the so-called *ilhas rasas* (flat islands) of Sal, Boa Vista and Maio. Here, the landscape ranges from the sand dunes, date palms and rocky moonscapes of Boa Vista to the near-savannah of the interior of Maio. Maio, in particular, has drawn the attention of international geologists who are finding evidence from this old land formation for an understanding of the early geological history of the Atlantic region.

Introduction

The principal feature of Cape Verde's climate, which is usually described as Sahelian, is its low and unreliable rainfall. The islands lie on the farthest margin of the inter-tropical convergence zone. In theory there is an annual 'monsoon', known as *as aguas* (the waters), lasting several days and occurring some time between July and October. Frequently, however, the rains fail or arrive at the wrong time of year and in insufficient quantities for the agricultural calendar. Some studies suggest that there may have been some long-term climatic changes resulting in a net drop of one half in recorded rainfall over the last one hundred years. Water shortages and *de facto* drought are a near-constant of Cape Verdean life, certainly during the last two hundred years.

The arrival of the rains transforms the islands' appearance for a short while. Barren rocky hills become shaded green and stony valley bottoms are changed temporarily into rivers. This brings its own problems of soil erosion for unless preventative action is taken, precious topsoil is washed out to sea. Accordingly, over the last twenty years soil conservation has been recognized as an urgent national priority. Barrages, dams and dikes have been constructed using appropriate technology and local labour. The most visible of the measures undertaken has been an ongoing and successful afforestation programme in which several millions of drought resistant acacia trees have been planted. As well as helping to prevent soil erosion these trees will eventually transform the appearance of the landscape and, it is estimated, make Cape Verde self-sufficient in fuelwood by the year 2000.

Vegetation and agriculture are conditioned by the two factors of water availability and altitude. The highest peaks have their own microclimates which generate enough humidity for a limited amount of coffee to be grown on Fogo, and for an unexpected area of coniferous woodland to survive on Santo Antão. However, vast areas of unirrigated land can barely support enough vegetation for the foraging goats. On the lower slopes of valleys irrigation is possible using water from underground sources. Bananas, mangos, breadfruit, yam, beans and sugar cane are all grown. Maize is the dietary staple and can be found cultivated even on the steepest slope in a painstakingly maintained system of terracing. Nevertheless, although Cape Verde is a predominantly agrarian society, agricultural production is completely inadequate to meet the food needs of the present population of 350,000.

It is not implausible to suggest that a proportion of Cape Verde's problems associated with agriculture and environmental management have their origins in the system and practices of the archipelago's original settlement. In the mid-15th century the Portuguese merchant-adventurers, who mastered the navigational difficulties of rounding Cape Bojador, became the first Europeans to encounter the lands and peoples of the Upper Guinea coast of West Africa. Blown off course, three different captains made claims to the discovery of the islands of Cape Verde around 1460. These were António de Noli, Diogo Gomes and Aluise da Cadamosto. Suggestions have been made, however, that Arab sailors had long known of the salt deposits on Sal and Maio, but there is no incontrovertible evidence for this. Certainly the islands were uninhabited when the Portuguese arrived.

To encourage settlement, and thus consolidate its power in the region, the Portuguese Crown gave large donations of land to favoured Europeans. Slaves were brought from the West African coast, the process of miscegenation began and the system of grossly unequal distribution of land was instituted. Santiago, the largest of the islands, was the first to be settled. Goats were introduced and often left to live wild on the uninhabited islands. They indubitably contributed to a process of environmental degradation. Food crops from around the known world were introduced, including maize. This was probably a poor choice of staple crop as it has a higher water demand than the Cape Verdean climate can usually satisfy.

The first Portuguese city in the tropics was founded at Ribeira Grande on Santiago. This was the seat of the Catholic Church's first diocese in West Africa. For perhaps one hundred and fifty years the city enjoyed relative prosperity as the hub of Portuguese colonial administration of its activities in West Africa.

The most lucrative of these activities was the booming slave trade which involved transporting peoples by ship from West Africa to the Americas. All such ships were supposed to put in at Santiago to pay Portuguese customs duties and the island became a veritable entrepôt for the slave trade. Slaves would spend several months undergoing 'latinization' as a means of enhancing their value. This was a cultural disorientation process in which they would learn Portuguese pidgin, be baptized and be prepared for a lifetime of servitude. Cape Verdeans were also active on the African mainland, particularly around the present-day country of Guinea-Bissau where they engaged in trade and forged links with the people of the region.

By the 17th century Cape Verde's importance was waning. Other European powers were establishing themselves in the region and the Portuguese Crown was unable to enforce its edicts. Moreover, pirates launched frequent attacks, with devastating effects: Sir Francis Drake's attack on Ribiera Grande in 1585 was particularly destructive and by the 17th century the city was virtually abandoned. Cape Verde's principal economic function became the provisioning of ships engaged in trans-Atlantic trade. Goat meat and salt were the staples on offer. In the 19th century coal bunkering under the control of British firms was of some importance to the town of Mindelo, São Vicente. Such was the weakness of the economy that for many years salt could be taken by passing ships simply for the cost of hiring the labourers, and goods traded in exchange for second-hand clothes. A curtain of colonial neglect descended.

Meanwhile, a language, a culture and a nation were being formed in Cape Verde. Its mixed race population was originally made up of members of diverse ethnic and language groups from West Africa together with a smaller number of Portuguese and other Europeans. These first inhabitants would probably have used the Portuguese pidgin of the slave trade as an interlanguage and this would have been the language of the big Portuguese-owned estates. When the children born into this environment used the interlanguage as their mother-tongue the language known as Crioulo was born. Five hundred years later it is the mother-tongue of all Cape Verdeans born in the archipelago. Lexical content is predominantly Portuguese, but structure and idiom are unique to Crioulo. The language was disparaged and distrusted by the Portuguese colonial authorities, but the late 20th century is presenting it with new challenges and opportunities. Increasing access to education and broadcast media are intensifying the population's exposure to Portuguese. At the same time, however, orthographic standards are being set for Crioulo, facilitating its use as a written language.

Another manifestation of the evolution of an autochthonous Cape Verdean culture is its rich literary tradition, both oral and written. Cape Verde's oral literature includes song forms such as the soulful *morna*, improvised verse and well-established narrative cycles – the most famous of which are the stories of Ti Lobo and Ŝibiño (Uncle Wolf and Nephew). Written literature experienced an astonishing renaissance with the publication of the cultural review *Claridade* in 1936. Since then poetry, short stories and novels have been published in surprising abundance, some experimenting with the use of Crioulo as a written literary language.

Through literature the question of a Cape Verdean cultural identity was put under examination. Inevitably, Cape Verde's political identity also came into question. The islanders held an ambiguous position within the Portuguese colonial structure: Cape Verdeans were not given the invidious legal identity of 'natives' as were the majority of the population of the Portuguese African possessions but neither were they given the privileged status of Metropolitan Portuguese. Educational standards, although poor, were relatively advanced compared with the rest of the Portuguese colonies, and numerous Cape Verdeans prospered elsewhere in the Empire as colonial functionaries. The poor and ill-educated, however, were encouraged to work as contract labourers in the nightmare cacao plantations of São Tomé and Príncipe. There was less ambiguity about the relationship between Portugal and the actual islands: this was one of neglect, and chronic underinvestment. A cynic might wonder whether a supply of cheap labour for other parts of the Empire was being deliberately created. There certainly came into existence a pool of labour which was only too desperate to emigrate when the inevitable famines struck.

During the 1950s there began to form nationalist movements for the liberation of the African nations under Portuguese colonial control. These often crystalized around African student groups in Lisbon. Amílcar Cabral, the founder and leader of the PAIGC (the African Party for the Independence of Guinea-Bissau and Cape Verde) emerged from this milieu. Cabral (1924–73) was born in Guinea-Bissau but was educated in Cape Verde until winning a scholarship to study agronomy at university in Lisbon. He was one of Africa's most original political thinkers and leaders, qualities which he combined with a pragmatic approach to the problems of winning the struggle for independence.

One of his aims was the eventual union of Guinea-Bissau and Cape Verde. The two countries are 600 miles apart, are very different in physical and human geography and had a very different experience of colonialism. Some links do exist however: some of the slaves brought to Cape Verde came from the area of present-day Guinea-Bissau; Portuguese administration linked the two countries for long periods; Cape Verdean traders and, later, colonial functionaries were active in Guinea-Bissau; Kriul, a language similar to Crioulo, is spoken in Guinea-Bissau alongside its indigenous languages.

Yet the most significant aspect of the relationship was probably that created by the PAIGC. Under Cabral's leadership the PAIGC led an extremely successful war of liberation in Guinea-Bissau and the liberation of Cape Verde was a constant objective. Many Cape Verdeans fought for the PAIGC on the mainland. When the fascist régime in Portugal was overthrown in April 1974 negotiations began for the decolonization of her empire. The Portuguese were hopeful that they might retain Cape Verde, but the PAIGC were adamant. Cape Verde achieved independence on 5 July 1975.

After independence the archipelago was governed by the Cape Verdean branch of the PAIGC. A *coup d'état* in Guinea-Bissau in November 1980 prompted the severance of this relationship and the Cape Verdean branch reconstituted itself as the PAICV (African Party for the Independence of Cape Verde). In January 1991 the first multi-party elections were held.

Since independence the archipelago's development has been the government's most important objective. Despite the paucity of

Introduction

natural resources other than its people and its rich fishing grounds, the country has made some remarkable achievements. Socioeconomic indicators compare favourably with those of other Least Developed Countries and Sahelian nations. However, domestic production is totally inadequate for the population of the islands: the economy is sustained by remittances from emigrants in the USA, Portugal and elsewhere; by revenues from the international airport situated on Sal; and by foreign aid. Given Cape Verde's reliance on the outside world, it is not surprising that it chooses to conduct a foreign policy of non-alignment combined with active involvement in appropriate regional and international organizations.

The bibliography

Material on Cape Verde is not easily available in abundance and what exists is overwhelmingly in Portuguese. Fortunately there are several key works in English which are outstanding by any standards. A significant body of scientific research has been published by Portuguese institutions such as the Junta de Investigações do Ultramar. The islands' history is surprisingly well documented: the dedicated work of the late António Carreira must be mentioned in this context. Cape Verdean literature has been widely disseminated, although too little exists in translation. Finally, the high quality of the work which has been published since independence by the Instituto Caboverdiano do Livro should be noted. It is hard to overestimate the importance of its role in supporting both creativity and research.

This bibliography cannot make any clams to providing comprehensive coverage of the field. I hope that it may serve as an introduction to˜this remarkable nation and perhaps give an indication of paths which others might find fruitful to follow. I feel unusually fortunate in my own discovery of Cape Verde and its people and hope that this bibliography may contribute towards wider recognition of the Cape Verdean people's history, extraordinary resilience and struggle for sustainable development.

Acknowledgements

I would like to thank the staff of the Biblioteca Nacional de Lisboa, the British Library and the Instituto Caboverdiano do Livro – institutions where most of my research was conducted – as well as my colleagues at the British Library of Political and Economic Science. I would also like to thank João Alves, Patrick Chabal, Keith Davis, Christopher Doutney, Loreto Todd and Richard Trillo, and for their wonderful support, both practical and moral, Mick Clementson and Cathy Shaw. All errors are, of course, my own.

Caroline S. Shaw
January 1991

The Country and Its People

1 **Arquipelago de Cabo Verde: estudo elementar de geographia phisica, economica e politica.** (Archipelago of Cape Verde: elementary study of physical geography, economics and politics.)
Ernesto Vasconcellos.   Lisbon: Centro Typographico Colonial, 1916. 126p. map. bibliog.
A compendium of the available data, which includes a description of culture and folklore. The work has a useful bibliography, and contains a compilation of statistics for the first years of the century.

2 **Cabo Verde. Cape Verde Islands. Cap Vert.**
National Development Fund, Ministry of Economic Coordination.
[Paris]: Éditions Delroisse, [1978]. 174p. 11 maps.
An introduction, in English, French and Portuguese, to the newly independent republic is followed by more than 150 stunning colour photographs by Michel Renaudeau. Arranged island by island, they show landscape, towns, villages, people, and scenes of everyday life.

3 **Cabo Verde: dez anos de desenvolvimento.** (Cape Verde: ten years of development.)
Fundo de Desenvolvimento Nacional.   Paris: Éditions Delroisse, [1985]. 217p. map.
Colour photographs by Christian Bossu-Picat of the islands are accompanied by text in English, French and Portuguese. The focus of the book is mainly on infrastructure, industry and other manifestations of the progress made towards development.

1

4 **Cabo Verde, Guiné, São Tomé e Príncipe: curso de extensão universitária, ano lectivo de 1965-1966.** (Cape Verde, Guinea, São Tomé and Príncipe: university extension course, academic year 1965-66.) Foreword by Adriano Moreira. Lisbon: Instituto Superior de Ciências Sociais e Política Ultramarina, Universidade Técnica de Lisboa, 1966. 1036p. 21 maps. bibliogs.

A collection of lectures of varying quality. Those relevant to Cape Verde cover the following subjects: physical and human geography (Raquel Soeiro de Brito); history from 1460 to 1580 (A. da Silva Rego); 15th-century history (João Ameal); names of people and places (António de Almeida); creoles from all three countries (Jorge Morais-Barbosa); the media (José Júlio Gonçalves); social services (Maria Palmira de Moraes Pinto Duarte); youth organizations (Alberto Feliciano Marques Pereira); the Roman Catholic Church (A. Ribeiro); missionaries (Joaquim Angélico de Jesus Guerra); nationalist organizations (João Baptista Nunes Pereira Neto); labour law (José Maria Gaspar); political and administrative structures (Armando M. Marques Guedes); Portuguese strategy in the Atlantic (Henrique Martins de Carvalho); strategic value (Luís Maria da Câmara Pina); economic structure (Vasco Fortuna); gross national product (GNP) (José Júlio Cravo Silva); foreign trade (José Pereira Neto); demography (Óscar Barata); agriculture (M. dos Santos Pereira).

5 **Cape Verde Islands.** London: Foreign Office, 1919. 44p. bibliog. (Handbooks Prepared under the Direction of the Historical Section of the Foreign Office, no. 124a).

A crisp summary, divided into sections dealing with geography, history, social and political conditions, economic conditions and general remarks. It contains the sort of information that a travelling businessman of the time might need to know – for example that water in Mindelo is so expensive that ships' captains distil their own; and that coal is cheaper in the Canaries. It also carries good advice on regulations affecting wages and conditions of employment.

6 **The Cape Verde story: a long road to liberation.** Félix Monteiro. *Ceres*, vol. 12, no. 3 (May–June 1979), p. 28-32. map.

Monteiro contributes a brief history of the islands' settlement and social structure and their legacy for contemporary Cape Verde for *Ceres*, the FAO (United Nations Food and Agriculture Organization) review on agriculture and development.

7 **5 Juillet 1975. L'indépendance du Cap-Vert: un nouveau pas vers l'unité avec la Guinée-Bissau.** (5 July 1975. The independence of Cape Verde: a new step towards unity with Guinea-Bissau.) *Afrique-Asie*, no. 86 (23-29 June 1975), p. 1-34.

A special issue devoted to Cape Verde's history, problems and future plans. Contributors include Simon Malley, Aristides Pereira, Luiz Cabral, Elisa Andrade, Pedro Pires, Basil Davidson, Jack Bourderie, Mário de Andrade, with texts from Amílcar Cabral, Baltasar Lopes, Ovídio Martins and Sukre d'Sal.

8 **Colóquios cabo-verdianos.** (Seminars on Cape Verde.)
Preface by Jorge Dias. Lisbon: Junta de Investigações do Ultramar, 1959.
182p. map. bibliogs. (Estudos de Ciências Políticas e Sociais, no. 22).

This volume on Cape Verdean culture and society contains several significant works: on literature by Manuel Lopes; social structure, Gabriel Mariano; bilingualism, Manuel Ferreira; education, Nuno Miranda; emigration, Luís Terry; physical anthropology, Almerindo Lessa; literary élites, Francisco Lopes; the economy, José Bacellar Bebiano. Many of the works are indexed elsewhere in this bibliography.

9 **Les îles du Cap-Vert.** (The Cape Verde Islands.)
Marie-Paule de Pina, preface by Claude Wauthier. Paris: Éditions Karthala, 1987. 216p. 8 maps. bibliog.

Marie-Paule de Pina is a journalist with a remarkable skill for identifying, expressing and investigating something of contemporary Cape Verde's unique quality. Her first chapter comes closest to being pure travel-writing. Island by island, she manages to summarize the essence of their individual characters. Two chapters then cover history from discovery to the present day, but the bulk of the book is based on interviews and visits carried out by de Pina. An interview with President Aristides Pereira discusses government policy, international cooperation and the fight against desertification. She is equally enthusiastic interviewing women working in garment factories and on road-building projects. An enormous amount of information, from economic development to foreign aid projects to airport operations is contained somewhere in the book. Acronyms abound. A chapter on cultural identity is a rare source on contemporary stars of the Cape Verdean music scene. She also mentions the work of the Centro Nacional de Artesenato (National Centre for Arts and Crafts) and the current position of the print and broadcast media. This is perhaps not the easiest of reference sources to use – there is no index – but it answers many of a newcomer's questions on the everyday workings of society, government and economy. Under the name of Paule-Nathalie Lefèbvre she has also published a collection of poems, *Cap-Vert: des îles, un peuple, un futur* (Cape Verde: some islands, one people, one future) (Paris: CCFD, 1986).

10 **Ilha da Boa Vista, Cabo Verde: aspectos históricos, sociais, ecológicos e económicos.** (The island of Boa Vista, Cape Verde: historical, social, ecological and economic aspects.)
Josef Kasper, translated from the German by Luís da Silva Madeira. Praia: Instituto Caboverdiano do Livro, 1987. 188p. 20 maps. bibliog.

This comprehensive study of the physical and human geography of an island whose population in 1980 was less than 3500 might seem of highly specialized interest. However, in the absence of complementary works on the other 'ilhas rasas' (flat islands) of Sal and Maio its findings can be considered relevant to these. In some more general aspects, such as the approach and methodology required to revitalize an economically and ecologically damaged community it is relevant to the rest of Cape Verde. Kasper covers climate, relief, geology, soil, flora, fauna, social structure and economic activity in their historical and actual contexts. This is all done with a view to the coexistent concerns of ecology and development needs: Kasper was sponsored by SWISSAID. Of greatest importance perhaps are the development of fishing and the successful work carried out to combat the spread of sand dunes – these were creeping down the main streets of the town of Sal-Rei. He also makes an interesting case for the utilization of purgeira (*Jatropha curcas* or Barbadosnut nettlespurge), a shrub which was traditionally used to provide lamp fuel and soap. He suggests that a small soap factory should be established to exploit one of the few natural resources which exist on the island.

11 **A ilha do Fogo e as suas erupções.** (The island of Fogo and its eruptions.)
   Orlando Ribeiro. Lisbon: Junta de Investigações do Ultramar, 1954.
   319p. 18 maps. bibliog. (Memórias. Série Geográfica, no. 1).

The first half of this book covers the physical and human geography of Fogo, an island which is also Cape Verde's live volcano. Chapters deal with relief, climate, human settlement, rural life and agriculture, home and social life, communications, commerce, economic crisis and emigration. The second half of the book is devoted to the island's volcanic eruptions. Accounts of eruptions before 1785 and those of 1785, 1799, 1816, 1847, 1852 and 1857 are collated and commented upon. J.S. Feijó's account of the 1785 eruption is transcribed. Ribeiro went to Fogo to study the eruption of 13 June 1951 and this is described in detail, with over forty black-and-white photographs to illustrate the text.

12 **Ilhas crioulas.** (Creole islands.)
   Augusto Casimiro. Lisbon: Editorial Cosmos, [1935]. 47p. (Cadernos Coloniais, no. 3).

Casimiro was a Portuguese political exile who spent some time on Cape Verde. He has written a very sympathetic portrait of the islands. Whilst lauding the Portuguese colonial ideals, he pleads for greater resources to be allocated to the islands. Chapters cover the principal features of Cape Verdean life: food crises, folklore, agriculture water shortage and emigration. See also his later work *Portugal crioulo* (Lisbon: Edições Cosmos, 1940. 280p.).

13 **Madeira, Cabo Verde e Guiné.** (Madeira, Cape Verde and Guinea.)
   João Augusto Martins, preface by Antonio de Lencastre. Lisbon: Livraria de Antonio Maria Pereira, 1891. 270p.

A solid contemporary account, whose facts and figures are enlivened by polemic and anecdote. Cape Verde appears on pages 57-234. Each island is covered individually including some of the uninhabited ones. There are also general observations on the economy, administration, culture and natural history. He is very critical of the Portuguese administration and also of the greed of the British business interests on São Vicente. Included in this volume are five attractive engravings, by different artists, of Santiago, São Vicente and Brava.

14 **Monografia sobre a província de Cabo Verde.** (Monograph on the province of Cape Verde.)
   João Baptista Amâncio Gracias. Praia: Imprensa Nacional, 1922. 128p. bibliog.

Prepared for the international exhibition in Rio de Janeiro in 1922, this otherwise unexceptional summary of the islands' history, geography, economy and government is distinguished by some picturesque black-and-white photographs.

15 **Monografia-catálogo da exposição de Cabo Verde.** (Monograph/catalogue
of the Cape Verde exhibition.)
Lisbon: Sociedade de Geografia de Lisboa, 1938. 61p. 2 maps. bibliog.
Destined for students and intended to be a catologue for the annual colonial exhibition
of the Sociedade de Geografia de Lisboa (the Geographical Society of Lisbon). Cape
Verde was the subject of the 1938 exhibition. The society manages to turn its apology
for the lack of exotic exhibits into an explanation of Portugal's 'civilizing' influence.
The first part of the text covers geography and history, with a little rather dubious
physical anthropology. The second part refers to items in the exhibition: there are
agricultural implements, extensive and interesting examples of medicinal plants and
traditional medical knowledge, housing, clothing and other expressions of everyday
life. The third part is a bibliography of 215 items compiled by João Faramhouse. A
general section is divided by subject; this is followed by an island-by-island listing. A
separate section lists sixty-six maps.

16 **Le moulin et le pilon: les îles du Cap-Vert.** (The mill and the pestle: the
Cape Verde Islands.)
Nelson Eurico Cabral, preface by Jacques Ruffié. Paris: Éditions
l'Harmattan; Agence de Coopération Culturelle et Technique, 1980.
185p. map. bibliog.
A very readable study of Cape Verdean society and culture, whose title refers to the
islands' mixed cultural heritage. In the preparation of maize, the staple diet, both the
Portuguese stone hand-mill and the African pestle can be found in use. Cabral begins
by examining the transition from slavery to semi-feudal agriculture: in slavery and in
the unequal distribution of land can be found the most important historical foundations
of Cape Verdean society. He continues with an interesting account of family life and
family structures: he finds some similarities with other West African cultures. His next
chapter covers religion, noting the varied and complex practices carried out within and
without the Roman Catholic Church. Next, he considers cultural manifestations,
covering education, publications, language, literature and folklore. He then looks at
the present economic situation and the history of drought, crisis and emigration.
Finally, he considers the political future and prospects for unity with Guinea-Bissau. A
continuing motif throughout this work is the history of peasant resistance and revolt,
something which can be overlooked in other works.

17 **Na asa do vento: o livro.** (On the wing of the wind: the book.)
Arnaldo Rocha Silva. [Praia]: The author, 1989. 113p.
A Brazilian working in Cape Verde as a co-operant, Silva contributed a weekly column
to the newspaper *Voz di Povo* (q.v.), giving his amused impressions of the Cape
Verdean way of life. A collection of the best of these articles is published in this
volume.

18 **Número dedicado a Cabo Verde e integrado nas comemorações do 5°
centenário do 'achamento' daquele arquipélago.** (Issue dedicated to Cape
Verde and integrated into the commemorations of the fifth centenary of
the 'discovery' of that archipelago.)
Garcia de Orta, vol. 9, no. 1 (1961), p. 11-165.
A collection of items on Cape Verdean society, past and present: items include a
history of cartography, by A. Teixeira da Mota; Cape Verde's food crises, H. Duarte
Fonseca; Gaspar Frutoso and the colonization of Cape Verde, A.H. de Oliveira

Marques; documentation and research in the colonies, N. Miranda; a glossary of vernacular plant-names, L.A. Grandvaux Barbosa; the socio-cultural situation, N. Miranda; endemic diseases, Manuel T.V. de Meira; the demographic evolution of Cape Verde, Nuno Alves Morgado; dances, Tomaz Ribas; 'Navigation de Lisbonne à l'île de São Tomé par un pilote portugais anonyme (vers 1545)' (q.v.); Cape Verde in Portuguese and foreign literature, N. Miranda: songs of Ana Procópio, Félix Monteiro.

19 **Santiago de Cabo Verde: a terra e os homens.** (Santiago, Cape Verde: the land and the people.)
Ilídio do Amaral. Lisbon: Junta de Investigações do Ultramar, 1964. 444p. 34 maps. bibliog. (Memórias, 2nd series, no. 48).
Santiago is the largest of all the islands of the archipelago, and has over half of the population. It is often considered distinct from the rest of Cape Verde. Slavery was more widespread here than on the other islands: slaves who had fled either their masters or the pirate attacks on coastal settlements lived in the interior of Santiago, separate from the rest of society. These were the so-called *badius* (literally, 'vagrants'), a name used to this day to describe people from Santiago. This volume is a reliable and much-cited work, covering physical geography, history, society, demography and economy. It has a valuable bibliography (p. 377-412) and seventy-one pages of photographs. Eleven sheet maps illustrate geological features, hydrological features, population, vegetation, and town plans of Assomada, Tarrafal and Praia.

20 **Ultramar português II: ilhas de Cabo Verde.** (Overseas Portugal II: the Cape Verde Islands.)
António Mendes Corrêa. Lisbon: Agência-Geral do Ultramar, 1954. 261p. 9 maps.
Aiming to be a comprehensive text-book of the islands, this dense and informative volume covers geology, landscape, climate, vegetation, fauna, human settlements, racial situation, demography, health, language, culture, education, politics, administration and the economy. The weight of all this information is alleviated somewhat by the numerous photographs, illustrations and tabulations. Each chapter has a summary in English.

The people of the Cape Verde Islands: exploitation and emigration.
See item no. 180.

Race, culture and Portuguese colonialism in Cabo Verde.
See item no. 212.

República de Cabo Verde: 5 anos de independência 1975-80.
See item no. 233.

Geography

General

21 **Cabo Verde: imagens e números.** (Cape Verde: pictures and numbers.)
António Costa. Lisbon: Centro de Estudos Geográficos, 1980, 1981.
2 vols. 56 maps. bibliog. (Estudos de Geografia das Regiões Tropicais,
Relatório nos 7-8 da Linha de Acção no. 5).

A poorly reproduced geographical scrapbook of photographs, statistical tables and
short extracts from a variety of sources. Volume one covers geology, relief, volcanic
activity, soil, vegetation, settlement, administrative districts and population. Volume
two covers agriculture, animal husbandry, fishing, industry, transport, commerce,
education, health and famine. Volume two also contains the bibliography, p. 88-92,
which is sadly short of material beyond the 1960s. It is divided between books and
articles, and statistics and climatic data.

22 **Dicionário corográfico do arquipélago de Cabo Verde.** (Geographical
dictionary of the Cape Verde Archipelago.)
Álvaro Lereno. Lisbon: Agência-Geral do Ultramar, 1952. 568p.

An alphabetical list of place-names, indicating the various administrative areas of each.
It was produced in response to the confusion found in place-names in official
documentation. Sometimes local names were being used, sometimes Portuguese ones.
Some places even found themselves being administered by two different districts. The
introduction to this work carefully describes the geographical limits of all the
administrative districts. Lereno's scrupulous approach to toponymy has not penetrated
everyday usage: many places are still commonly called by more than one name.

A ilha do Fogo e as suas erupções.
See item no. 11.

A bibliography of African ecology: a geographically and topically classified list of books and articles.
See item no. 473.

Climate

23 **O balanço hidrológico na ilha de Santiago (Cabo Verde).** (The hydrological balance on the island of Santiago [Cape Verde].)
F. Reis Cunha. *Garcia de Orta*, vol. 9, no. 2 (1961), p. 359-79. 3 maps. bibliog.

Calculations, explained in the article, have been made to determine rates of evaporation. By comparing this with rainfall measurements the amount of moisture entering the soil can be estimated. Even in rainy years, coastal regions can be considered arid, although inland areas can have a water surplus from August to October. The three maps show 'contours' indicating areas of water deficit and surplus – information of great importance for agricultural planning. There is a summary in English.

24 **As crises de Cabo Verde e a chuva artificial.** (The Cape Verdean crises and artificial rain.)
H. Duarte Fonseca. *Garcia de Orta*, vol. 4, no. 1 (1956), p. 11-34; vol. 4, no. 2 (1956), p. 191-213. 5 maps.

Fonseca studies the weather patterns of Cape Verde, and in particular the behaviour of the northeast trade winds, the Harmattan and the South Atlantic monsoons. He identifies four weather patterns which may precipitate drought. He makes a particular study of rainfall and winds between August and October of 1941, when there was an overall drought, and again between August and October of 1944 when there was a drought in Barlavento. He concludes that even in drought years the South Atlantic monsoon air masses may pass nearby. These are humid, and could provide 'artificial' rain if stimulated.

25 **Étude bioclimatique de l'archipel des Canaries.** (Bioclimatic study of the Canary Islands.)
J.J. de Granville. *Cahiers ORSTOM, Série Biologie*, vol. 15 (April 1971), p. 29-60. 8 maps. bibliog.

As the title suggests, this work is mainly concerned with the Canary Islands. However, data on precipitation, evaporation and air temperature are compared from Madeira, the Azores, Cape Verde and neighbouring points on the African coast. It is concluded that whilst the other Atlantic archipelagos have a Mediterranean climate, Cape Verde's is tropical. There is a summary in English.

26 **Meteosat looks at the general circulation: II. hurricane formation near the Cape Verde Islands.**
N.E. Davis. *Weather*, vol. 35, no. 5 (1980), p. 134-40. map.
Davis, from the European Space Agency, has been studying the inter-tropical convergence zone. Dramatic satellite photographs show the formation of cyclone Flossie.

27 **Monitoring and critical review of the estimated source strength of mineral dust from the Sahara.**
Ruprecht Jaenicke. In: *Saharan dust: mobilization, transport, deposition*, edited by Christer Morales. Chichester, England: John Wiley & Sons, 1979 (SCOPE, no. 14), p. 233-42. bibliog.
Dust-laden northeast winds from the Sahara are a well-known feature of Cape Verde's climate and Sal has become the site for a ground-based monitoring site. Jaenicke explains the reasons for Sal's suitability. In this chapter he also explains the importance of the work being carried out there to determine seasonal variation in dust transport. See also Ruprecht Jaenicke and Lothar Schütz, 'Comprehensive study of physical and chemical properties of the surface aerosols in the Cape Verde Islands region' (*Journal of Geophysical Research*, vol. 83, no. C7 [20 July 1978], p. 3585-99. map. bibliog.), which contains information on Sal's climate; and 'Water-soluble potassium, calcium and magnesium in the aerosols over the tropical North Atlantic', by D.L. Savoie and J.M. Prospero (*Journal of Geophysical Research*, vol. 85, no. C1 [20 January 1980], p. 385-92. map. bibliog.). Toby N. Carlson and Richard S. Caverly 'Radiative characteristics of Saharan dust at solar wavelengths' (*Journal of Geophysical Research*, vol. 82, no. 21 [20 July 1977], p. 3141-52. bibliog.), calculates the amount of solar energy absorbed by dust from the Sahara as it is transported across the Atlantic. Measurements were taken at Sal and Barbados.

28 **Le point en 1982 sur l'évolution de la sécheresse en Sénégambie et aux îles du Cap-Vert. Examen de quelques séries de longue durée (débits et précipitations).** (The view in 1982 on the evolution of the drought in Senegambia and the Cape Verde Islands. Examination of some long-term time series [discharge and precipitation].)
J.C. Olivry. *Cahiers ORSTOM – Série Hydrologie*, vol. 20, no. 1 (1983), p. 47-69. bibliog.
Using rainfall measurements from Saint-Louis (Senegal), Banjul (The Gambia) and Praia, and also measuring the discharge of the River Senegal, Olivry attempts to estimate climate evolution in the region. He notes the persistence of drought. Rainfall data from Praia (1875-1982) and Ribeira Brava, São Nicolau (1940-82) is tabulated and shows that, despite irregularites, net precipitation has halved over the last one hundred years. Olivry makes the important comment that there is not always a direct correlation between lack of rainfall and famine: it can be the case that rain occurs, but at the wrong time of year for the maize crop.

Soils

29 **Dificuldades na desagregação e dispersão de alguns solos de Cabo Verde.**
(Difficulties in the disaggregation and dispersion of some soils from Cape
Verde.)
Maria Luísa da Franca. *Garcia de Orta, Série de Estudos Agronómicos*,
vol. 4, nos 1-2 (1977), p. 19-30. bibliog.
Using new techniques of laboratory analysis the author finds that the proportion of
detected clay in soils from Cape Verde is significantly higher than previously thought.
João Tiago Mexia contributes an appendix 'Dificuldades na desagregação e dispersão
de alguns solos de Cabo Verde – interpretação estatística' ('Difficulties in the
disaggregation and dispersion of some soils from Cape Verde' – statistical
interpretation) (*Garcia de Orta, Série de Estudos Agronómicos*, vol. 4, nos 1-2 [1977],
p. 31-8).

30 **Em defesa da terra.** (In defence of the land.)
Amílcar Cabral. *Cabo Verde: Boletim de Propaganda e Informação*,
vol. 1, no. 2 (Nov. 1949), p. 2-5; vol. 1, no. 6 (March 1950), p. 15-17;
vol. 2, no. 14 (Nov. 1950), p. 19-22; vol. 2, no. 15 (Dec. 1950), p. 6-8.
These four chapters have as introduction the earlier article 'Algumas considerações
acêrca das chuvas' (Some thoughts on the rains) in the same journal, vol. 1, no. 1 (Oct.
1949), p. 5-7. This was written just as four years of drought were ending and it explains
the importance which should be given to stabilizing agricultural conditions. The
sprouting corn is 'indispensável, insubstituível, é pai e mãe, marido e esposa, irmão e
irmã das gentes caboverdeanas' (indispensable, without substitute, it is the father and
mother, the husband and wife, the brother and sister of the Cape Verdean people). As
a newly graduated soil scientist Cabral, in 'Em defesa da terra', explains the causes of
soil erosion in Cape Verde and its fundamental role in generating agricultural disaster.
Explaining that removal of natural vegetation cover has left the soil vulnerable to
massive erosion particularly during the rains, he describes as misplaced the joy at the
rains' arrival: the valleys are soon filled with yellow water carrying soil out to the sea.
In turn the denuded land loses its capacity to retain water and this leads to floods and
the drying up of springs. He makes several proposals to halt this process, amongst
them terracing, dykes, contour cultivation and reafforestation. It is interesting to note
in these articles a hint of Cabral's political development as he comes to the realization
that the political will necessary for these measures to be carried out would have to
come from Cape Verdeans themselves.

31 **Estudo da fertilidade quanto ao fósforo de alguns solos de Cabo Verde,
Guiné e Timor.** (Study of the fertility of the phosphate system in some
soils from Cape Verde, Guinea-Bissau and Timor.)
Maria Luísa R. Santos, José N.N. Vicente. *Garcia de Orta. Série de
Estudos Agronómicos*, vol. 2, no. 2 (1975), p. 65-78. bibliog.
Using the Larsen-Cunha parametric complex, the authors find that their samples of
alluvial soils from Cape Verde are very rich in phosphates, and that these phosphates
are easily available to plants. There is a summary in English.

32 **Os solos da ilha da Boavista.** (The soils of Boa Vista Island.)
Mateus Nunes. *Garcia de Orta*, vol. 16, no. 2 (1968), p. 225-42.
2 maps. bibliog.
Boa Vista does not display much variety in soil type: sand and salinity are the key features of this less-favoured island. Nunes classifies and describes the soils, which are mainly reddish-brown soils, clay and halomorphic types. This is illustrated by a 1:100,000 soil map of the island. A brief introduction to Boa Vista's physical and human geography is also provided.

33 **Os solos da ilha de Santiago.** (The soils of Santiago Island.)
Fernando Xavier de Faria.   Lisbon: Junta de Investigações do Ultramar, 1970. 157p. map. bibliog. (Estudos, Ensaios e Documentos, no. 124).
A general survey of all aspects of the geography of Santiago is followed by a classification and description of the island's soils. The author also includes some reflections on soil use in Santiago. The principal problems are erosion and soil types which do not retain water. Despite the social consequences he believes that the situation is serious enough to warrant the end of *sequeiro* (unirrigated) cultivation where the soil is not really appropriate to agriculture. *Regadio* (irrigated) cultivation should be further developed. Whilst outlining the methodology used for this study de Faria notes that he encountered cartographic problems which necessitated the use of aerial photographs from 1957. These are reproduced in this volume to form a map of an approximate scale of 1:50,000, with superimposed markings to illustrate the location of different soil types. There is a summary in English.

34 **Os solos da ilha de São Nicolau (arquipélago de Cabo Verde).** (The soils of São Nicolau Island [Cape Verde Archipelago].)
Mateus Nunes.   Lisbon: Junta de Investigações do Ultramar, 1962. 108p. 8 maps. bibliog. (Estudos, Ensaios e Documentos, no. 94).
São Nicolau is an agricultural island, but it has been one of the worst affected by drought of all of the archipelago. In response to this, Nunes' study is concerned with the agricultural application of each soil type as well as its classification and description. He suggests methods to overcome the problem of erosion, including increasing the amount of terracing along contour lines and removing the goats which graze in the mountains. An introductory chapter gives a general summary of São Nicolau's physical and human geography. Soil mapping is illustrated on a 1:30,000 aerial photograph of the island. Four supplementary tracings of this map are provided, which show land types, soil groups, agricultural suitability and crop distribution. There is a summary in English.

35 **Os solos da ilha do Fogo.** (The soils of Fogo Island.)
Fernando Xavier de Faria.   Lisbon: Junta de Investigações Científicas do Ultramar, 1974. 146p. map. bibliog. (Estudos, Ensaios e Documentos, no. 129).
A general survey of Fogo's physical and human geography precedes a classification and description of the different soil types. His findings are illustrated on a 1:100,000 map of the island. Attention is given to the difficulties of dealing with rocky areas in a study of this type. The uses and practical qualities of these soils are outlined.

11

Estudos sobre a fertilidade dos solos de Cabo Verde (ilha de Santiago). IV –
Deficiências na nutrição mineral da bananeira.
See item no. 321.

Maps and mapping

36 **Atlas de Portugal ultramarino e das grandes viagens portuguesas de
descobrimento e expansão.** (Atlas of Portuguese overseas territories and
the great Portuguese voyages of discovery and expansion.)
Garcia de Orta, vol. 2, no. 2 (1954), p. 257-61.
An index to the atlas, with twenty maps referring to Cape Verde.

37 **Cartas geográficas e hidrográficas das províncias ultramarinas.**
(Geographical and hydrographic maps of the overseas provinces.)
Garcia de Orta, vol. 2, no. 2 (1954), p. 247-56.
A list of maps either published or held by the Junta das Missões Geográficas e de
Investigações do Ultramar (Board of Geographical Missions and Overseas Research).
Items relevant to Cape Verde appear on pages 247-8.

38 **Estratégia alimentar de Cabo Verde, 1982. Food strategy of Cape Verde,
1982.**
ITC. The Netherlands: [n.p.], [1982].
A series of maps of each of the inhabited islands on a scale of 1:100,000. Rainfall,
catchment areas and infrastructure are indicated, including the location of planned
development projects such as harbours and factories. There are annotations in
Portuguese and English.

39 **A evolução da geodesia e a ocupação geodésica do ultramar português em
África.** (The development of geodesic mapping in the Portuguese
colonies in Africa.)
José Farinha da Conceição. Lisbon: Junta de Investigações do
Ultramar, 1970. 81p. 7 maps. bibliog. (Estudos, Ensaios e Documentos,
no. 127).
A general introduction to the practice of geodesic mapping is followed by reports on
the work undertaken in the colonies: Cape Verde is discussed on pages 61-2. A
1:1,000,000 map of the archipelago shows the results of these measurements.

40 **Exposição de cartographia nacional (1903-4): catálogo.** (Exhibition of national cartography [1903-4]: catalogue.) Edited by Ernesto de Vasconcellos. Lisbon: Sociedade de Geographia de Lisboa, 1904. 279p.

A useful source for early maps. Thirty-seven entries, with detailed annotations, are listed for Cape Verde (p. 143-8).

41 **Mindelo: planta da cidade.** (Mindelo: map of the city.) Edited by Gabriel E. Évora. São Vicente, Cape Verde: Gráfica, [1985].

A 1:5,000 coloured street map of Mindelo giving names of the principal streets and indicating points of interest for the visitor, such as the police station, bank, markets and bars. An inset map shows the road network for the island of São Vicente. Also included are useful phone numbers and days of local festivals.

42 **Praia – Santiago: plantas da cidade e ilha.** (Praia – Santiago: maps of the city and the island.) Edited by Gabriel E. Évora, Lúcio Santos. São Vicente, Cape Verde: Gráfica, 1986.

This one sheet contains four different maps. A 1:9,000 map of Praia as a whole names the city districts, principal roads and institutions. Symbols indicate places of interest for the visitor, and roads and distances to other parts of Santiago are marked. The Platô is Praia's commercial centre and a 1:3,500 map shows this area in detail with street names and important institutions and places of interest marked. Cidade Velha (formerly known as Ribeira Grande) lies fifteen kilometres from Praia, which replaced it as Cape Verde's capital in 1770. Its many interesting ruins of former colonial glory are marked on a map of what is now merely a village. A 1:500,000 map of the island of Santiago shows the road network. As well as maps, this document provides some brief facts and figures about Praia and the island as a whole. Useful phone numbers and Transcor bus destinations are given.

43 **Relatório da missão hidrográfica do arquipélago de Cabo Verde.** (Report of the hydrographic team of the Cape Verde Archipelago.) Teixeira de Aragão. *Anais. Junta de Investigações do Ultramar*, vol. 13, no. 2 (1958), p. 77-110. 7 maps.

A report of mapping work carried out in 1958 at various locations around the Cape Verdean coastline. Details of geodesic measurements, elevations, sea depths and tide range from selected locations are given. Studies of Porto dos Mosteiros (Fogo), Porto do Maio (Maio), Porto do Curralinho (Boa Vista) and Porto Ferreira (Boa Vista) are accompanied by panoramic black-and-white photographs.

44 **República de Cabo Verde.** (Republic of Cape Verde.) Lisbon: Serviço Cartográfico do Exército Português. 1968- .

A series of 1:25,000 maps of the entire landmass of the archipelago, whose scale allows an enormous amount of detail to be shown – 10m contours, vegetation, buildings, roads and paths. Begun in 1968 by the mapping service of the Portuguese army, the series has continued since independence under a cooperative mapping agreement with the Cape Verdean government. Most of the maps of the major islands have now been completed.

Geography. Maps and mapping

45 **World mapping today.**
R.B. Parry, C.R. Perkins. London: Butterworths, 1987. 583p.
Information on the current state of mapping and useful addresses for Cape Verde can be found on pages 515-16.

Cartografia portuguesa antiga.
See item no. 109.

Cartas das ilhas de Cabo Verde de Valentim Fernandes (1506-1508).
See item no. 116.

Geology

General

46 **Bibliografia geológica do ultramar português.** (Geological bibliography of the Portuguese overseas territories.)
Francisco Gonçalves, Jaime Caseiro. Lisbon: Junta de Investigações do Ultramar, 1959. 272p.
Entries usually appear with a brief abstract, are arranged by author and are indexed by geographical area, author and subject. One hundred and twenty-eight entries refer to Cape Verde.

47 **Geochemistry of the Cape Verde Islands and Fernando de Noroñha.**
Bernard M. Gunn, Norman D. Watkins. *Geological Society of America Bulletin*, vol. 87 (Aug. 1976), p. 1089-100. 3 maps. bibliog.
Chemical analyses taken from seven of the Cape Verde islands and from Fernando de Noroñha (situated to the west of the Mid-Atlantic Ridge) show that these islands are the most alkaline parts of the oceanic crust.

48 **A geologia do arquipélago de Cabo Verde.** (The geology of the Cape Verde Archipelago.)
J. Bacelar Bebiano. Lisbon: Ministério das Colónias, 1932. 275p. 11 maps.
Also published in *Communicações dos Serviços Geológicos de Portugal*, vol. 18 (1932), this is a seminal work in its field. Two introductory chapters summarize the geological publications and give a brief geographical description. The main body of the work is divided into two parts: the first covers the islands of Barlavento, with chapters on São Vicente, Santo Antão, São Nicolau, Sal, Boa Vista and the uninhabited islands of Santa Luzia, Branco and Razo; the second part covers Sotavento, with chapters on Maio, Santiago, Fogo, Brava and the uninhabited Ilhéus Secos. Each chapter gives a very detailed description of mineral water and rock types, but the author considers that there are no mineral resources of any economic value. His conclusion includes some

15

Geology. General

thoughts on what the islands' origins may have been. The volume contains maps of Santa Luzia and the nine inhabited islands on a scale of between 1:100,000 and 1:140,000, shaded to illustrate different rock types, and 135 black-and-white photographs. Appended are 'Subsídios para a petrologia do Archipélago de Cabo Verde (Ilha de S. Vicente)' (Elements for the petrology of the Cape Verde Archipelago [São Vicente Island]) by Amílcar Mário de Jesus who provides a chemical analysis of some rock samples supplied by Bebiano (p. 245-63) and 'Notas hidrológicos (Ilha de Santo Antão)' (Hydrological notes [Santo Antão Island]) (p. 265-8) reproduced from the *Boletim Oficial da Província de Cabo Verde*, no. 16 (19 April 1913).

49 **Géologie Africaine / African Geology.**
Orléans, France: Centre International pour la Formation et les Échanges Géologiques, 1976- . quarterly.
Produced in cooperation with UNESCO Earth Science Division, Paris and the Musée Royal de l'Afrique Centrale, Tervuren, Belgium, this bulletin publishes brief abstract of current work, arranged geographically. Works on Cape Verde are listed as part of the Atlantic Ocean region.

50 **Outline of the geology of the Cape Verde Archipelago.**
Raoul C. Mitchell-Thomé. *Geologische Rundschau*, vol. 61, no. 3 (1972), p. 1087-109. 3 maps. bibliog.
This is probably the most readable geological source, giving detailed descriptions of the geological characteristics of the whole archipelago, but always in the context of being a general survey. It is indubitably a starting-point for any more specialized study Mitchell-Thomé explains the forces which have made the Cape Verdean landscape principally vulcanism and erosion by wind and sea. He gives special attention to the volcano on Fogo and also to a study of igneous rock.

51 **Petroquímica do arquipélago de Cabo Verde e comparação do vulcanismo cabo-verdiano com o da Renânia.** (Petrology of the archipelago of Cape Verde and comparison of Cape Verdean vulcanism with that of the Rhineland.)
C. Burri, translated from the German by N.F. Grossman. *Garcia de Orta, Série de Geologia*, vol. 1, no. 2 (1973), p. 1-26. map. bibliog.
Originally published under the title 'Petrochemie der Capverden und Vergleich des Capverdischen Vulkanismus mit demjenigen des Rheinlandes' in the *Schweizerische Mineralogische und Petrographische Mitteilungen*, vol. 40 (1960), this is a study of Cape Verde's igneous rocks. It suggests a general similarity between vulcanite rock from both Cape Verde and the Rhineland. The substantial bibliography includes many works in German.

52 **Volcanic rocks from the Cape Verde Islands.**
Gerald M. Part. *Bulletin of the British Museum (Natural History) Mineralogy*, vol. 1, no. 2 (1950), p. 25-72, 2 maps, bibliog.
The rock collections at the British Museum of Natural History are the basis for this study. A general survey of works on Cape Verdean geology precedes a petrographical description of the different rock types with accompanying diagrams. The results of chemical analyses are tabulated.

16

53 **Die Vulcane von Capverden und ihre Produkte.** (The volcanoes of Cape Verde and their products.)
Cornelius Doelter. Graz, Austria: Leuschner u. Lubensky, 1882. 171p. 5 maps.

A study of the topography and petrology of the islands of Santo Antão, São Vicente, Santiago and Maio. The volume contains some attractive black-and-white line drawings of the Cape Verdean landscape.

Islands

54 **A achadinha da Praia (Cabo Verde): um caso típico de inversão de relevo vulcânico.** (The Praia *achadinha* [Cape Verde]: a typical case of inversion of volcanic morphology.)
António Serralheiro. *Garcia de Orta*, vol. 19, nos 1-4 (1971), p. 279-88. map.

A striking feature of Praia's landscape is the *achadas* (elevated plains) on which the different districts of the city are built. Serralheiro describes the forces of vulcanism and erosion which formed them. Black-and-white photographs illustrate landscape and geological detail. There is a summary in English.

55 **Alguns aspectos geomorfológicos do litoral da ilha de Santiago (arquipélago de Cabo Verde).** (Some geomorphological aspects of the coastline of the island of Santiago [archipelago of Cape Verde].)
Ilídio do Amaral. *Garcia de Orta, Série de Geologia*, vol. 2, no. 1 (1974), p. 19-28. map. bibliog.

A description of the various features of the Santiago coastline – cliffs, shingle and sandy beaches – and the processes of their formation. Of particular interest are the raised littoral platforms, which are affected by water-level weathering rather than marine abrasion. There is a summary in English. António Serralheiro has made a study of the fossils which can be found on the raised littoral platforms of Santiago, São Vicente and Maio in 'Sobre as praias antigas de algumas ilhas de Cabo Verde' (On the ancient beaches of some of the Cape Verde Islands) (*Garcia de Orta*, vol. 15, no. 1 [1967], p. 123-38. 3 maps. bibliog.).

56 **Carta geológica de Cabo Verde, notícia explicativa da folha da ilha Brava e dos ilhéus Secos (na escala 1/50000).** (Geological map of Cape Verde, explanatory notes on the sheet referring to Brava Island and the Seco Islets [on the scale of 1:50,000].)
F. Machado, J. Azeredo Leme, J. Monjardino, M.F. Seita. *Garcia de Orta*, vol. 16, no. 1 (1967), p. 123-30. map. bibliog.

The 1:50,000 map shows the uninhabited islets of Grande, Luiz Carneiro and Cima (collectively known as either the Secos or Rombos) and Brava. It is coloured to indicate nine different kinds of rock: the text is a geological description of these islands to accompany the map. Brava's most interesting geological feature, the partial ring structure which may represent the ancient ocean floor, is described in 'O complexo sienito-carbonatítico da ilha Brava, Cabo Verde' (The syenite-carbonatite intrusion of Brava Island, Cape Verde), by F. Machado, J. Azeredo Leme, and J. Monjardino (*Garcia de Orta*, vol. 15, no. 1 [1967], p. 93-8. map.). For more information on the Secos or Rombos, see 'Petrografia do ilhéu Grande (ilha Brava, Cabo Verde)' (Petrography of Grande Islet [Brava Island, Cape Verde]), by L. Aires Barros (*Garcia de Orta*, vol. 16, no. 2 [1968], p. 249-58. bibliog.) and 'Litofácies do arquipélago de Cabo Verde II. Calcaritos dos ilhéus Rombos' (Lithofacies of the Cape Verde archipelago II. Calcites of the Rombo Islets) by C. Romariz (*Garcia de Orta*, vol. 18, nos 1-4 [1970], p. 247-52).

57 **As erupções do Fogo e a vida da ilha.** (Fogo's eruptions and the life of the island).
Orlando Ribeiro. *Cabo Verde, Boletim de Propaganda e Informação*, no. 41 (1953), p. 13-15.

A description of the 1951 eruption – the first in ninety-four years – and its effects. Ribeiro briefly assesses possible future risks: he believes that only a very limited area of the island is in danger.

58 **Estudo geológico. petrológico e vulcanológico da ilha de Santiago (Cabo Verde).** (A study of the geology, petrology and vulcanism of the island of Santiago [Cape Verde].)
C.A. Matos Alves, João Rocha Macedo, L. Celestino Silva, A. Serralheiro, A.F. Peixoto Faria. *Garcia de Orta, Série de Geologia*, vol. 3, nos 1-2 (1979), p. 47-74. 3 maps. bibliog.

A detailed study of the geological features of the island and the formation of its different regions. It is accompanied by a 1:100,000 coloured geological map and a summary in English. There are several studies of particular rocks from Santiago contained in *Garcia de Orta, Série de Geologia*. More recent works in English include M.O. Figueiredo and Silva, 'Alkaline-calcic metasomatic undersaturated rocks associated with alkaline-carbonatitic complexes of Santiago (Cape Verde Islands)' (vol. 1, no. 4 [1976], p. 33-142); Figueiredo and Silva, 'Note on the occurrence of niobium-rich zirconolite in carbonatitic rocks of Santiago Island (Cape Verde Republic)' (vol. 4, nos 1-2 [1980], p. 1-6); and M. Hermínia Mendes and Silva, 'Preliminary note on the occurrence of peridotite nodules in Santiago (Cape Verde Islands)' (vol. 6, nos 1-2 [1983], p. 175-8).

59 **Geologia da ilha de Maio (Cabo Verde).** (Geology of Maio Island [Cape Verde]).
António Serralheiro. Lisbon: Junta de Investigações do Ultramar, 1970. 103p. 2 maps. bibliog.

Maio is one of the older of the archipelago's islands and this work is directed towards an understanding of their origins. There is a very detailed geological description of the island and Serralheiro concludes that the archipelago emerged from one of the later phases of the opening of the Atlantic Ocean. The volume includes a 1:30,000 map of Maio, colour-coded for different rock types and forty-eight black-and-white photographs. There is an English summary.

60 **The geological history of Maio, Cape Verde Islands.**
C.J. Stillman, H. Furnes, M.J. LeBas, A.H.F. Robertson, J. Zeilonka.
Journal of the Geological Society of London, vol. 139 (1982), p. 347-61.
2 maps. bibliog.

The authors aim to establish a geological time-scale for Maio and thus to reach a greater understanding of the evolution of Atlantic islands. Maio has attracted much attention because it has an 'abundant exposure of Mesozoic fossiliferous marine sediments'. Some of the findings, and by extension the mapping, of *Geologia da ilha de Maio (Cabo Verde)* (q.v.) are questioned, and this article accompanies a re-mapping of the island. The new geological map is on a scale of 1:50,000, with shading to illustrate the location of different rock types. See also 'Mesozoic deep-water and Tertiary volcaniclastic deposition of Maio, Cape Verde Islands: implications for Atlantic paleoenvironments and ocean island volcanism', A.H.F. Robertson (*Geological Society of America Bulletin*, vol. 95 [April 1984], p. 433-53. 3 maps. bibliog.). Using new mapping, petrography, chemical analysis and microfossil study Robertson's detailed work finds that Maio provides some clues to the early history of Atlantic islands and their paleoenvironments. Another recent work is 'The geochemistry and petrology of an alkaline lamprophyre sheet intrusion complex on Maio, Cape Verde Republic', by H. Furnes and C.J. Stillman (*Journal of the Geological Society of London*, vol. 144 [1987], p. 227-41. 2 maps. bibliog.). This studies the sheet intrusions into the Mesozoic and Tertiary basement complex to determine whether they are from a single magma source. There seems to have been volcanic activity at different times and thus different degrees of erosion.

61 **Nota explicativa da carta geológica da ilha de S. Nicolau (Cabo Verde) na escala de 1:50000.** (Explanatory note on the geological map of São Nicolau [Cape Verde] on the scale of 1:50,000.)
J. Rocha de Macedo, António Serralheiro, L. Celestino Silva. *Garcia de Orta, Série de Geologia*, vol. 11, nos 1-2 (1988), p. 1-32. map. bibliog.

A lengthy essay describes the geology of the island and explains the probable process of its formation. This is to accompany the 1:50,000 map, which is lavishly coloured to indicate different geological features. The authors also provide an index of geographical names. An earlier study of São Nicolau is 'Estudo estratigráfico dos sedimentos do Campo da Preguiça ilha de S. Nicolau (Cabo Verde)' (Stratigraphical study of sediments from Campo da Preguiça, island of São Nicolau [Cape Verde]) by António Serralheiro and M. Lourdes Ubaldo (*Garcia de Orta, Série de Geologia*, vol. 3, nos 1-2 [1979], p. 75-82. 2 maps. bibliog.). This found fossilized Foraminifera from the Upper Miocene period. These are also found on the distant islands of Maio and Santiago, which helps date general volcanic activity in the archipelago as a whole.

62 **Note préliminaire sur la géologie de l'île de Boa Vista (Cap-Vert).** (Preliminary note on the geology of Boa Vista Island [Cape Verde].)
A. Serralheiro, C.A. Matos Alves, João Rocha de Macedo, L. Celestino Silva. *Garcia de Orta, Série de Geologia*, vol. 1, no. 3 (1974), p. 53-60. map.

A description of geological characteristics and the processes of their formation. Boa Vista is notable for its razed plains: the highest altitude is 400m. This essay is accompanied by black-and-white landscape photographs and a 1:100,000 geological map. For more detailed studies of some of the rocks found on Boa Vista see de Macedo and Silva, 'Sobre a existência de rochas vítreas na ilha da Boavista (Cabo

Verde)' (On the existence of vitreous rocks on Boa Vista Island [Cape Verde])
(*Garcia de Orta, Série de Geologia*, vol. 1, no. 4 [1976], p. 117-24. map. bibliog.)
and Silva and F.J.A.S. Barriga, 'Primary analcime megacrysts up to 20cm in
phonolitic and basaltic rocks, Boa Vista, Cape Verde Islands' (*Garcia de Orta,
Série de Geologia*, vol. 10, nos 1-2 [1987], p. 1-10. map. bibliog.).

63 **Noticia sobre algumas aguas mineraes da ilha de Santo Antão
(archipélago de Cabo Verde).** (Report on some mineral waters from the
island of Santo Antão [archipelago of Cape Verde].)
F.F. Hopffer. Lisbon: Lallemont Frères, 1883. 20p.

Hopffer was the former head of the Cape Verdean health service, and he was very
interested in the reputed healing properties of two springs in the Ribeira Grande area
of Santo Antão. These properties are reflected in the names 'Fonte do Doutor' (the
doctor's source) and 'Nascente do Doutor' (the doctor's spring). He describes their
location, estimates their rate of flow and makes a tentative chemical analysis.

64 **Petrologia e vulcanismo da ilha do Fogo (Cabo Verde).** (Petrology and
vulcanism of Fogo Island [Cape Verde]).
C.F. Torre de Assunção, F. Machado, L. Conceição Silva. *Garcia de
Orta*, vol. 15, no. 1 (1967), p. 99-110. map. bibliog.

An analysis of different ages of lava flow from Fogo's volcano shows very little
difference other than that the more recent lava is found to have fewer alkalis, less
aluminium, and more magnesium. A study of the viscosity and porosity of lava from
the 1951 eruption can be found in F. Machado's 'Estudo reológico de uma lava do
vulcão do Fogo (Cabo Verde)' (Study of lava from the Fogo volcano [Cape Verde])
(*Garcia de Orta, Série de Geologia*, vol. 1, no. 1 [1973], p. 9-14).

65 **Preliminary geothermal investigations in Cape Verde.**
Verónica Carvalho Martins. *Geothermics*, vol. 17, nos 2-3 (1988),
p. 521-30. 4 maps. bibliog.

Research has been taking place on Fogo to investigate the viability of utilizing
geothermal energy for electricity generation. At present Fogo is supplied by small
diesel generators, but where there is no electricity supply wood, butane and kerosene
are used. It is estimated that around 60 per cent of Cape Verde's energy consumption
is from biomass. However, Fogo does have geothermal potential. Rainwater filters
through the permeable volcanic rock and reaches underground reservoirs. Volcanic
activity means that water samples taken during investigations have been found to have
temperatures of 200–300°C.

66 **Stratigraphy, facies, and significance of late Mesozoic and early Tertiary sedimentary rocks of Fuerteventura (Canary Islands) and Maio (Cape Verde Islands).**
Alastair F. Robertson, Daniel Bernoulli. In: *Geology of the Northwest African continental margin*, edited by U. von Rad, K. Hinz, M. Sarnthein, E. Seibold. Berlin; Heidelberg, Germany; New York: Springer-Verlag, 1982, p. 498-525. 8 maps. bibliog.
Layers of deep water sedimentary rock exposed in volcanic rock help to date and document the early Atlantic Ocean and the history of the formation of these islands.

67 **Sur les terrains sédimentaires de l'île de Sal. Avec remarques sur les îles de Santiago et de Maio (archipel du Cap-Vert).** (On the sedimentary formations of the island of Sal. With some remarks on the islands of Santiago and Maio [archipelago of Cape Verde].)
Georges Lecointre. *Garcia de Orta*, vol. 11, no. 2 (1963), p. 275-89. map. bibliog.
The principal geological features of Sal are its sedimentary formations, its raised beaches containing fossils, and deposits of grit from the African continent.

68 **Vulcanismo das ilhas de Cabo Verde e das outras ilhas atlânticas.** (Vulcanism of the Cape Verde Islands and of the other Atlantic Islands.)
Frederico Machado. Lisbon: Junta de Investigações do Ultramar, 1965. 83p. 14 maps. bibliog. (Estudos, Ensaios e Documentos, no. 117).
A readable work which studies the volcanoes of Fogo, the Canaries and the Azores. The history of their eruptions is outlined, and a pattern seems to exist whereby eruptions in the Canaries are followed by ones in Fogo and then in the Azores. Crater formation and types of lava are described. A tentative explanation of the eruptive process of the Fogo volcano is suggested. Fogo may lie on a north–south tectonic fault, which could cause pressure on a layer of magma which lies just ten kilometres beneath the island. The volume is illustrated by a number of dramatic black-and-white photographs. There is a summary in English.

Flora and Fauna

Plants

69 **Beiträge zur Flora der Cap Verdischen Inseln.** (A study of Cape Verdean flora.)
Johann Anton Schmidt. Heidelberg, Germany: Akademische Buchandlung von Ernst Mohr, 1852. 356p.
An old but still much-cited work. A long essay is followed by a detailed listing of plants by family, noting when and where recorded. The plants are indexed by Latin name.

70 **Études Macronésiennes. 1. Géographie des cryptogrames vasculaires.** (Macronesian studies. 1. The geography of vascular cryptograms.)
Pierre Dansereau. *Agronomia Lusitania*, vol. 23 (1961), p. 151-81, map. bibliog.
The article intends to contribute to a greater understanding of plant migration, focusing on the four Atlantic archipelagos of Madeira, the Azores, the Canary Islands and Cape Verde. Eighty-eight plant species are studied and the results tabulated in such a way that comparisons between the four locations are easy to make. It is interesting to note that Cape Verde is quite distinct from the others, with its bias towards tropical rather than temperate species.

71 **Les îles du Cap Vert. Géographie, biogéographie, agriculture. Flore de l'archipel.** (The islands of Cape Verde. Geography, biogeography, agriculture. Flora of the archipelago.)
Auguste Chevalier. *Revue de Botanique Appliquée et d'Agriculture Tropicale*, nos 170-1 (Oct.-Nov. 1935), p. 733-1090. map. bibliog.
Widely considered to be the most comprehensive work on Cape Verdean vascular plants, this is a scholarly amalgam of previous studies and the results of Chevalier's own enthusiastic fieldwork on all the inhabited islands except Brava and São Nicolau. The inventory of plants gives Latin name, vernacular name when known, where found

22

and by whom. Some entries are accompanied by short essays. Items are indexed by Latin name and by vernacular name. As a preface, Chevalier supplies substantial and useful essays on the geography and botany of the islands. He gives a history and review of previous works in this field, of which only Schmidt's 'incomplete' *Beiträge zur Flora der Cap Verdischen Inseln* (q.v.), is considered of any value. Much space is devoted to his thoughts on the plant colonization of Cape Verde. Flora is typically insular, in that it comes from a variety of places, carried by sea, wind, birds and insects. The three important elements in this colonization are Mediterranean/Atlantic island species, Ethiopian/tropical African species and those brought by man. Geographical conditions which affect plant life are outlined. Altitude seems to be the determining feature for plant location, and of course drought influences plant adaptations. Chevalier also includes an essay on Cape Verdean agriculture, observing the techniques employed and the types of crop which are grown.

72 **Nota sobre a composição das sementes de *Cucumis ficifolius* de Cabo Verde.** (A note on the seed composition of the *Cucumis ficifolius* of Cape Verde.)
José E. Mendes Ferrão, Ana Maria B.C. Ferrão. *Garcia de Orta, Série de Estudos Agronómicos*, vol. 8, nos 1-2 (1981), p. 11-16. biblog.
The fatty acid content of wild cucumber seeds from Santiago is analysed. The plant's distribution and economic potential as a human foodstuff are also discussed. There is a summary in English.

73 **Plantas úteis da África Portuguesa.** (Useful plants of Portuguese Africa.)
F. de Mello de Ficalho, edited and with a foreword by Ruy Telles Palhina. Lisbon: Agência Geral das Colónias, 1947. 2nd ed. 301p.
This is a substantial improvement on the Conde de Ficalho's first edition of 1884 simply by virtue of the addition of a list of plant families and an index which includes plant names in Portuguese and African languages as well as in Latin. The Conde's introduction includes a short history of cultivated plants in Africa, noting the role of introduced species. He details the expeditions which called in at Cape Verde and did some collecting (p. 60-1). The main body of the work is not a rigorous scientific treatise: each plant has a layman's working description, note of medical, culinary or other usage, general origin and, occasionally, a historical reference.

74 **Purgueira da ilha do Fogo. Composição da semente e algumas características da gordura.** (*Jatropha curcas* of Fogo Island. Seed composition and some fatty acid characteristics.)
José E.M. Ferrão, Ana Maria B.C. Ferrão, Maria Teresa S. Patrício. *Garcia de Orta, Série de Estudos Agronómicos*, vol. 10, nos 1-2 (1983), p. 175-8.
Jatropha curcas (Barbadosnut nettlespurge) is a drought-resistant plant, once widely used in Cape Verde for household lighting. As well as analysing the seeds' chemical composition and fatty acid content, the authors also consider the plant's economic potential. There is a summary in English.

75 **Subsídios para um dicionário utilitário e glossário dos nomes vernáculos das plantas do arquipélago de Cabo Verde.** (Elements for a working dictionary and glossary of the vernacular names of the plants of the Cape Verde Archipelago.)
L.A. Grandvaux Barbosa. *Garcia de Orta*, vol. 9, no. 1 (1961), p. 37-94. bibliog.
This work arose from botanical exploration undertaken in 1955-56 to assess Cape Verde's suitability for cotton growing, a project without a positive outcome. Barbosa begins with a description of previous botanical missions to Cape Verde and the collections and publications which they produced. He notes that attention has not been given evenly to all the islands, some of which need further study. The listing of vernacular names to Latin names (p. 49-61) is divided by island, since each speaks its own variety of Crioulo. Only the islands of Barlavento (Santo Antão, São Vicente, Santa Luzia, São Nicolau and Sal) are covered. The final section of this work lists plants by their Latin name, giving vernacular names, location and brief (non-scientific) description. There are fifty-one black-and-white photographs of specimens.

Agroforestry in the West African Sahel.
See item no. 317.

Birds

76 **A field guide to the birds of West Africa.**
Gérard J. Morel, William Serle. London: Collins, 1977. 351p.
Although nothing surpasses the Bannermans' *History of the birds of the Cape Verde Islands* (q.v.), this is a much more convenient guide for use in the field. There are 515 species illustrated – 335 in colour by Wolfgang Hartwig; a checklist of species; a list of scientific and vernacular names (Portuguese not included, but the Spanish may be of some assistance); and indexes of scientific and English names. The authors aim to cover all the birds known to have been found in West Africa. Of the 1097 birds recorded in the area covered (roughly bounded by Mauritania, Chad and Congo and including Cape Verde), 726 are dealt with in the body of the text. Description covers visual identification, voice, distribution and habitat, nesting and a note of allied species where appropriate. The other 371 species are briefly annotated in the checklist of species.

77 **History of the birds of the Cape Verde Islands.**
David A. Bannerman, W. Mary Bannerman, introduction by Leão de Tavares Rosado do Sacramento Monteiro. Edinburgh: Oliver and Boyd, 1968. 458p. 5 maps. bibliogs. (Birds of the Atlantic Islands, vol. 4).
The distinguished ornithologist David Bannerman confesses to becoming 'engrossed by the birds of Cape Verde as early as 1913. The general conclusion of his researches is that the birds are largely of the Palaearctic region. As a result of their visit in 1966 he and his wife became so enthusiastic about Cape Verde in general that they decided to expand the scope of the intended volume. The core feature, nevertheless, is the 'Systematic list by families and species', p. 151-450. This is an annotated list, with field notes, which aims to include all the birds ever reported in Cape Verde. Each bird may have several pages of notes. These give names in English, Latin and Portuguese (all of

which feature in the indexes), a full description, an ornithological history and the authors' own observations. This can include, for example, a detailed description of the white-headed kingfisher (*Halcyon leucocephala acteon*) killing and eating a mouse in a disgusting manner. Bannerman also sets the record straight on birds which he believes have been erroneously reported form the islands. There are colour and black-and-white illustrations. Resident, migratory and breeding birds, totalling 105 species, are listed on pages xv-xix and xxiv. An example of the Bannermans' scholarship is the chapter 'Explorers of the bird-life since 1784', p. 16-44. This contains notes on previous ornithological research by João da Silva Feijo (1784-89), Charles Darwin (1832), Carl Bolle (1851-52), John Macgillivray (1852), H. Dohrn (1865), J.G. Keulemans (1865), Boyd Alexander (1897), Leonardo Fea (1897-98), Robert Cushman Murphy (1912), José Gonçalves Correia (1922), G.F. Simmons (1923-24), W.R.P. Bourne (1951) and René de Naurois (1961-). T...e Bannermans make proposals for the conservaton of bird life, p. 44-7: they suggest that Razo should be made a sanctuary. Razo is the home of the unique Razo lark (*Alauda razae*) and the rumoured home of the probably extinct giant skink (*Macroscincus coctei*). There is an ornithological bibliography of fifty-six items (p. xxv-xxxi). In addition to this material on birds there is a general geographical introduction, p. 1-6; an essay on the discovery of Cape Verde, p. 7-16; an essay on vegetation by L. Grandvaux Barbosa, p. 58-61; and notes on the butterflies of Cape Verde by N.D. Riley, p. 62-5. Both the Bannermans provide lively accounts of their stay in Cape Verde. David Bannerman's is mainly concerned with his observations of the islands' natural history, p. 66-117. Good bird-watching sites are noted. His wife describes domestic and social life, p. 118-50.

As aves em algumas superstições indígenas da Guiné e de Cabo-Verde.
See item no. 415.

Insects

78 **'Conspectus' da entomofauna cabo-verdiana.** (A comprehensive survey of Cape Verdean insects.)
Alberto Coutinho Saraiva. Lisbon: Junta de Investigações do Ultramar, 1961. 189p. 16 maps. bibliogs. (Estudos, Ensaios e Documentos, no. 83).

Saraiva is setting out to pull together the various studies of Cape Verdean insects, from 1758 to 1960. His first chapter describes the biogeography of the islands, lavishly supplemented by a 1:750,000 map of the whole archipelago showing prevailing winds and coloured to illustrate the different biogeographical zones. Chapter two discusses previous studies, with particular praise for the work of Håkan Lindberg of Finland in 1953-54 (see *Ergebnisse der zoologischen Forschungsreise von Prof. Dr. Håkan Lindberg nach den Kapverdischen Inseln im Winter 1953-54*). Chapter three is a systematic listing of the insects found in the islands, giving physical description, notes on distribution both in Cape Verde and abroad, information on the collectors and comparative remarks with regard to the Canary Islands and the West African coast. In a short concluding essay Saraiva uses the data on insects to disprove theories that Cape Verde was once joined to the African continent by a land bridge. There is a summary in English.

79 **Ergebnisse der zoologischen Forschungsreise von Prof. Dr. Håkan Lindberg nach den Kapverdischen Inseln im Winter 1953-54.** (Results of the voyage of zoological research of Prof. Dr. Håkan Lindberg in the Cape Verde Islands during the winter of 1953-54.) Håkan Lindberg, Robert Mertens, P. Wygodzinsky, N.C.E. Miller, A. Luther, Max Vachon, Jacques de Beaumont, Eduard Wagner, Adrien Roudier, Michel Ferragu, B. Tjeder, Curtis W. Sabrosky, Claude Herbulot, A. Villiers, Reinhard Remane, Lucien Chopard, Viking Nyström, Pierre Viette, Samuel Panelius, Richard Frey, B. Herting, F.I. van Emden, Erwin Beyer.   *Societas Scientiarum Fennica Commentationes Biologicae,* vol. 15, nos 5, 11 (1955); vol. 15, nos 16, 19-21 (1956); vol. 16, nos 1-2, 7-11, 13-14 (1957); vol. 17, nos 3, 7-8 (1958); vol. 18, nos 3-4, 7 (1958); vol. 19, nos 1-2 (1958); vol. 20, no. 1 (1958); vol. 20, no. 4 (1959). map. bibliogs.

These twenty-five articles contain the results of Lindberg's expedition to Cape Verde: it probably remains the most important work on Cape Verdean insect life, and it also covers molluscs and reptiles. Many new species were found, and an international team of zoologists examined the collection. The reports which they sent back to Helsinki are in German, French and English. Mostly consisting of scientific descriptions and diagrams of the items, they also often contain short essays and bibliographies. The most substantial piece of work is Lindberg's 'Hemiptera Insularum Caboverdensium' (Hemiptera of the Cape Verde Islands) (vol. 19, no. 1 [1958]). This is a 246-page ground-breaking contribution to the field, complete with bibliography (p. 244-6) and numerous black-and-white illustrations.

80 **Insectos de Cabo Verde.** (Insects of Cape Verde.) M.L.G. Alves.   In: *Estudos de Zoologia.*   Lisbon: Junta de Investigações Científicas do Ultramar, 1974, p. 209-34. (Memórias da Junta de Investigações Científicas do Ultramar, no. 58, 2nd series).

In many ways a complementary work to Saraiva's *'Conspectus' da entomofauna cabo-verdiana* (q.v.), as Alves is using Saraiva's 1960-61 collection as well as that of a 1969-70 expedition conducted by the Missão de Estudos Zoológicos do Ultramar (the Overseas Zoological Studies Mission). He gives detailed descriptions and information about specimens of *Heteroptera* and *Coleoptera*. There is a summary in English.

81 **Os mosquitos de Cabo Verde (*Diptera: culicidae*): sistemática, distribuição, bioecologia e importância médica.** (The mosquitoes of Cape Verde [*Diptera: culicidae*]: taxonomy, distribution, bio-ecology and medical importance.) H. Ribeiro, Helena da Cunha Ramos, R. Antunes Capela, C. Alves Pires.   Lisbon: Junta de Investigações Científicas do Ultramar, 1980. 141p. 18 maps. bibliog. (Estudos, Ensaios e Documentos, no. 135).

This major work is the result of a field survey carried out in 1977 as part of the Agreement for Scientific and Technical Cooperation between Portugal and the Republic of Cape Verde. All nine inhabited islands were investigated and 5,000 specimens of mosquitoes collected from the 178 survey sites. Earlier research on mosquitoes is briefly summarized, and the bibliography (p. 133-41) is a great contribution to knowledge on this subject. The survey made many new sightings, concluding that there are eight species and sub-species in the islands. There is a guide to identifying adults and fourth instar larvae, followed by a very detailed description of each. This gives their previous record in Cape Verde, their world and local distribution and body measurements. From these observations it is concluded that there is now a specifically Cape Verdean form of *Anopheles (Cellia) gambiae* Giles, 1902. The origins of the mosquitoes are considered: the Ethiopian and Sinantropic predominate over the Palaearctic. Human activity is thought to have been influential. Finally, the medical implications of mosquitoes are studied. Santiago has long had a bad reputation for malaria and suitable means for its control are considered. There is a summary in English.

As lagartas polífagas – *Heliothis armigera* (Hübner) e *H. peltigera* (Schiff) – no arquipélago de Cabo Verde.
See item no. 322.

Marine life

82 **Big fish from salt water.**
John Goddard.   London: Ernest Benn, 1977. 244p. bibliog.
A well-illustrated guide to 'tackle, techniques and species in British, European and African waters' which in covering the Azores, Madeira, the Canary Isles and Sierra Leone can be taken as a guide to what might be found in Cape Verdean waters.

83 **Céphalopodes de l'archipel du Cap-Vert, de l'Angola et du Mozambique.**
(Cephalopods of the Cape Verde Archipelago, Angola and Mozambique).
William Adam.   In: *Estudos de Biologia Marítima.*   Lisbon: Junta de Investigações do Ultramar, 1962, p. 1-64. bibliog. (Memórias da Junta de Investigações do Ultramar, no. 33, 2nd series).
Adam gives a detailed physical description for each species, noting distribution and where, when and by whom each sample was recorded. Some of his information dates back to 18th-century studies. His main research seems to have taken place in Angola, but it can be deduced that Cape Verde is rich in *Octupus vulgaris*, a popular local dish.

84 **Contribuição para o conhecimento dos formaníferos actuais da ilha de Maio (arquipélago de Cabo Verde).** (A contribution towards the understanding of the Foraminifera of Maio Island, archipelago of Cape Verde.)
G. Mateu, A. Tavares Rocha.   Luanda, Angola: Instituto de Investigação Científica de Angola, 1971. 108p. 3 maps. bibliog.
A detailed micropalaeontological report on research work carried out in 1964 and 1965 on samples from beaches and dunes on Maio. Fifty-four species of Foraminifera were found. Other recent studies in this field are cited. There is a summary in English.

85   **Seashells from Cape Verde Islands.**
     Luis Pisani Burnay, António Antunes Monteiro.   Lisbon: The authors,
     1977. 85p. 3 maps. bibliog.
     The authors wished to help clear up taxonomic confusion in this area. The differen
     islands have very different marine environments, and the richness of Cape Verde';
     marine life is reflected in the variety of malacological fauna. The authors carried ou
     work on Sal, São Vicente and Santo Antão. Shells are listed in family order (p. 19-56
     with detailed description, and sixty-six black-and-white photographs are included. Th
     authors' enthusiasm is everywhere manifest: even the occasion of a *Conus ermineu*.
     sting on Mrs Burnay is made the opportunity for a detailed observation of the painfu
     effects. This perhaps explains the book's curious dedication, 'to both our wives, An;
     and Helena. They did not protest too much.' The valuable bibliography (p. 81-5
     contains 122 items.

Le *Gérard Tréca* aux îles du Cap-Vert.
See item no. 326.

**Proceedings of the symposium on the living resources of the Atlantic
continental shelf between the Straits of Gibraltar and Cape Verde.**
See item no. 327.

Tourism and Travel Guides

86 Atlantic Islands: Azores, Madeira, Canary and Cape Verde Islands.
RCC Pilotage Foundation, compiled by Anne Hammick, Nicholas Heath,
foreword by O.H. Robinson.   St. Ives, Cambridgeshire, England: Imray
Laurie Norie & Wilson, 1989. 220p. 118 maps. bibliog.

A guidebook for yachts, this book gives practical advice on navigation, facilities and
regulations. Routes to and from the Atlantic Islands are discussed, taking into account
season and prevailing wind. Cape Verde is covered in detail on pages 187-210 as a
practical place to break a transatlantic passage. There is sensible advice on tides,
anchorages, weather, beacons and potential hazards for yachts and those sailing in
them. In particular, Hammick warns of the dangers of Boa Vista. She advises yachts to
keep a five-mile distance from the island, which is thought to lie at least two miles east
of its charted position and to be in a zone of reefs and magnetic anomalies. There is a
map for each island and each potential anchorage. In general, Hammick repeats the
sailor's familiar comment that the Canary Islands are cheaper and have better facilities.

87 Cabo Verde e o turismo. (Cape Verde and tourism.)
Bento Levy.   *Ultramar*, vol. 7, nos 27-8 (1967), p. 147-52.

Not a very imaginative or enticing summary of Cape Verde's attractions and tourist
facilities, really approaching enthusiasm only when describing the potential for sport
fishing – see also *Big fish from salt water*.

88 A guide to the Cape de Verd Islands.
John Rendall.   London: C. Wilson, 1856. 30p.

Rendall was the British Consul in Mindelo, São Vicente, at a time when the British
interest in the natural harbour of Porto Grande, Mindelo, was increasing. It was an
important refuelling stop for coal-fired ships crossing the Atlantic, and several British
coaling companies were established in Mindelo. The guide reflects these maritime
concerns in its descriptions of such things as Customs regulations and the various
hazards each island might present to the seaborne.

Tourism and Travel Guides

89 **Roteiro do archipelago de Cabo Verde.** (Chart of the Cape Verde Archipelago.)
Christiano José de Senna Barcellos.   Lisbon: Typographia do Jornal Colonias Portuguezas, 1892. 100p. 10 maps.

As a Portuguese Navy lieutenant Barcellos had noticed deficiencies in the cartography of the archipelago, something he attempts to remedy in this book for mariners. He comments bitterly on the lack of official assistance he received. The result is an island-by-island description of port facilities, sea-depths, winds and currents, with accompanying maps. There is also a note of shipping regulations, tables of winds and distances between the islands, and the co-ordinates and reach of the lighthouses.

90 **Tourismus in der dritten Welt: von der Kritik zur Strategie: das Beispiel Kapverde.** (Tourism in the Third World: from critique to strategy: the case of Cape Verde.)
Silke May.   Frankfurt, Germany: Campus Verlag, 1985. 416p. 3 maps. bibliog.

The first half of this encyclopaedic volume is concerned with tourism in the Third World in general. May covers the history of tourism, its development, economic importance, and often damaging social and cultural impact. The second half is devoted exclusively to Cape Verde, based on research carried out in the early 1980s. A very detailed description of the islands' tourist facilities gives information on hotels, airports, flights, other aspects of the infrastructure, planning and legislation. There is a lack of facilities of an international standard, although in many respects Cape Verde is relatively favoured for tourist development. May considers future options for tourism in Cape Verde. Noting that facilities are often overloaded by demand from visiting emigrants and local people working or visiting away from their home towns and islands, she believes that as a first step this 'internal tourism' should be developed and thus multinational involvement might be avoided. The bibliography (p. 400-17) contains some background works on Cape Verde, but is mostly concerned with Third World tourism in general.

91 **West Africa: a travel survival kit.**
Alex Newton.   South Yarra, Australia: Lonely Planet Publications, 1988. 459p. 79 maps.

Cape Verde appears on pages 131-46. This is a reasonably accurate and informative travel guide, although it covers little beyond Praia, Mindelo and the Fogo volcano. There is good information on hotels, restaurants and clubs in and near these locations, and travellers should take particular note of Newton's comments on the reservations policy of TACV (Transportes Aereos de Cabo Verde), the national airline.

92 **West Africa: the rough guide.**
Jim Hudgens, Richard Trillo.   London: Harrap Columbus, 1990. 1232p. 130 maps. bibliog. (Rough Guide Series).

A practical guide to travelling in West Africa. Chapter nine is devoted to Cape Verde, making this probably the best work of its kind. There is reliable information on how to get to the islands and, once there, how to travel between them. There are suggestions on places to stay, places to eat, and places to drink and listen to music. The islands of Santiago, Fogo, Santo Antão, São Vicente, São Nicolau and Sal are covered in some detail. In addition to maps of these islands there are town plans for Mindelo and Praia. Supplementing the practical details are a lengthy background essay on Cape Verdean history and society, and some useful Crioulo phrases. There is a bibliography for the volume as a whole which is divided by country.

Cape Verde Islands.
See item no. 5.

Travellers' Accounts

93 **Account of a voyage to the islands of the Canaries, Cape de Verde and Barbadoes, in 1721.**
George Roberts. In: *A new general collection of voyages and travels, volume 1*, collected by Thomas Astley. London: Frank Cass, 1968, p. 599-627.

Entertaining and perceptive, this is an account of an almost farcically unlucky voyage. Roberts left London in 1721 bound for Virginia. After numerous calamities Roberts' troubles really started when he accidentally arrived at São Nicolau. Here he encounters pirates. As he comes out on deck, unprepared and half dressed, he is greeted with the strange and fearsome cry, 'You Dog! you son of a b—! you speckled shirt dog!' There follows a tense and exciting first-hand account of Roberts' protracted dealings with the pirates, who were led by Edmund Loe and John Russel (or Lopez). The pirates – described as 'although bad, yet generous' – were clearly frustrated at finding so little to plunder either on ship or on land. Roberts finally gets his ship back, but without crew, provisions or seaworthy sails. Even the Cape Verdean stowaways decide they want to abandon him when his mainsail splits. He manages to find harbour on Santo Antão where he is treated very kindly. A bad storm completely wrecks his sloop, and he is stranded at the foot of a rocky cliff on Brava. Undeterred, and not for the last time, he cobbles together a new boat from the wreck. Here begins many months of plying between the islands – all of which he visits – conducting a little trade, repairing the boat and trying to find a passing ship to take him home. He is thus a well-qualified commentator on Cape Verdean life and culture. Only in 1725 does he manage to return to London.

94 **Black and white make brown.**
Archibald Lyall. London; Toronto: Heinemann, 1938. 303p. 2 maps.

Lyall wrote on diverse topics, producing works of fiction, sociology, travel and philology. All these interests come together in this enthusiastic account of his travels to Cape Verde and Guinea-Bissau in 1936 and 1937. This seems to have been a journey undertaken simply in order to go where few others had been. Entertaining on the expatriate social circle which embraces him, his detailed observations cover many aspects of Cape Verdean society. He notes the presence of political deportees: this was a phenomenon of several centuries' standing. Cape Verde's penal role was approaching its culmination in the building of the Tarrafal prison camp, from which, he remarks, the locals expected economic benefits. He is also witness to the flowering of Cape Verdean poetry in the *claridoso* movement, meeting Manuel Lopes, Jorge Barbosa and Pedro Cardoso. He gives fair translations of several poems and *mornas*. His subsequent travels in Guinea-Bissau are a useful reminder of the connections which existed between that country and Cape Verde. He notes the large Cape Verdean presence there as being a class of officials, functionaries and small traders who far outnumbered the Portuguese.

95 **Esmeraldo de situ orbis**. (About the emerald place of the world.).
Duarte Pacheco Pereira. Lisbon: Imprensa Nacional, 1892. 125p.

A commemorative edition, with some facsimiles, taken from a 17th-century copy of Pereira's manuscript of the late 15th or early 16th century. An introduction gives a history of the manuscript and a biography of Pereira, a navigator, fighter and writer who took part in the exploration of the west coast of Africa. The manuscript is a geographical and historical treatise. Cape Verde is mentioned on pages 48-9. Its geographical position is given in such a way as to be helpful to mariners and there is a brief description of the islands. This notes the presence of goats, cotton, and the fact that agriculture is possible only by irrigation. The text is in Portuguese.

96 **Journal of an African cruiser: comprising sketches of the Canaries, the Cape de Verds, Liberia, Madeira, Sierra Leone, and other places of interest on the West coast of Africa.**
Horation Bridges, edited by Nathaniel Hawthorne. London: Wiley & Putnam, 1845. 179p.

Bridges was an officer in the US navy who visited São Vicente and Santo Antão in 1843. His account of that visit gives evidence of his compassionate and generous nature. He notes the importance of Cape Verde for the US whaling fleet, but also sees that the revenue does not seem to have benefited the inhabitants. He is critical of the Portuguese administration, and comments that in the famine of 1832 the Portuguese merely shipped a few cargoes for sale, whereas 'America fed the starving thousands, gratuitously, for months'. He is also distressed by the political exiles: 'It is a melancholy thought, that many an active intellect – many a generous and aspiring spirit – may have been doomed to linger and perish here, chained as it were, to the rocks, like Prometheus, merely for having dreamed of kindling the fire of liberty in their native land.' On a trip to Santo Antão, he notes the dancing, the dangerous roads and the great beauty of the *ribeiras* (valleys).

97 **Navigation de Lisbonne à l'île São Tomé par un pilote portugais anonyme (vers 1545).** (Voyage from Lisbon to the island of São Tomé by an anonymous Portuguese pilot [circa 1545].)
Edited by Serge Sauvageot, notes by T. Monoud, R. Mauny. *Garcia de Orta*, vol. 9, no. 1 (1961), p. 123-38. map. bibliog.

A facsimile of the anonymous pilot's report in Italian to the Veronese Count Rimondo della Torre is appended to this modern French translation. The pilot visited Cape Verde on his journey, and gives a convincing account of what he found. Indeed, modern historians consider him to be an eminently reliable source. He notes the quantity of salt to be found on Maio and Sal and the quality of the goat-meat, but is most valuable in his description of the city of Ribeira Grande, Santiago. He finds it full of fruit trees, well-constructed houses and around 500 households.

98   **A new general collection of voyages and travels. Volume 1.**
Collected by Thomas Astley.   London: Frank Cass, 1968. 680p.
11 maps. (Travels and Narratives, no. 47).

A facsimile of the original edition of 1745, this volume contains several works relevant
to Cape Verde. The first of these is Walter Wren's 'The voyage of Captain George
Fenner to the islands of Cape Verde, in 1566, with three ships and a pinnace' (p. 185-
91). Fenner visited Boa Vista, Maio, Santiago and Fogo. Boa Vista was notable for its
population of exiles and goats. Annual rent for the island was 40,000 goatskins. Fenner
attempted to trade at Santiago, but was treated very treacherously: he describes the
Portuguese as 'these Christian barbarians'. An English translation of Cadamosto's 'The
second voyage of Aluise da Cada Mosto to the coast of Africa, in 1456, in which the
Cape de Verde Islands were discovered' appears on pages 592-6. George Roberts'
'Account of a voyage to the islands of the Canaries, Cape de Verde and Barbadoes, in
1721' (q.v.) is on pages 599-627. 'A description of the Cape de Verde Islands' appears
on pages 627-80. This is a compilation of the accounts of many different travellers, with
sources acknowledged in footnotes. Some of the travellers' anecdotes are retold and
there are some observations on Cape Verdean life, but the main area of interest is in
the islands' products and coastline. There is, for example, a lot of detail on how to load
salt at Maio: not surprising, when every year over a hundred English ships came to
collect salt, free of all charge except that of labour. There is a map based on George
Roberts' cartography, and two striking engravings of Fogo and São Vicente from
originals by John Nieuhoff.

99   **A new voyage round the world.**
William Dampier, introduction by Albert Gray.   London: Adam &
Charles Black, 1937. 2nd ed. 376p.

Dampier sailed from Virginia to Sal in August 1683, and reports fairly unfavourably on
the people he met in Cape Verde (p. 56-61). Apart from flamingoes, Sal was inhabited
by 'Portuguese banditti' whom he suspects of having sold him goat dung instead of
ambergris. It should be noted that Dampier gave only old clothes in exchange. The
ship's hull was cleaned at São Nicolau and water taken on board. They could not land
on Maio because some English pirates under Captain Bond of Bristol had taken the
governor and some other men captive the previous week. Dampier's previous
experience of Santiago leads him to describe the people there as thieves. Nevertheless,
he gives a fine description of Fogo: 'It is all of it one large mountain of a good height,
out of the top whereof issues Flames of Fire, yet only discerned in the Night: and then
it may be seen a great way at Sea'.

100   **Six years of a traveller's life in Western Africa. Volume 1.**
Francisco Travassos Valdez.   London: Hurst & Blackett, 1861. 354p.

Valdez, a keen exponent of Portugal's civilizing mission in Africa, was sent to Luanda
as a government arbitrator in 1852. On his journey from Lisbon he was instructed to
report on the West African coast and the Cape Verde islands. Chapters II and III (pp.
32-162) cover Cape Verde, island by island, including the uninhabited. He describes
topography, anchorages and harbour facilities, settlements, agriculture and other
features of economic potential. There are snippets of the social customs of Santiago –
weddings, funerals and *batuque* (a traditional form of music, dance and song) – and
interesting news of a slave rebellion on Boa Vista in 1811. Nevertheless the principal
value of this report is the author's detailed assessment of what he sees in terms of
potential for the islands' economic development. No natural resource is too slight –
salt, cattle, cotton, weaving, orchil, purgueira, indigo, dragon's blood (a resin from the
dragon tree *Dracoena draco*), cochineal, maize, tobacco, seabirds (for lamp oil), jet,

fish, saltpetre or vegetables. He sees the need for better port facilities, makes an unusual argument for Sal-Rei, Boa Vista to become the new capital and strongly criticizes the *morgadio* system of land tenure on Santiago as a terrible brake on agricultural development. Coloured no doubt by Valdez's enthusiasm for governmnent service this report stands out from others of the period, not only for its detail, but also for its view of the islands as a relatively busy and resourceful place.

101   The voyage of the *Beagle*.
Charles Darwin, edited by Janet Browne, Michael Neve. Harmondsworth, England: Penguin, 1989. 432p. 2 maps.
Darwin's first landfall after leaving England was Santiago and his visit to the island in January 1832 is recorded (p. 41-7). He was enthusiastic about what he found, 'The island would generally be considered as very uninteresting; but to any one accustomed only to an English landscape, the novel prospect of an utterly sterile land possesses a grandeur which more vegetation might spoil.' He is also struck by the beauty of the vegetation of the *ribeiras* (valleys), the dancing girls, geological features and the behaviour of sea slugs, octopus and cuttlefish. This is a shortened version of the first edition of 1839: the editors provide an introduction. Darwin refers to Cape Verde in *The origin of species* (Harmondsworth: Penguin, 1968. 476p.) as an example of islands which are stocked from a neighbouring continent.

102   West African Islands.
Alfred Burden Ellis.   London: Chapman & Hall, 1885. 352p.
Ellis was a major in the British army, who visited São Vicente and Santo Antão on a journey to the Gold Coast. His account is heavily coloured by his fierce prejudices against the Portuguese and missionaries, not to mention Africans. He describes a meal in Mindelo as being uneventful 'except that a mulatto waiter considered himself grossly insulted by being called Sambo instead of José'. The reader can only rejoice at Ellis's disastrous encounters with rickety furniture and fleas in the overpriced hotels. There is evidence of significant borrowings from Bridges's *Journal of an African cruiser: comprising sketches of the Canaries, the Cape de Verds, Liberia, Madeira, Sierra Leone, and other places of interest on the West coast of Africa* (q.v.).

Madeira, Cabo Verde e Guiné.
See item no. 13.

Listen! the wind.
See item no. 302.

Viagem a Cabo Verde.
See item no. 307.

35

History

The Portuguese empire

103 **A new history of Portugal.**
Harold Victor Livermore. Cambridge, England: Cambridge
University Press, 1976. 2nd ed. 408p. 7 maps.
A convenient and straightforward reference work for those events in Portugal which
had their distant repercussions in Cape Verde.

104 **Portugal and Africa 1815-1910: a study in uneconomic imperialism.**
Richard J. Hammond. Stanford, California: Stanford University
Press, 1966. 384p. 7 maps. (Food Research Institute, Studies in
Tropical Development).
A controversial work which claims that between 1815 and 1910 Africa yielded Portugal
no economic rewards. Although Cape Verde's experience of colonialism was somewhat
different from that of the African continent, this is nonetheless an interesting approach
to Portugal's colonial activity.

105 **Portugal in Africa: the last hundred years.**
Malyn Newitt. London: C. Hurst, 1981. 278p. 6 maps. bibliog.
Covering the period 1870 to 1974, this is a readable, coherent and reliable study.
Although mostly concerned with the continent of Africa and general concepts of
Portuguese colonialism during this period, there is a chapter devoted to 'Portugal's
islands' (p. 201-18). This contains useful information on the cocoa plantations of São
Tomé and Príncipe and the Cape Verdean contract labourers. There is also some detail
on Cape Verde itself, with particular reference to the islands' economic history. Crisis,
emigration, decline in traditional trading products such as salt and cloths and 20th-
century colonial economic management are covered. Newitt has also found
information on the British in Mindelo, and the social and economic effects of their
control of the coal-bunkering trade.

106 **Portuguese Africa.**
Ronald H. Chilcote. Englewood Cliffs, New Jersey: Prentice-Hall, 1967. 149p. 4 maps. bibliog. (The Modern Nations in Historical Perspective: African Subseries).
Although obviously a little dated, chapter five, 'Portuguese Guiné, the Cape Verde Archipelago and São Tomé and Príncipe' (p. 83-104) contains some brief, but pertinent, notes on Portuguese nationalism, Luso-tropicality, and resistance movements.

107 **The Portuguese seaborne empire 1415-1825.**
Charles Ralph Boxer, introduction by J.H. Plumb. London: Hutchinson, 1969. 426p. 7 maps. bibliog. (The History of Human Society).
Within the time-scale of Boxer's study the emphasis is naturally drawn to those areas of the globe more lucrative to the Portuguese, such as Brazil and the spice-yielding lands of the East, rather than Cape Verde and West Africa. Nevertheless this is a useful souce of information on the remarkable Portuguese expansion down the West African coast and beyond. The second section of the book describes the Portuguese methods of colonization, discussing features of administration, trade, and attitudes to race. Even though not specifically applied to Cape Verde, these issues are relevant.

Discovery

108 **António de Noli e a colonização das ilhas de Cabo Verde.**
(António de Noli and the colonization of the islands of Cape Verde.)
Charles Verlinden. *Revista da Faculdade de Letras* (Lisbon), vol. 3, no. 7 (1963), p. 28-45.
António de Noli and Diogo Gomes claimed to have discovered the islands in 1460 when their ships were blown off course. Verlinden describes the immediate circumstances of this event and discusses Alvise da Cadamosto's rival claim (see *The voyages of Cadamosto and other documents on Western Africa in the second half of the fifteenth century*). Verlinden provides useful information about de Noli's relationship with the Portuguese Crown, the technicalities of the system of captaincy and the Crown's authority over its conquests in the period 1460–1500. See also *Primórdios da ocupação das ilhas de Cabo Verde* (Origins of the occupation of the Cape Verde Islands) by Orlando Ribeiro (Lisbon: Universidade de Lisboa, 1955, 35p. and also in *Revista da Faculdade de Letras* [Lisbon], 2nd series, vol. 21, no. 1 [1955]). This is of interest with regard to the means by which settlement was established. Particular attention is given to the introduction of food crops such as maize and coconuts, and the islands' role as an 'experimental station' for plants being transported across the world at this time.

109 **Cartografia portuguesa antiga.** (Early Portuguese cartography.)
Armando Cortesão. Lisbon: Comissão Executiva das Comemorações
do Quinto Centenário da Morte do Infante D. Henrique, 1960. 195p.
bibliog. (Colecção Henriquina).

Some references can be found to fifteenth-century representations of Cape Verde.
Intriguingly, Cortesão mentions 'The Nautical Chart of 1424' (p. 71) which shows some
islands south of the Canaries named 'himadoro'. It is very tempting to imagine that
they might be the Cape Verde Islands. The first authenticated appearance of Cape
Verde is on Benincasa's map of 1468. Benincasa uses Alvise de Cadamosto's
nomenclature, which suggests that Cadamosto was his source of information (see *The
voyages of Cadamosto and other documents on Western Africa in the second half of the
fifteenth century*). The British Museum contains a fine collection of these beautifully
illuminated early maps. The islands are usually shown as a tumbling stack of rather
misshapen oblongs.

110 **Diogo Gomes. As relações do descobrimento da Guiné e das ilhas dos
Açores, Madeira e Cabo Verde.** (Diogo Gomes. Reports of the
discovery of Guinea and the islands of the Azores, Madeira and Cape
Verde.)
Gabriel Pereira. *Boletim da Sociedade de Geographia de Lisboa*, vol.
17, no. 5 (1898-99), p. 267-93.

Pereira presents a translation from the Latin of Gomes' chronicle, and gives his own
commentary. Gomes – together with Cadamosto and António de Noli – is one of
three who claimed to be the first to discover Cape Verde. Pereira comments on
Gomes' claims: he considers him a bit of a braggart tending to inflate his own
achievements at the expense of his companions' (one of whom was de Noli himself).
Gomes insists that de Noli reaped the glory – and the captaincy of Cape Verde –
simply because he was the first to return to Portugal and inform Alfonso V of their find.
Notwithstanding this, Gomes' description of Santiago (a name he gave to the island) is
a classic of New World utopias: white sand, rivers of fresh water, green pasture,
strange fruits and tame birds. It is tempting to wonder whether Gomes is again
exaggerating his achievements or whether the settlement of the islands was more
destructive to the ecological balance than has been previously considered. For the
document in English, see *The voyages of Cadamosto and other documents on Western
Africa in the second half of the fifteenth century*, p. 91-102.

111 **Les navigations médiévales sur les côtes sahariennes antérieures à la
découverte portugaise (1434).** (Medieval navigation along the Saharan
coast before the Portuguese discoveries [1434].)
Raymond Mauny. Lisbon: Centro de Estudos Históricos Ultramarino,
1960. 151p. 5 maps. bibliogs.

The problems of climate, geography and ship technology for Arab and European
navigators are explained, prior to the point where they were overcome by the
Portuguese and Gil Eanes rounded Cape Bojador in 1434. Explorations, both real and
fabled, are described. Maundy believes that the Arabs could not have reached the
Cape Verde Islands. See also N. Levitzion and J.F.P. Hopkins (eds) *Corpus of early
Arabic sources for West African history* (Cambridge: Cambridge University Press,
1981. 492p.). Sixty-five pre-sixteenth-century Arabic texts which contain knowledge
from the Arab world of West Africa are presented in English translation with
annotations. There appears to be no evidence of knowledge of the Cape Verde Islands.
The editors take references to Al-Jaza'ir al-Khalidat (the 'Immortal Isles') to refer to

the Canary Islands: the Arabs probably had not been there, but included them out of respect for Ptolemy's world geography. Awlil is mentioned in several texts as a source of salt, but the editors believe that this is a reference to the Trarza salt deposits on the coast of southern Mauritania, which at times of flooding by the River Senegal can appear to be an island.

112 **The voyages of Cadamosto and other documents on Western Africa in the second half of the fifteenth century.**
Gerald Roe Crone.   London: Hakluyt Society, 1937. 154p. 3 maps. bibliog. (Works issued by the Hakluyt Society, 2nd series, no. 80).
Despite its relatively advanced age, this is still an infallible starting-point for the study of the discovery of the islands of Cape Verde. English translations, with annotations by Crone, of the 'Voyages of Cadamosto' (p. 1-84) and the 'Voyages of Diogo Gomes' (p. 91-102) contain what are probably the earliest written notices of the islands of Cape Verde. Crone's forty-five-page introduction helps clarify the otherwise rather confusing evidence on Portuguese activity on the West African coast (1448-90) and his vivid biography of Alvise da Cadamosto and the background to his voyage illustrates the pull of the Portuguese court for the ambitious European men who took part in these voyages. Crone's main area of interest, however, is in adjudicating on the rival claims of Alvise da Cadamosto and Diogo Gomes to having discovered the islands in either 1458 or 1460 respectively. He notes the unsatisfactory nature of the documentation surrounding Diogo Gomes' voyage, which was recorded from an oral statement made several years after the events described. He also notes the challenges which have been made by historians to Cadamosto's claim. Certainly, Cadamosto's account causes some problems. He mentions rivers which do not exist, and impossible wind directions for his chance arrival there. Crone makes a very good defence for him, and sensibly points out that Cadamosto's importance is not in his discovery, but his careful, informative and unsensational narrative.

General

113 **Alguns aspectos da administração pública em Cabo Verde no século XVIII. (Some aspects of public administration in Cape Verde in the 18th century.)**
António Carreira.   *Boletim Cultural da Guiné Portuguesa*, vol. 27, no. 105 (1972), p. 123-203.
Some of the particular problems facing the public authorities during this period were the shortfall in shipping using the islands' port facilities, attacks by pirates, lack of public finance and bad relations with Lisbon, not to mention the involvement of local officials and clergymen in smuggling. Carreira also provides information on the methods of raising revenue. Contemporary documents are reproduced on pages 165-203.

114 **Atlantic Islands: Madeira, the Azores and the Cape Verdes in seventeenth-century commerce and navigation.**
T. Bentley Duncan. Chicago; London: University of Chicago Press, 1972. 291p. 9 maps. bibliog. (Studies in the History of Discoveries).

T. Bentley Duncan outlines in his introductory chapter the thesis of this excellent and highly recommended study – 'that the mid-Atlantic islands, in the days of sailing ships, played an important, an influential, and, in certain areas and times, even an indispensable and vital role in oceanic trade, transport and communications'. The discovery of the islands is summarized in the second chapter. Chapter eight, p. 158-94, 'The Cape Verdes: crossroads of the Atlantic', uses contemporary reports to describe the islands' role and value as a supply station. The development of settlements, the nature of the shipping which used the islands and the types of products supplied are covered. Chapter nine, p. 195-238, 'The slave trade in the Cape Verdes', is an important contribution to the interpretation of the inadequate records of Cape Verde's role as an entrepôt in this traffic. As well as discussing legal and commercial aspects, the acculturation process undergone by enslaved peoples arriving in Santiago is described. His concluding chapter looks briefly at the importance of the islands to 19th-century shipping, and at Cape Verde's potential strategic importance in the 20th century. Four appendices cover geographical data, historical demography, Portuguese weights and measures and Portuguese money. An excellent bibliography is to be found on pages 267-79. Manuscript sources are listed on pages 267-9; general works on pages 270-2 and works on Cape Verde on pages 276-9.

115 **A capitania das ilhas de Cabo Verde: organização civil, eclesiástica e militar, séculos XVI-XIX – subsídios.** (The captaincy of the islands of Cape Verde: civil, ecclesiastical and military organization, 16th–19th centuries – foundations.)
António Carreira. *Revista de História Económica e Social*, no. 19 (Jan.–April 1987), p. 33-76.

With his usual close attention to source material Carreira describes the administrative structure of Cape Verde. State personnel were divided into three categories for budgetary purposes – civil, ecclesiastical and military. In fact, the clergy made up as much as half of the total number. Some of the administrative links between Cape Verde and Guinea-Bissau are discussed.

116 **Cartas das ilhas de Cabo Verde de Valentim Fernandes (1506-1508).** (Valentim Fernandes' maps of the Cape Verde Islands [1506-8].)
A. Fontoura da Costa. Lisbon: Agência Geral das Colónias, 1939. 110p. 8 maps. bibliog.

One of several early descriptions of Cape Verde comes from Fernandes: this volume describes his life and work and reproduces part of the latter. Fernandes (d. 1518/19) was a printer, cartographer and intellectual from Moravia who, like many others, was attracted to Lisbon by the Portuguese expansionary activities. He collected written and oral information on the discoveries: this in turn was collected by Conrado Peutinger (1465-1547) and formed part of the 'Munich Manuscript'. His description of the islands, together with numerous annotations, appears on pages 43-53. It is interesting to note the rapid and successful colonization of the archipelago by goats: almost every island receives the same comment, 'Povoada de cabras e não de gente' (populated by goats and not people). This volume also discusses the developments taking place in the mapping of the islands. Reproductions demonstrate the increasing knowledge, and comparisons are made between Fernandes' maps and those of the present day. The changes in nomenclature of the islands is also noted.

117 **As companhias pombalinas.** (The Pombaline companies.)
António Carreira. Lisbon: Editorial Presença, 1983. 2nd ed. 426p. map. bibliog.

A revised version of the 1969 edition which was published under the title of *As companhias pombalinas de navegação, comércio e tráfico de escravos entre a costa africana e o nordeste brasileiro* (The Pombaline companies of navigation, commerce and the slave traffic between the African coast and northeast Brazil). This second edition takes advantage of further documentary evidence unearthed by Carreira. He first describes the earlier Portuguese companies operating in the area. The Marques de Pombal was concerned to ensure Portuguese control over the colonies and in 1755 the Companhia do Grão-Pará e Maranhão was formed. This maintained a monopoly of Cape Verdean trade as part of its remit to develop the Brazilian regions of Pará and Maranhão by importing slave labour. Cape Verde's limited involvement in this phase of the slave trade is described, as is the trade in *urzela* (a dye-yielding lichen) and *panos* (woven cotton cloths). A similar company, the Companhia Geral de Pernambuco e Paraíba was in existence between 1761 and 1787, but had little connection with Cape Verde. Carreira appends transcripts of several of the relevant documents, including the 'Petição' (petition) of 14 November 1757, in which the company asks for a monopoly of all Cape Verdean commerce, free from any payment of duty. Carreira points out that these are extraordinary rights to be given by a monarch to a private organization.

118 **Conflitos sociais em Cabo Verde no século XVIII.** (Social conflicts in 18th-century Cape Verde.)
António Carreira. *Revista de História Económica e Social*, no. 16 (July-Dec. 1985), p. 63-88.

Against a background of economic decline, weak government, corruption and lawlessness Carreira documents and describes a society of feuding family dynasties who used their slaves to perpetuate internecine violence. His research focuses on three of these murders and the ensuing judicial cases.

119 **Descrição corográfica e estatística das ilhas e capitania de Cabo Verde. Parte 2ª, capítulo 5° da ilha do Maio.** (Geographical and statistical description of the islands and captaincy of Cape Verde. Part two, chapter five, the island of Maio.)
António Marques da Costa Soares, edited by Félix Monteiro. *Raízes*, nos 5-6 (1978), p. 121-41. map.

A previously unpublished report dated 1830, this document gives a contemporary description of Maio. The valuable notes supplied by Monteiro are really an essay on the history of Maio, which achieved a degree of importance for the supply of salt to passing shipping. Monteiro notes many sources for travellers' accounts of the island.

120 **Descrições oitocentistas das ilhas de Cabo Verde.** (Nineteenth-century descriptions of Cape Verde.)
Edited by António Carreira. [Lisbon]: Edição patrocinada pela Presidência da República de Cabo Verde, 1987. 275p.

Carreira provides an introduction, transcription and annotations for eleven documents from the late 18th century to the first thirty years of the 19th century. There are three texts by Aniceto António Ferreira. The first of these is a description of Boa Vista's agricultural, maritime and general economic activity. The other two concern the agriculture and development of the islands in general: one proposal is for the capital to be moved from Santiago to Fogo to better please the European businessmen. Manuel Alexandre de Medina e Vasconcelos is represented by his list of proposals for the regeneration of the islands, which shows just how neglected they had become. Seven of António Pusich's works are included. Pusich (1760-1838) was born in Dalmatia: polymath and polyglot, he was made governor of Cape Verde in 1818 and applied himself to its study. This volume contains, amongst others, his description of the coastline and his comments on the administrative and judicial systems. The majority of these documents are reproduced in facsimile at the back of the volume.

121 **Dissertação sobre as ilhas de Cabo Verde 1818.** (Treatise on the islands of Cape Verde 1818.)
Manuel Roiz Lucas de Senna, edited by António Carreira. [Lisbon]: Edição patrocinada pela Presidência da República de Cabo Verde, 1987. 377p.

A lively and fascinating document of the daily life of the islands in the early 19th century, produced by a Portuguese army officer stationed in Santiago. There is a lengthy section on local products, which includes information on the preparation of indigo dye, the agricultural techniques used and the preparation of certain foods. He also describes the practice of slavery, the state of crafts and technology, weaving, landscape and water resources, local illnesses and their cures, birth, religion, death, women, weddings and churches. Carreira provides introduction, transcription and annotations. A facsimile of the original document is appended (p. 111-377).

122 **Documentos para a história das ilhas de Cabo Verde e 'Rios de Guiné' (Séculos XVII e XVIII).** (Documents for the history of the Cape Verde Islands and the 'Guinea Rivers' [17th and 18th centuries].)
António Carreira. Lisbon: The author, 1983. 306p. 4 maps.

This selection of original documents transcribed and annotated by Carreira contains material on 17th-century trading contracts with the Portuguese crown. There is also José António Pinto's report, p. 141-271, on the political, military and commercial situation in Guinea and Cape Verde, dating from 1793 to 1797. He writes about agriculture, the military garrison, weaving, smuggling, livestock and *purgueira*. The text is also reproduced in facsimile.

123 **The English in the Atlantic Islands c. 1450-1650.**
Geoffrey Vaughan Scammell. *Mariner's Mirror*, vol. 72, no. 3 (Aug. 1986), p. 295-317. bibliog.

English adventurers and traders realized the importance for both commerce and plunder of the Iberian-controlled Atlantic islands. Cape Verde was the least favoured of the archipelagos because of its insalubrious climate. Nevertheless, the English exported Cape Verdean horses to Barbados and sent iron bars to Cape Verde for use in the purchase of slaves.

124 **Ensaio e memórias económicas sobre as ilhas de Cabo Verde (século XVIII).** (Essay and economic memoirs on the Cape Verde Islands [18th century].)
João da Silva Feijó, edited by António Carreira. Praia: Instituto Caboverdiano do Livro, 1986. 83p. (Estudos e Ensaios).

Feijó (1760-1824) was a military instructor and geographer born in Rio de Janeiro. This collection of works was first published in 1797, and is reprinted here with Carreira's scholarly annotations. There are three essays which could be broadly described as political studies, one of which Carreira suspects has been plagiarized by António Pusich. He includes both versions. The remaining essays are on *urzela*, a dye-yielding lichen, and on the production of indigo dye on Santo Antão. These were clearly important contemporary economic ventures.

125 **The first imperial age: European overseas expansion c. 1400-1715.**
Geoffrey Vaughan Scammell. London: Unwin Hyman, 1989. 281p. 6 maps. bibliog.

In this thematic rather than chronological approach to the period, Scammell addresses such issues as the motives for expansion, the reasons for the varying degrees of success, the methods of exploitation and the creation of new types of societies. Although Cape Verde is mentioned on barely a dozen occasions the themes of this work are pertinent and the broad perspective extremely useful. The suggestions for further reading (p. 257-61) are also very helpful.

126 **A Guiné e as ilhas de Cabo Verde: a sua unidade histórica e populacional.** (Guinea and the Cape Verde Islands: their historical and populational unity.)
António Carreira. *Ultramar*, vol. 8, no. 32 (1968), p. 70–98.

The focus of this article is on the links which were forged between the two countries by the slave trade. From unspecified source material, Carreira enumerates the ethnic groups which were brought to Cape Verde, and gives a brief description of their history in Guinea-Bissau.

127 **História da Guiné e ilhas de Cabo Verde.** (The history of Guinea and the Cape Verde Islands.)
PAIGC. Porto, Portugal: Edições Afrontamento, 1974. 182p. 17 maps.

Probably more relevant to Guinea-Bissau than Cape Verde, but nevertheless interesting from the point of view of anti-colonial historiography.

128 **História geral de Cabo Verde. Corpo documental. Volume 1.** (A general history of Cape Verde. Documentary body. Volume 1.) Introduction by Luís de Albuquerque, Instituto de Investigação Científica Tropical and Direcção-Geral do Património Cultural de Cabo Verde. Lisbon: Imprensa Nacional. 1988. 323p.

The Centro de Estudos de História e Cartografia Antiga (the Centre for the Study of Early History and Cartography) within the Instituto de Investigação Científica Tropical (the Institute for Tropical Scientific Research) and the Direcção-Geral do Património Cultural de Cabo Verde (the Directorate for Cape Verdean Cultural Heritage) are preparing a history of Cape Verde. Prior to its publication they have decided to publish the documentary evidence which will be supporting the work. This volume contains documents from the 15th century to the early 16th century, all of which relate directly to Cape Verde. Of human interest are the many reports of the cases of offenders exiled to the islands. Some have already been published, while others are previously unpublished material from the archives of the Centro de Estudos de História e Cartografia Antiga. They have been transcribed and appear with full cataloguing details. An index will appear in a later volume.

129 **Historical dictionary of the Republic of Cape Verde.** Richard Lobban, Marilyn Halter. Metuchen, New Jersey; London: Scarecrow Press, 1988. 2nd ed. 171p. map. bibliog. (African Historical Dictionaries, no. 42).

This is the useful and comprehensive 'basic reference tool' which it sets out to be. Subject entries, arranged in alphabetical order, cover the period 4000 BC to 1987. A point is made of including references to the African peoples whose descendants contribute to the present population of Cape Verde, an aspect of Cape Verdean history which is often overlooked. The second edition is an updated and expanded version of the relevant entries in the *Historical dictionary of the Republics of Guinea-Bissau and Cape Verde*, published in 1979 (African Historical Dictionaries, No. 22). There is an introductory essay and chronology of key-dates. The excellent forty-five-page bibliography is orientated toward more recent works in English and includes a section on Cape Verdeans in America.

130 **A history of the Upper Guinea Coast, 1545 to 1800.** Walter Rodney. New York, London: Monthly Review Press, 1980. 283p. 5 maps. bibliog.

Although using mainly European source material, this excellent history of the area between The Gambia and Cape Mount, Sierra Leone seeks to portray European activity in the region only in relation to its impact on African peoples. The chapter 'Portuguese activity (1550-1600)', p. 71-94, covers the settlement of Cape Verde and the role of Cape Verdeans in trading activity on the mainland. Subsequent chapters cover relevant aspects of European commerce.

131 **As insolências do Capitão Domingos Rodrigues Viegas e do seu irmão Belchior Monteiro de Queiroz contra as autoridades da ilha de Santiago (1653-1665).** (Insults committed against the authorities of the island of Santiago by Captain Domingos Rodrigues Viegas and his brother Belchior Monteiro de Queiroz [1653-65].)
Daniel A. Pereira. *Revista de História Económica e Social*, no. 16 (July-Dec. 1985), p. 31-61.
According to received wisdom and Senna Barcelos's *Subsídios para a história da Cabo Verde e Guiné* (q.v.), these two brothers were the *mestiço* (mixed race) leaders of a robber band of as many as 200 black slaves and white criminals. Pereira looks again at legal documents and the social and racial history of this period to give a less swashbuckling account of events. His analysis concludes that the brothers were wealthy and powerful men, acting on the margins of the law and with no respect for any authority other than their own. Slave-owning societies are subject to this kind of abuse.

132 **Portuguese attempts at monopoly on the Upper Guinea Coast, 1580-1650.**
Walter Rodney. *Journal of African History*, vol. 6, no. 3 (1965), p. 307-22.
The crowns of Spain and Portugal were united between 1580 and 1640, during which time the Portuguese were heavily involved in exporting slaves from the Upper Guinea coast to the Spanish West Indies. Cape Verde was the hub of the Portuguese administration of this trade and Rodney provides interesting information on the islands' role. All ships loading slaves were supposed to pay dues at Santiago and it was a source of discord that the Spanish often avoided this tax.

133 **A primeira visita de um governador das ilhas de Cabo Verde à Guiné (António Velho Tinoco c. 1575).** (The first visit by a governor of the Cape Verde Islands to Guinea [António Velho Tinoco c. 1575].)
A. Teixeira da Mota. Lisbon: Junta de Investigações do Ultramar, 1968. 15p. (Agrupamento do Estudos de Cartografia Antiga, no. 23).
Although mostly concerning the mainland, this study shows how Cape Verde functioned as a defensive base, dispatching naval resources for the Portuguese in the Upper Guinea region. It also refers to Tinoco's plan to bring Jesuits to Cape Verde and from there to carry out evangelical work in the Guinea region.

134 **Regimento que deve observar o feitor da ilha de São Vicente, Vicente das Neves Caio (1752).** (Compulsory instructions for the administrator of São Vicente, Vicente das Neves Caio [1752].)
Daniel A. Pereira. *Revista de História Económica e Social*, no. 17 (Jan.-June 1986), p. 89-101.
A summary of some of the events of the very early stages of the settlement of São Vicente. Before any permanent settlers arrived people from Santo Antão, São Nicolau and Boa Vista kept goats and donkeys on the island: eradicating this practice was a priority of the first settlement projects. In the 1740s Francisco de Lima e Mello transported forced labour to the island to gather *urzela* (a dye-yielding lichen). He also avoided paying taxes, hence the *regimento*, transcribed here by Pereira, was given to Caio to try to ensure that the crown received all the profit it should from the development of São Vicente. Incidentally. Pereira adds that one of his aims in

publishing this article is to counter the received opinion that the Arquivo Histórico de Cabo Verde (Historical Archive of Cape Verde) is in an unworkable state, but rather that it is a potentially rich source of material.

135 **Secas e fomes em Cabo Verde (achegas para o estudo das de 1845-1846 e de 1889-1890).** (Droughts and famines in Cape Verde [supplementary material for the study of those of 1845-46 and 1889-90].)
António Carreira. *Revista de História Económica e Social*, no. 15 (Jan.-June 1985), p. 135-50.

Carreira publishes two documents which he considers to be of importance. The first (p. 138-40) is 'Ofício no. 109', an official letter sent by the Junta Geral de Fazenda (General Council of the Treasury) to the Ministério da Marinha e Ultramar (the Naval and Overseas Ministry) on 18 March 1846. It describes the terrible crisis which was afflicting the islands. The second (p. 141-50) is the 'Relatório do inspector das obrás públicas' (report of the inspector of public works) dated 26 July 1890, written by Claudino Augusto Carneiro de Sousa e Faro. It gives the amounts which had been spent on public works during the crisis, and proposes a rationalization of the service together with a programme of reafforestation and water conservation measures. Sadly, but unsurprisingly, these proposals appear not to have been acted upon.

136 **Sir Francis Drake's West Indian voyage 1585-86.**
Edited by Mary Frear Keeler. London: Hakluyt Society, 1981. 358p. 4 maps. bibliog. (Works issued by the Hakluyt Society, 2nd series, no. 148).

Drake, for the English, is a national hero: to other nations he was a pirate. All three of his encounters with Cape Verde, in 1566, 1577 and 1585, involved piracy or plunder. Most spectacular was his interlude on Santiago between 17 and 29 November 1585 on his way to the West Indies. He arrived at the then capital Ribeira Grande, and a textbook attack involving 1,000 soldiers was launched. The city had, however, been abandoned by all but a few invalids and old women, and the only plunder was food, wine, cannon and church bells. Information, possibly obtained by torture, led him to São Domingos a dozen miles away, where it was thought the governor and bishop might be hiding. It too was deserted, and so was set on fire, as were Praia and Ribeira Grande. The island's revenge came a week after the English left: 300 men died of fever. This volume contains four lively contemporary records of the events: included are accounts of some disciplinary problems and the execution of a ship's steward for buggery. Keeler supplies helpful annotations and three contemporary sketches of Ribeira Grande which show the position of buildings, ships and troops. See Richard Hakluyt's *Voyages and discoveries*, edited by Jack Beeching (Harmondsworth, England: Penguin, 1972. 443p.) for a description of Maio when Drake called there in 1577 on his circumnavigation of the globe. On this occasion they boarded a Portuguese ship and stole sherry and madeira. See also G. M. Thompson's *Sir Francis Drake* (London: Futura, 1976. 358p.).

137 **Subsídios para a historia de Cabo Verde e Guiné.** (Contributions towards the history of Cape Verde and Guinea.)
Christiano José de Senna Barcellos. *Historia e Memorias da Academia Real das Sciencias de Lisboa. Nova Serie 2ª Classe Sciencias Moraes e Politicas, e Bellas Lettras*, vol. 8, part 2, no. 54 (1900); vol. 9, part 1, no. 55 (1902); vol. 10, part 2, no. 58 (1906); vol. 12, part 1, no. 61 (1910); vol. 13 (1913).

The seven sections of this masterly work keep to a strict chronological arrangement: the first part covers 1460-1640 (246p.); part two, 1640-1750 (305p.); part three, 1750-1833 (403p.); part four, 1833-42 (316p.); part five, 1843-53 (281p.); part six, 1853-61 together with a fairly detailed summary of events up to the time of writing (305p.); part seven (103p.) is a collection of indexes, one by subject and one by name for each of the six sections. It is easy to see why Barcellos is so admired by António Carreira: they both share the same respect for primary sources. Despite the relative age of this work, it is still worth consulting for its scholarship with regard to the use and discussion of sources, and its sheer size, scope and volume of 'facts'. Despite these laudable aspects it is a remarkably readable work. The author covers economic and social issues as well as administrative matters, and is not adverse from the inclusion of entertaining anecdotes. Some facsimile plans of buildings and settlements are also to be found, including a street plan of Mindelo from 1858 on which only eighteen buildings are marked.

138 **Subsídios para o estudo dos 'lançados' na Guiné.** (Contributions towards the study of the *lançados* in Guinea.)
Maria da Graça Garcia Nolasco da Silva. *Boletim Cultural da Guiné Portuguesa*, vol. 25, no. 97 (Jan. 1970), p. 25-40; vol. 25, no. 98 (April 1970), p. 217-32; vol. 25, no. 99 (July 1970), p. 397-420; vol. 25, no. 100 (Oct. 1970), p. 513-60.

The *lançados* were traders of European descent who operated more or less illegally in the Upper Guinea region. This well-documented study of early commercial history is obviously mainly concerned with events in Guinea, but it also touches upon an aspect of 15th- and 16th-century Cape Verdean history. Many of the *lançados* were from Cape Verde, and inasmuch as the Portuguese could be said to administer Guinea then, it was administered from Cape Verde.

139 **Tratado breve dos rios de Guiné do Cabo-Verde.** (Brief treatise on the rivers of the Guinea of Cape Verde.)
André Alvares d'Almada. Porto, Portugal: Diogo Köpke, 1841. 108p. map.

Captain Alvares d'Almada, from Santiago, wrote this account of the peoples of the Upper Guinea coast in 1594. He travelled from the River Senegal to Sierra Leone, in the trading zone open to the inhabitants of Santiago. This work can be seen as a guide for traders, and incidentally gives evidence of Cape Verdean activity on the mainland. In the area around the Cap Vert peninsula (Senegal) trading links between Cape Verde and the Wolof kingdom of Budumel are noted. Also noted is the presence of *lançados* in the area of São Domingos (Guinea-Bissau). Some of the problems faced by the bishop of Cape Verde in dealing with this area are illustrated. Further south, trade in salt and slaves takes place.

140 **West Africa: quest for God and gold 1454-1578.**
John W. Blake. London: Curzon; Totowa, New Jersey: Rowman &
Littlefield, 1977. 2nd ed. 246p. bibliog.
First published under the title *European beginnings in West Africa 1454-1578* in 1937,
Blake has made several revisions. It remains an impressive study of Portuguese activity
in the region and the attempts by Spain, France and England to rival her commercial
monopoly. Cape Verde's importance to European commerce during this period is
striking. Inhabitants of Santiago were granted special privileges in Upper Guinea
which enabled them to dominate trade in the area. The islands' wealth – or, more
specifically, that of the shipping passing through them – led to numerous pirate attacks
by Spanish, French, Dutch and English. The Portuguese fortified the lively city of
Ribeira Grande. The French may have been the worst: on occasion they entered
harbours, laid waste to the ships already there, then just lay in wait for the next ones to
arrive. This volume gives a clear picture of the commercial and political forces which
were changing West Africa, and creating a nation in the islands of Cape Verde.
Another work covering this period, although giving less of an overall perspective, is
Foundations of the Portuguese empire by Bailey W. Diffie and George D. Winius (St.
Paul, Minnesota: University of Minnesota Press, 1977. 533p. bibliog.).

141 **Yankee traders, old coasters & African middlemen.**
George E. Brooks. [Boston, Massachusetts]: Boston University Press,
1970. 370p. 3 maps. bibliog. (African Research Studies, no. 11).
Excluding the slave trade, this is a history of the rise and fall of American 'legitimate'
trade with West Africa in the 19th century, in which Cape Verde played a minor role.
Americans participated in the trade of salt with the mainland, for limes from The
Gambia for example. Big profits could be made during times of famine. For several
years from 1818 Samuel Hodges, in partnership with the powerful Cape Verdean
commercial figure Manuel António Martins, used the islands as an entrepôt for
smuggling operations. By the end of the century Europeans had effectively ousted the
Americans from the region's trade, and many of their ships had been taken over by
Cape Verdean seamen.

**Ilhas de Cabo Verde: origem do povo caboverdiano e da diocese de Santiago
de Cabo Verde.**
See item no. 199.

**Jesuit documents on the Guinea of Cape Verde and the Cape Verde Islands
1585-1617 in English translation.**
See item no. 200.

Monumenta missionaria africana. África ocidental.
See item no. 201.

Slavery

142 **The Atlantic slave trade: a census.**
Philip D. Curtin. Madison, Wisconsin: University of Wisconsin Press,
1969. 338p. 25 maps. bibliog.

The aim of this exceptional work of scholarship is to bring together information from
many and disparate sources so as to measure the massive forced movement of peoples
in the Atlantic region. Although the book's value is in looking at the trade as a whole,
Cape Verde is referred to.

143 **Cabo Verde: formação e extinção de uma sociedade escravocrata (1460-
1878).** (Cape Verde: formation and extinction of a society based on
slavery [1460-1878].)
António Carreira. [Praia]: Instituto Caboverdiano do Livro, 1983.
2nd ed. 549p. map. bibliog.

With his accustomed close reference to source material, Carreira studies several
aspects of Cape Verdean life during these four centuries of slavery. He covers the early
land donations and contracts with the Portuguese crown and the early social groups of
the *lançados* (Cape Verdeans traders in Upper Guinea of European descent),
tangomaus ('latinized' Africans who often worked with the *lançados*), converted Jews
and nobles. He then discusses the earlier phases of the slave trade, including the means
used by Europeans and Africans to obtain slaves, the prices of slaves and the goods
used in the trade. He then moves on to the evolution of the system of commerce. Also
covered are sociological aspects of the effects of slavery on Cape Verde, including the
treatment of slaves; 'latinization' (which implies baptism and the acquisition of
Portuguese behaviour and language); pirate attacks and the consequent flight of slaves
into the interior; and the social system prior to abolition. Abolition itself is covered in
discussion of the treaties signed between Portugal and Great Britain, and the
consequent rise in illegal trafficking in Cape Verde. At the same time, slavery as an
institution was disappearing from the islands. A census of slaves taken in 1856 is given
close attention. Seventeen documents are appended. Amongst the most interesting of
these are those concerning a slave revolt in 1835, and the freeing of slaves by writs or
wills.

144 **Notas sobre a tráfico português de escravos.** (Notes on the Portuguese
slave trade.)
António Carreira. Lisbon: Universidade Nova de Lisboa, 1983. 2nd
ed. 108p. map. bibliog.

A summary of the trade and the institution of slavery in West Africa and Brazil, which
includes Cape Verde within its remit. The role of Cape Verdean traders and the
lançados (backwoods traders in Guinea of Cape Verdean origin) is noted, as is the
importance of trade goods such as dyes and cloths from the islands. The cruelties of
slave-owners are revealed: examples come from Cape Verde as well as Brazil and
Angola. Carreira provides a useful glossary of Portuguese terminology associated with
slavery and the slave trade.

145 **O tráfico clandestino de escravos na Guiné e em Cabo Verde no século XIX.** (The clandestine traffic in slaves in Guinea and Cape Verde in the 19th century.)
António Carreira. *Raízes*, nos 5-6 (1978), p. 3-34.
Carreira discusses the effects on Cape Verdean businessmen of the treaty of 1815 which abolished the slave trade north of the Equator. This had been forced on other European nations by the British after the Congress of Vienna. In 1836 the trade was banned in all parts of the Portuguese empire. However there seems to have been a small, but much abused, loophole allowing limited movements between Cape Verde and Guinea-Bissau. Carreira's information comes in part from the Boa Vista seat of the Portuguese and British Mixed Commission which was set up in 1842 to monitor adhesion to the abolition of the trade. The Spanish appear to have been particularly active in smuggling.

Portuguese attempts at monopoly on the Upper Guinea Coast, 1580–1650.
See item no. 132.

Towns

146 **Um aspecto original no processo de urbanização da cidade de S. Filipe.** (A novel aspect of the urbanization process in the town of São Filipe.)
António Jorge Delgado. *Magma*, vol. 1, no. 1 (April 1988), p. 4-8.
The development of the towns of Ribeira Grande (Santo Antão), Mindelo and Praia are described. Despite differences, all three contain a recognizable central zone. São Filipe (Fogo) however has followed a different path. An early schism in the ruling class, the author suggests, led to the polarization of the town. It is separated into Bila Baxo and Bila Riba: residents strongly identify with their particular zone in this town of 7,000 inhabitants.

147 **Marcos cronológicos da Cidade Velha.** (Chronological landmarks for Cidade Velha.)
Daniel A. Pereira. Praia: Instituto Caboverdiano do Livro, 1988.
151p. (Estudos e Ensaios).
Extracts from documentary material, maps, plans and photographs of the present-day ruins are used to give a strictly chronological guide (1456-1884) to the rise and fall of the first 'tropical' city of the Portuguese empire. Originally Ribeira Grande was the capital of the islands but it was the victim of repeated attack by pirates and was virtually abandoned. It is now known as Cidade Velha ('the old city') and contains impressive ruins of forts and churches. This volume is not very readable, but contains much useful information about source material.

148 **Novos subsídios para a história da fundação de Mindelo (Cabo Verde).**
(New material for a history of the foundation of Mindelo [Cape
Verde].)
José de Oliveira Boléo.   *Garcia de Orta*, vol. 1, no. 2 (1953), p. 229-
42.

In 1835 Queen Maria II had ordered Mindelo to become the new capital of the islands.
Material from the Arquivo Histórico do Ultramar (Overseas Historical Archive) is
reproduced, including some of the instructions and decrees sent by the Visconde Sá da
Bandeira relating to the town's construction and population. The author gives some of
the background to the political upheavals then taking place in Cape Verde and
Portugal. An administrator's report made in 1882, 'A ilha de São Vicente de Cabo
Verde, relatório de Joaquim Vieira Botelho da Costa' (São Vicente Island, Cape
Verde, report of Joaquim Vieira Botelho da Costa) is published, with extensive notes
by Félix Monteiro, in *Raízes*, nos 7-16 (July 1978–Dec. 1980), p. 127-213. This covers
life on the island – which is dominated by Mindelo – in great detail, even to the
number of bars, and gives an indication of the rapid growth of the town.

149 **'Vilas' et 'cidades': bourgs et villes en Afrique lusophone.** ('Vilas' and
'cidades': towns and cities in Portuguese-speaking Africa.)
Organization by Michel Cahen, preface by Catherine Coquery-
Vidrovitch.   Paris: Éditions l'Harmattan, 1989. 299p. 15 maps.
bibliogs.

This multi-authored volume contains two contributions to the study of Cape Verde's
towns and cities. Elisa Silva Andrade's 'La formation des villes au Cap-Vert' (The
formation of Cape Verde's cities), p. 23-41, looks at Ribeira Grande (Santiago), Praia
and Mindelo. She concludes that Praia never matched Ribeira Grande's splendour,
and that although Praia and Mindelo show many of the features of the 18th- and 19th-
century European city, they also demonstrate aspects of the underdeveloped colonial
country. João Estêvão contributes 'Peuplement et phénomènes d'urbanisation au Cap-
Vert pendant la période coloniale, 1462-1940' (Settlement and features of urbanization
in Cape Verde during the colonial period, 1462-1940), p. 42-59. This gives a
chronology for the settlement of the inhabited islands, and a brief history of urban
formation with particular reference to Ribeira Grande and Mindelo. Both chapters
provide bibliographies.

Liberation movements and decolonization

150 **The African liberation reader.**
Edited by Aquino de Bragança, Immanuel Wallerstein.   London: Zed
Press, 1982. 3 vols.

Selected articles, speeches and other ephemeral materials from African nationalist
movements, assembled by the editors in 1974, are published in English. Probably best
used in parallel with the more specific *Emerging nationalism in Portuguese Africa:
documents* (see item no. 153).

151 **Declaração do Conselho Superior da Luta.** (Declaration of the Supreme Council of the Struggle.)
PAIGC. Bissau: Imprensa Nacional da Guiné-Bissau, 1975. 11p.
A declaration made on 25 June 1975 calling upon the community of nations to recognize the coming independence of Cape Verde (5 July 1975) and to provide material aid. The aim of unity with Guinea-Bissau is emphasized.

152 **Developments in Angola, Cape Verde and São Tomé and Príncipe.**
Decolonization, vol. 2, no. 4 (March 1975), p. 32-7.
The text of the 18 December 1974 agreement between the Portuguese government and the PAIGC is reproduced. This provided for a transitional government of five members, three appointed by the PAIGC, two appointed by the Portuguese government, under a High Commissioner also appointed by the Portuguese government. Elections would be held on 30 June 1975 for a Constituent Assembly. *Decolonization* is produced by the United Nations Department of Political Affairs, Trusteeship and Decolonization.

153 **Emerging nationalism in Portuguese Africa: a bibliography of documentary ephemera through 1965.**
Ronald H. Chilcote. Stanford, California: Hoover Institution on War, Revolution and Peace, 1969. 114p. (Hoover Institution Bibliographical Series, no. 39).
Covers material issued by the Portuguese African nationalist movements and their militants collected between 1959 and 1965 and stored on microfilm at the Hoover Institution library. Portuguese Africa in general can be found on pages 1-9: the most important of the organizations concerned is probably CONCP, the Conferência das Organizações Nacionalistas das Colónias Portuguesas (Conference of the Nationalist Organizations of the Portuguese Colonies). 'Portuguese Guiné, Cape Verde, São Tomé and Príncipe' (p. 64-80) is a good source for material on Amílcar Cabral and the PAIGC. UN material can be found on pages 93-110. A complementary volume is Chilcote's *Emerging nationalism in Portuguese Africa: documents* (Stanford, California: Hoover Institution Press, 1972. 646p.). This contains English translations of some of the documents mentioned in the bibliography and an introduction. Although there is little that is specific to Cape Verde, the chapter 'African nationalism in Portuguese Guiné, São Tomé and Príncipe and the Cape Verde Archipelago', p. 297-381, contains several of Cabral's works. See also 'Cabo Verde is African too', 1960, p. 312-15: Henri Labéry of the Frente pela Libertação da Guiné Portuguesa e Cabo Verde (Front for the Liberation of Portuguese Guinea and Cape Verde) – says the Cape Verdean 'must disregard the European blood running in his veins'.

154 **Liberation movements in Lusophone Africa: serials from the collection of Immanuel Wallerstein.**
Chicago: Center for Research Libraries, Cooperative African Microforms Project, 1976, 1977. microfilm. 3 reels.
The struggle in Africa for independence from Portugal produced a number of serials and ephemeral materials. This microfilm collection is probably the most convenient way to approach the material. Reel one covers Angola. Reel two covers Mozambique and Guinea-Bissau. Material relevant to Cape Verde can be found in several of the serials. *PAIGC Actualités* (PAIGC News), although mainly concerned with reporting the war in Guinea-Bissau, often contains news items from Cape Verde. There are reports of famine, strikes and the work of nationalists there. *PAIGC Actualités* was

published monthly in French by the PAIGC in Conakry from 1969 to 1974. A quarterly edition appeared in English from 1971. The microfilm holds the French issues from no. 1 (Jan. 1969) to no. 49 (Jan. 1973) and the English issues from nos 27-9 (March-May 1971) to nos 30-3 (June-Sept. 1971). The microfilm also contains some relevant PAIGC communiqués. Similar items are published in the PAIGC's *Libertação: Unidade e Luta* (Liberation: Unity and Struggle) ([Conakry?]: irreg.), which the microfilm holds for July 1962 to August 1965. Reel three covers 'General Lusophone Africa'. Of relevance, albeit minor, is *Bulletin d'Informations* (News Bulletin), published in French in Rabat, Morocco from 1961. The microfilm holds up to no. 6 (May 1962). *Guerrilheiro*, published in London bi-monthly in English by the Committee for Freedom in Mozambique, Angola and Guiné from 1970 [to 1975?] is held on this reel from no. 3 (Jan.-Feb. 1971) to no. 23 (Jan.-March 1975).

155 **No fist is big enough to hide the sky: the liberation of Guinea-Bissau and Cape Verde.**
Basil Davidson, preface by Aristides Pereira. London: Zed Press, 1981. 187p. map. bibliog.

This is a considerably expanded version of Davidson's book *The liberation of Guiné* (Harmondsworth, England: Penguin, 1969). In addition to the earlier work's lively journalistic account of the PAIGC's armed struggle in Guinea-Bissau, this volume contains four new chapters to bring the chronicle of events up to date. There is also a new preface by Aristides Pereira. The new chapters contain information on the decolonization process in Cape Verde, much of which can be found in Davidson's more recent work, *The Fortunate Isles* (q.v.). However, these accounts of the war in Guinea-Bissau are of interest, since many Cape Verdeans participated. Conversely, they also emphasize the different experiences of the two nations: the contemporary account in *The liberation of Guiné* strikes the reader for the very absence of Cape Verde from these events.

156 **Programa do partido.** (The party programme.)
[PAIGC]. Bissau: Edições PAIGC, 1979. 11p.

A document produced before independence which refers closely to the history of Cape Verde and Guinea-Bissau for its theoretical foundations. Emphasis is laid on the unity of the two peoples, and on the unification of the two nations after independence. Details will be established by legitimate representatives of the people.

157 **Sobre a situação em Cabo-Verde.** (On the situation in Cape Verde.)
PAIGC. Lisbon: Livraria Sá da Costa, 1974. 52p. (Cadernos Livres, no. 3).

Abílio Duarte presented this report to the UN Decolonization Committee at its 970th session on 29 April 1974. It is an argument for Cape Verdean independence, and should be seen in the light of Portuguese attempts to treat Cape Verde differently from the other African colonies. Portuguese administrative control is described as government imposed from outside the islands. The achievements and international respectability of the PAIGC are outlined: in contrast, the Portuguese government is criticized for defying the 1960 UN resolution on decolonization, and for allowing famine in Cape Verde, mismanaging the economy and using the islands as a military base. They are also accused of inciting emigration: conditions for emigrants in São Tomé and Príncipe and Lisbon are described. The declaration of independence in Guinea-Bissau on 24 September 1973 is considered relevant to Cape Verde as the constitution links itself to Cape Verde's struggle for independence. Duarte's final point is that the PAIGC are willing to negotiate with Portugal, but are equally willing to fight for independence.

The Fortunate Isles: a study in African transformation.
See item no. 231.

Manual político do PAIGC.
See item no. 236.

Independência.
See item no. 454.

Works on Amílcar Cabral

158 **Amílcar Cabral.**
Aquino de Bragança.   Lisbon: Iniciativas Editoriais, 1976. 34p.
(Pontas de Vista, no. 31).
Amílcar Cabral (1924-73) was the founder and leader of the PAIGC. Pragmatic in his approach to the armed struggle for the liberation of Guinea-Bissau and Cape Verde, he was also a political thinker of great originality. The first half of this work by de Bragança. a journalist and friend of Cabral, is a summary of the Cabral's political views and tactics in the liberation of Guinea-Bissau. The second half is a dramatic account of the events of 20 January 1973, the day of Cabral's assasination. The text is in Portuguese. Another work by a companion of Cabral is the memoirs of his brother Luís Cabral, *Crónica da libertação* (Chronicle of liberation) (Lisbon: Edições *O Jornal*, 1984. 464p.). This is a record of both Cabral and the independence struggle in Guinea-Bissau.

159 **Amílcar Cabral: a bio-bibliography of his life and thought, 1925-1973.**
Ronald H. Chilcote.   *Africana Journal*, vol. 5, no. 4 (Winter 1974), p. 289-307.
Intended to be comprehensive, this is a valuable bibliographical resource. Works by Cabral are covered in three sections: books, monographs and pamphlets; articles; ephemera. Studies of Cabral and his work are divided between books and articles. The many petitions and statements which Cabral presented to the UN are listed in French rather than English and may appear under the heading 'PAIGC'.

160 **Amílcar Cabral: essai de biographie politique.** (Amílcar Cabral: an essay of political biography.)
Mário de Andrade.   Paris: François Maspero, 1980. 167p. (Petite Collection Maspero).
As its title suggests this is very much a political study, tracing the development of Cabral's political thinking.

161 **Amílcar Cabral: revolutionary leadership and people's war.**
Patrick Chabal. Cambridge, England: Cambridge University Press,
1983. 272p. 4 maps. bibliog. (African Studies Series no. 37).
Chabal has produced the first full biography of Cabral, together with a history of the
modern nationalist movement of Guinea-Bissau. He has had remarkable access to
private papers and involved individuals and this must be the most reliable and coherent
work on the subject. Cabral was born in Guinea-Bissau of Cape Verdean parents,
settling in Cape Verde at the age of ten. The PAIGC policy of unity between the two
countries was Cabral's own and Chabal devotes some thought to its origins and
problems. The two countries were not viewed homogeneously by the Portuguese and
propaganda was used to try to create tension within the PAIGC on this issue. Chabal
suggests however that this was not a cause of the 1973 coup attempt which killed
Cabral, nor the November 1980 coup in Guinea-Bissau. He points out how
uncompromising the PAIGC were on this issue when, after the April 1974 revolution
in Portugal, General Spínola tried to negotiate a separate status for Cape Verde within
a Portuguese constitution along the lines of that of the Azores or Madeira. Despite the
separation of Cape Verde and Guinea-Bissau after the November 1980 coup Cabral's
thought informs the present-day PAICV. This study is therefore an invaluable aid to
understanding contemporary government in Cape Verde. Chabal's highly regarded
bibliography is on pages 240-69. Primary sources are divided into Cabral's agricultural
works, his political works, PAIGC documents, official documents from the republics of
Cape Verde and Guinea-Bissau, other documents, interviews, and newspapers and
periodicals.

162 **Continuar Cabral: simpósio internacional Amílcar Cabral, Cabo Verde
17 a 20 de Janeiro de 1983.** (Continuing Cabral: an international
conference on Amílcar Cabral, Cape Verde, 17-20 January 1983.)
[PAICV]. [Praia]: Grafédito; Prelo-Estampa, 1984. 705p.
These are the collected papers from this major conference on the political thought and
legacy of Amílcar Cabral. The contributions – in Portuguese, French, English or
Spanish – are gathered together in five sections. The first, on the figure of Cabral in the
context of his time, contains works by Leopold Sédar Senghor, O.V. Martichyne, Basil
Davidson and Ário Lobo de Azevedo. The second, on Cabral's revolutionary theory,
has works by Jean Suret-Canale, Ronald Chilcote, José Medeiros Ferreira and
Nzongola-Ntalaja. The third, the cultural dimension in Cabral's work, has papers by
Dulce Duarte, Manuel Alegre, François Houtart, Geneviève Lemercinier, Marcela
Glisenti and the Cuban Centre for African and Middle Eastern Studies. The fourth,
Cabral's revolutionary practice, has works by Luís Moita, Bernard Magubane, Sérgio
Ribeiro, Mohamed T. Diawara, V.G. Solodovnikov, Babakar Sine, Olívio Pires and
Gérard Chaliand. The fifth section, the universality of Cabral's theory, has works by
Yves Benot, Immanuel Wallerstein, Paulette Pierson-Mathy, Lucio Luzzatto, Imre
Marton, Sylvia Hill, Bosgra Sietse and Jean Ziegler. Similar versions of the papers by
Chilcote, Davidson, Nzongola-Ntalaja, Duarte (English version), Hill and Benot
(English version) can be found in 'Unity and struggle: reassessing the thought of
Amílcar Cabral', a special issue of *Latin American Perspectives*, issue 41, vol. 11, no. 2
(Spring 1984), p. 3-96.

163 **Unity and struggle.**
Amílcar Cabral, translated by Michael Wolfers, introductions by Basil
Davidson, Mário de Andrade. London: Heinemann Educational
Books, 1980. 298p. (African Writers Series).
A good selection of Cabral's most important speeches and writings, chosen by the
PAIGC. Mário de Andrade contributes a biographical note, p. xviii-xxxv. Divided into
two sections, 'The weapon of theory' and 'Revolutionary practice', the texts reflect
both Cabral's political thought and revolutionary pragmatism. Although there is little
in this collection specific to Cape Verde, the 'New Year's message' (January 1973), p.
288-98, comments on the first clashes between troops and Cape Verdeans in Praia in
September 1972, and urges the improvement of the islands' clandestine organization.
An overlapping collection of texts in English is *Return to the source: selected speeches
of Amílcar Cabral*, edited by the Africa Information Service (New York; London:
Monthly Review Press, 1973. 110p. bibliog.).

Em defesa da terra.
See item no. 30.
Emergência da poesia em Amílcar Cabral: 30 poemas.
See item no. 398.

56

Population

164 **Aspectos demográficos do arquipélago de Cabo Verde.** (Demographic aspects of the archipelago of Cape Verde.)
António A. Mendes Corrêa. *Garcia de Orta*, vol. 1, no. 1 (1953), p. 3-15.
A survey of the 20th-century demographic trends, inclusive of the results of the 1950 census. Corrêa gives much attention to the unusual sex distribution of births: in Portugal the male to female ratio is 106:100; in Cape Verde it is 101:100.

165 **Demografia caboverdeana.** (Cape Verdean demography.)
António Carreira. [Praia]: Instituto Caboverdiano do Livro, 1985. 56p. map. bibliog.
A clear and concise study which deals with statistics from 1807 to 1983. Carreira points out that population statistics for Cape Verde are surprisingly good. From the 17th century onwards, church records for births and deaths are reliable indicators and from the beginning of the 19th century populational censuses were taken. This volume provides tables and interpretation for six demographic features. First there are population totals for 1807 to 1980: these show a trend for growth, but one which is markedly affected during periods of drought. Secondly, there is the average population by island for 1807 to 1980: this also gives the percentage of total Cape Verdean population of each island, showing the rising importance of Santiago, São Vicente and Sal. Births and deaths, by sex, from 1860 to 1983 are given: during the famine period of 1940 to 1949 90,354 deaths are recorded and Carreira believes the total may be higher, given that the overwhelming number of deaths precluded official burials. Next, birth and death rates are calculated for 1860 to 1983: the 1980 growth rate was 2.4 per cent, and would no doubt be higher still were it not for emigration. Registered still-births for 1926 to 1983 are given. Finally, births and deaths by island are given for 1974 to 1983. In conclusion, Carreira discusses the available statistical sources and expresses his anxiety about the rising population. Tables appended give the annual figures from which the tables in the main body of the text were produced.

Population

166 **Determinantes da evolução demográfica de Cabo Verde.** (Determining factors in the demographic evolution of Cape Verde.)
J.T. Mexia, Rosa M. Matias. *Garcia de Orta*, vol. 17, no. 3 (1969), p. 263-70.

Amounts of corn and bean imports and the rainfall totals in Praia and Mindelo in any given year and the two years preceding are used to calculate demographic change. The authors set out the mathematical formula devised to do this, which they hope will be of use in determining food stock policy. There is a summary in English.

167 **A evolução demográfica de Cabo Verde.** (The demographic evolution of Cape Verde.)
António Carreira. *Boletim Cultural da Guiné Portuguesa*, vol. 24, no. 94 (April 1969), p. 475-500.

Carreira – with his usual meticulous care in the use, and indication of use, of original source material – has collated demographic evidence from 1469 to 1964. The results are presented in two tables. The first covers Cape Verde as a whole from 1469 to 1964. Totals are broken down by sex, and the rate of change in population is given. Lengthy footnotes for each of the seventy-two different dates indicate the information source. The second table gives population totals from 1582 to 1960 for each island.

168 **Inventory of Population Projects in Developing Countries Around the World.**
New York: UN Fund for Population Activities, 1973/1974- . annual.

Each issue contains country-by-country reports, which include Cape Verde, giving statistics and news of government initiatives and relevant aid programmes. A second section covers regional, interregional and global programmes while a third section indicates information sources.

169 **A população de Cabo Verde no século XX.** (The population of Cape Verde in the 20th century.)
Eduíno Brito. Lisbon: Agência-Geral do Ultramar, 1963. 79p. map.

With the support of numerous statistical tables and figures Brito covers migratory movements, population density, population structure by race, age and sex. Birth and death rates are calculated, and the soundness of the statistical methods used is illustrated by the remarkably accurate forecast made of the 1990 population total.

170 **O primeiro 'censo' de população da capitania das ilhas de Cabo Verde (1731).** (The first 'census' of the population of the captaincy of the Cape Verde Islands [1731].)
António Carreira. *Revista de História Económica e Social*, no. 13 (Jan.-June 1984), p. 51-66.

Under instructions from Lisbon, D. Frei José de Santa Maria de Jesus, the bishop of Cape Verde, produced in 1731 the first detailed demographic document of the era. It gives population statistics by island or administrative district, by sex, by marital status, and by social class or race. The four categories which define social class or race are *branco* (white), *mestiço* (mixed race), *preto* (black) and *escravo* (slave). Carreira tabulates the information and provides annotations.

171 **1° recenseamento geral da população e habitação 1980.** (The first general census of population and housing 1980.)
Direcção de Recenseamentos e Inqueritos, Secretaria de Estado da Cooperação e Planeamento. Praia: The author, 1983. 6 vols. map.
The first volume covers the current resident population, shown by sex, for each local administrative district. Family size is also indicated. Volume two gives population structure, showing such data as marital status by age and district, internal population movements, educational attainment, and number of live births by mother's age. Volume three deals with the active population, and shows such factors as age, sex, type of work, unemployment and education. Volume four covers housing, indicating the size, age, facilities and material of construction of the housing stock. Volume five is the 'Recenseamento geral da população – 1970. População global e estrutura da população' (General population census – 1970. Total population and population structure). This gives population totals by age, sex, marital status and district. Volume six is an analysis of the data presented in the other volumes. Projections of future demographic trends are made.

172 **Seroantropologia das ilhas de Cabo Verde. Mesa redonda sobre o homen cabo-verdiano.** (Physical anthropology of the Cape Verde islands. Round table on Cape Verdean man.)
Almerindo Lessa, Jacques Ruffié. Lisbon: Junta de Investigações do Ultramar, 1957. 153p. (Estudos, Ensaios e Documentos, no. 32).
The first chapter deals with the results of an experiment into Cape Verdean genetic origins. Tests on blood, colour blindness and taste sensitivity to phenylthiocarbamide were carried out in Portugal, the different islands of Cape Verde and amongst peoples from the neighbouring areas of West Africa. Collated on scatter diagrams, some interesting results emerge. Sotavento and Barlavento are distinct from each other, but closer genetically to the littoral peoples of West Africa (Fulas, Biafadas, Papeis, Peul, Manjacos and Bijagós) than to Portugal. The second chapter is a transcript of a wide-ranging round-table discussion, which attempts to anchor cultural themes in biology. As always, the question of origins provokes stirring debate. Similar to the first part of this work is Lessa's 'O homen cabo-verdiano. Suas raízes, sua multiplicação, suas doenças' (Cape Verdean man. His origins, his multiplication, his diseases), in: *Colóquios cabo-verdianos* (q.v.), p. 113-30.

Emigration

173 Angola under the Portuguese: the myth and the reality.
Gerald Bender. London: Heinemann Educational Books, 1978. 287p.
2 maps. bibliog.
This history of Angola reveals a little known aspect of Cape Verdean emigration.
Throughout the 20th century the Portuguese government had sponsored the planned
rural settlement of Portuguese peasants in Angola. Bender describes this programme
as a 'colossal failure' on which over $100,000,000 was spent in the last twenty years of
Portuguese rule alone. In 1961 it was decided to recruit Cape Verdeans as well as
Portuguese, in the belief that their intermediary racial status would contribute to multi-
racial harmony in the *colonatos* (settlements). Of course nothing of the sort happened.
The Cape Verdeans were almost as badly selected as the Portuguese settlers. They
tended to be relatively old, illiterate and were often fishermen rather than farmers.
Little or no technical agricultural assistance was given. The Cape Verdeans did not
ease race relations: Bender expresses no surprise that they 'manifest antipathy towards
Africans in their attempt to identify with the ruling white sector'. In fact they seemed
to have gained a reputation for drinking and fighting. In 1968 their recruitment was
stopped. A lengthy footnote to page 203 describes racial antagonism between Cape
Verdeans and Portuguese in Portugal and the USA.

174 Barbadians in the Amazon and Cape Verdeans in New England:
contrasts in adaptations and relations with homelands.
Sidney M. Greenfield. *Ethnic and Racial Studies*, vol. 8, no. 2 (April
1985), p. 208-32. 5 maps. bibliog.
Greenfield contrasts the very different emigrant experiences of Barbadians in Pôrto
Velho, Rondônia and Cape Verdeans in New Bedford, Massachusetts. The former
have become completely integrated into Brazilian life and no longer maintain contacts
with Barbados. The Cape Verdeans however remain a distinct ethnic group with strong
emotional and financial links with their homeland. Greenfield explains in some detail
the actual and historical circumstances which have resulted in this situation. He notes
the different types of Cape Verdean emigration to New England, distinguishing the
emigration from Brava of crewmen recruited for the whaling fleet and the very poorly
remunerated seasonal labourers taken from Santiago to work in the cranberry bogs.

The Brava men continued to work at sea on New England boats, gradually bringing wives and families to New England and forming a small, self-contained Cape Verdean colony. The Santiago men generally could not afford to do so and were looked down upon by the others. Isolation from mainstream American life was increased by the racism of white America and Bravense reluctance to integrate with black Americans. Greenfield goes on to describe the effects of 20th-century US immigration laws and independence in Cape Verde. The policy of the post-independence government has been to stimulate emigrants' interest in Cape Verde and to maintain good relations with the USA.

175 **Cabo Verde: 72 ano quinto de seca.** (Cape Verde: 1972 fifth year of drought.)
Händel de Oliveira.   Lisbon: Tipografia António Coelho Dias, 1973. 228p.

Two collections of articles published in the Lisbon newspaper *Diário de Notícias* (Daily News) are reproduced in book form. The first, from 1 to 6 August 1972, deals with the phenomenon of Cape Verdeans living in Lisbon. The situation in Cape Verde is explained for the benefit of those citizens who have been wondering about the strange people congregating in Campo de Ourique (an inner-city district of Lisbon). Emigrants are interviewed who speak positively about their life in Portugal. The Church proves to be important for the emigrants – who receive no medical protection for the first year of their stay. These articles are followed up by those from 14 to 26 November 1972 which report on de Oliveira's visit to Cape Verde. They are of less interest than the first collection, except perhaps as an example of propaganda for the colonial government's management of the drought. There is some evidence here of the government's intention to encourage emigration to Portugal rather than to other destinations. Horror stories from Holland tell of Cape Verdeans who are never heard of again, and, somewhat improbably, of the accumulation of money taking six times as long in Holland as in Portugal.

176 **Cape Verdean Americans.**
Deirdre Meintel Machado.   In: *Hidden minorities: the persistence of ethnicity in American life*, edited by Joan H. Rollins.   Lanham, Maryland; London: University Press of America, 1981, p. 227-50. bibliog.

The multiple social identities claimed by Cape Verdean Americans are also discussed in Greenfield's 'In search of social identity: strategies of ethnic identity management amongst Capeverdeans in Southeastern Massachusetts' (q.v.), but Machado's specialist and intimate knowledge of Cape Verdean culture makes a particularly interesting contribution to the subject. She points out the Cape Verdean's difficulties with the American binary racial categories of 'black' and 'white': the Cape Verdean system is infinitely more sophisticated, and can be a social as well as racial terminology. Although subject to racism, and notably so when outside the New England communities, the Cape Verdeans have generally avoided being identified with African Americans. They define themselves culturally by their food, their music and their language – Crioulo: these things separate them from the black community as much as from the white. Machado notes some of the modifications which these cultural markers have undergone in the US. Marriage within the community is also important: Machado suggests that the need for a Cape Verdean bride is one reason for the close links maintained for so long between Cape Verdean Americans and the islands. Interviews illustrate the problems of racial identity.

Emigration

177 Emigração em Cabo Verde: solução ou problema? (Cape Verdean emigration: solution or problem?).
Deirdre Meintel. *Revista Internacional de Estudos Africanos*, no. 2 (June-Dec. 1984), p. 93-120.

Meintel's first comments are a salutary reminder that the commonly cited causes of emigration – drought and a high birth rate – are not necessarily the complete picture. She suggests that these became 'causes' only when capitalist development elsewhere created new labour needs, specifically, in US industry and the cocoa plantations of São Tomé. Portuguese colonialism did nothing to make Cape Verde viable, preferring it to remain as a pool of potential emigrant labour. The author then goes on to consider the ways in which emigration actually causes problems. Firstly, she considers some of the economic problems. It can happen that families lose touch with their emigrant breadwinners and this increases the burdens on women and the domestic economy. Cash remittances monetarize the economy and increase the need for residents to obtain money. Secondly, emigration changes social patterns, particularly with regard to marriage and household norms. Either, households are composed of women and children, with men as transitory sexual partners who rarely contribute financially; or, households are run by women, but the usually male breadwinner abroad has final authority. Finally, a 'cultural dependence' is established whereby cultural traits from abroad are considered to be prestigious. Meintel concludes that emigrants should be encouraged to become involved in national development. There is a summary in English.

178 In search of social identity: strategies of ethnic identity management amongst Capeverdeans in Southeastern Massachusetts.
Sidney M. Greenfield. *Luso-Brazilian Review*, vol. 13, no. 1 (Summer 1976), p. 3-18. bibliog.

Possibly the key work in the study of Cape Verdean emigrants in the USA: its conclusions seem to be confirmed time after time. Greenfield first describes the history of Cape Verdean emigration. Unlike other immigrants in the USA they seemed to reject assimilation: to avoid being absorbed into the discriminated group of the African Americans they asserted their own ethnic identity. Greenfield identifies four strategies adopted: the 'Cape Verdean-Portuguese' was hampered by the racism of Portuguese immigrants; the 'Cape Verdean-Black' emerged during the 1960s civil rights movements, but caused conflict with other Cape Verdeans; the 'Cape Verdean-African' was a response of solidarity to the African independence movements, although many immigrants were very dubious about the post-independence links between Cape Verde and Guinea-Bissau; the 'Cape Verdean-American' wishes to be considered as a distinct ethnic group within the USA.

179 Labour in Portuguese West Africa.
William Cadbury. London: George Routledge & Sons; New York: E.P. Dutton, 1910. 2nd ed. 187p. map.

Rumours of conditions of neo-slavery on the cacao plantations of São Tomé and Príncipe prompted the investigations of the cocoa manufacturers Cadburys, Fry and Stollwerk, who subsequently boycotted the product. The book is a compilation of various reports carried out between 1907 and 1909 and was intended to pressurize the Portuguese government into reforming both conditions on the plantations and the system of recruiting labour. Many Cape Verdeans were recruited to the plantations as contract labourers – a traumatic memory which persists. Yet the reports note a distinction between the treatment of Cape Verdean and Angolan workers, an indication of the ambiguous status of the Cape Verdean in the Portuguese colonial hierarchy. The book was reprinted in 1969 (New York: Negro Universities Press).

180 **The people of the Cape Verde Islands: exploitation and emigration.**
António Carreira, translated from the Portuguese and edited by
Christopher Fyfe.   London: C. Hurst; Hamden, Connecticut: Archon
Books, 1982. 224p. 2 maps. bibliog.

This is a history of the Cape Verdean diaspora. Emigration is an integral part of the social experience, and the mixed feelings which it arouses are equally manifest in literary culture. Carreira uses a wide range of source materials including demographic and trade statistics, legislation, governors' reports and eye-witness accounts. He notes the problems caused by the chaotic state of the Lisbon archives and the dubious record-keeping of the Portuguese. Given that emigration is such a central part of Cape Verdean life, the background explanation which Carreira gives of its causes is actually a very useful and depressing account of economic stagnation and ecological crisis. He defines two types of emigration – 'voluntary' and 'forced'. The voluntary flow was first, in the wake of the American whaling fleet, to the east coast of the USA. Later Europe became an important destination, with a lesser flow to Guinea-Bissau. The forced migration was to the cacao plantations of São Tomé and Princípe. This was the colonial solution to famine in Cape Verde and labour shortages in the plantations. Conditions of service were horrific; see *Labour in Portuguese West Africa*. Carreira also quotes from Jerónimo Paiva de Carvalho – the curator for labourers in São Tomé – *Alma negra: depoimento sobre a questão dos serviçais de S. Tomé* (Black soul: testimony on the question of contracted workers in São Tomé) (Porto, 1912).

181 **A Portuguese colonial in America: Belmira Nunes Lopes. The
autobiography of a Cape Verdean-American.**
Maria Luisa Nunes.   Pittsburgh, Pennsylvania: Latin American
Literary Review Press, 1982. 215p. 3 maps. (Discoveries).

In 1976 Maria Luisa Nunes taped these interviews recording the autobiography of her aunt, Belmira Nunes Lopes. She was born in Harwich, Massachusetts in 1899: her father was from Fogo, her mother from Brava. This is a rare account, not only of an indomitable woman, but of the Cape Verdean immigrant experience. The account begins by establishing the family origins in Cape Verde. These stretch back to her great-grandparents: the account of social relations in the mid-19th century is of great interest. Race is an important factor in these inherited memories of Cape Verde. Childhood on Cape Cod is a portrait of the Cape Verdean community, and the difficulties of being black, poor and Roman Catholic in the USA. For several years the family picked cranberries, strawberries and blueberries: her father, a former whaler, chopped wood. In towns they experienced racism, but at least were amongst the Cape Verdean community, and the festivities, music and wakes (wakes are an important part of Cape Verdean culture: see *Race, culture and Portuguese colonialism in Cabo Verde*). Lopes took full advantage of the US education system and became a teacher. In 1967, at the Portuguese government's expense, she visited Angola and Mozambique. She met many Cape Verdean officials in Luanda, and in Lourenço Marques (Maputo) she records an unofficial meeting with the poet Gabriel Mariano. In 1973 she visited Cape Verde, and movingly describes this as 'one of the highlights of my life. I felt I was going home'. Her attitudes to ethnicity closely reflect 'In search of social identity: strategies of ethnic identity management amongst Capeverdeans in Southeastern Massachusetts' (q.v.): part of her efforts to mobilize the Cape Verdean community in the USA has been to campaign for Cape Verdeans to be recognized as a distinct ethnic group.

Emigration

182 **O problema da emigração cabo-verdiana.** (The problem of Cape Verdean emigration.)
Luís Terry. In: *Colóquios cabo-verdianos.* Lisbon: Junta de Investigações do Ultramar, 1959, p. 97-112.
The demographic pressure to emigrate is summarized, and some of the negative effects of emigration are outlined. The main theme of the essay is that emigration, if it is necessary, should be kept within the Portuguese empire.

Language

183 **Cabo Verde: contribuição para o estudo do dialecto falado no seu arquipélago.** (Cape Verde: contribution towards the study of the dialect spoken in its archipelago.)
Maria Dulce de Oliveira Almada. Lisbon: Junta de Investigações do Ultramar, 1961. 166p. bibliog. (Estudos de Ciências Políticas e Sociais, no. 55).
Crioulo, a creole language, is the Cape Verdean mother-tongue. This volume covers the history, phonetics, morphology and syntax of Crioulo and was originally submitted as a thesis. Almada readily admits that the publication of Baltasar Lopes' *O dialecto crioulo de Cabo Verde* (q.v.) made this work somewhat redundant. Nonetheless it remains of value for the comparative clarity of its phonetic transcription and the author's intimate knowledge of the Crioulo variant of São Vicente and, to a lesser extent, of São Nicolau.

184 **Les créoles portugais.** (Portuguese creole languages.)
Alain Kihm. *Bulletin des Études Portugaises et Brésiliennes*, vol. 46-47, (1986-87), p. 61-87. bibliog.
A succinct survey of Portuguese creole languages around the world, which is summarized by a genealogical tree that rather contentiously shows 16th-century vernacular Portuguese as sole progenitor. A useful bibliography is included on pages 84-7.

185 **O crioulo de Cabo Verde: surto e expansão.** (The creole of Cape Verde: rise and growth.)
António Carreira. Mem Martins, Portugal: The author, 1983. 2nd ed. 95p. 2 maps. bibliog.
A historical and sociological study, as opposed to a linguistic work, this volume sets out the conditions for the development of Crioulo and its expansion into Guinea-Bissau. His principal conclusion is that Kriul (Guinea-Bissau) could not have arisen independently of Crioulo (Cape Verde). He points out the weakness of the Portuguese

Language

presence in Guinea-Bissau: the only foreigners who had any success there were the Crioulo-speaking *lançados* (backwoods traders) from Cape Verde. Conversely, the social conditions in Cape Verde were ripe for the formation of an autochthonous creole language. He describes the relevant demographic and social aspects of the early years of the islands' settlements. References to Crioulo from many different sources are assembled.

186 **The development of Atlantic creole languages.**
William Washabaugh, Sidney M. Greenfield. In: *The social context of creolization*, edited by Ellen Woolford, William Washabaugh. Ann Arbor, Michigan: Karoma, 1983, p. 106-19.

The authors piece together a picture of the social system of sugar plantations which began in the 12th century in Cyprus. They were characterized by the use of imported labour. The system was transplanted by the Portuguese to the Atlantic islands, including Cape Verde. These were the societies in which people from many different linguistic groups were forced together and, by necessity, creole languages evolved. Social and political influences on creole language formation are considered, with an interesting discussion of the demands of the Portuguese nation-state to propagate national identity in its new territories. Excluding African slaves from full participation in this identity could have promoted the creation of a separate cultural identity, expressed in the creole languages.

187 **O dialecto crioulo de Cabo Verde.** (The creole dialect of Cape Verde.) Baltasar Lopes da Silva. Lisbon: Imprensa Nacional/Casa da Moeda, 1984. 2nd ed. 391p. bibliog. (Escritores dos Países de Língua Portuguesa, no. 1).

First published in 1957, since which time it has been the bedrock of later studies of Cape Verdean Crioulo, the present edition is a facsimile of the first. It begins with a lengthy essay by Rodrigo de Sá Nogueira, giving what might be called the Portuguese perspective on the formation of creole languages within the Portuguese colonies. Lopes' own introduction considers the origins of Crioulo, and the linguistic, cultural and population connections with the West African mainland. However, he places greatest emphasis on the influence of Portuguese, and the survival in Crioulo of archaic forms and usages of Portuguese. The main body of the work which follows is probably the most comprehensive analysis of Crioulo phonetics, morphology and syntax. This covers all varieties of the language, but annotations indicate differences between Barlavento, Sotavento or individual island varieties. Similarities with varieties of Portuguese are also illustrated. Lopes uses a consistent, but very complex, system of phonetic transcription which is set out on pages 47-52. A valuable Portuguese-to-Crioulo lexicon can be found on pages 193-388. More of Lopes' ideas on Crioulo can be found in his earlier essay, 'Uma experiência romanica nos trópicos' (A Romance experience in the tropics) in *Claridade*, no. 4 (Jan. 1947), p. 15-22; no. 5 (Sept. 1947), p. 1-10. In this he refers closely to Gilberto Freyre's *O mundo que o português criou* (preface by António Sérgio. Rio de Janeiro: Livraria José Olympio Editora, 1940. 164p.).

188 **Diskrison strutural di lingua kabuverdianu.** (Structural description of
the Cape Verdean language.)
Manuel Veiga, preface by Dulce Almada Duarte. [Praia]: Instituto
Caboverdiano do Livro, 1982. 163p.

To date, probably the most useful of all the works on the Crioulo language. Although
a preliminary description of the language and not a 'grammar', it is a consistent,
professional and reliable study. Perhaps its major virtue is that it is conducted in terms
of Crioulo itself rather than being a comparison with some Portuguese ideal of
language. The orthography used, based on the International Phonetic Alphabet, is
explained (p. 13-14). Duarte's preface discusses the social and political issues which are
raised by creole languages: she sees political implications in this book's revelation that
Crioulo has a very different structure to that of the Portuguese language. She hopes
that this work will lead eventually to a Crioulo grammar for use in schools and thus
facilitate mother-tongue education. Veiga's introduction outlines the aims of the study
and explains the use of the Santiago variant of Crioulo in the main body of the work
(only the prefaces are in Portuguese). His research was based on a Greenberg-
Tervuren Welmers questionnaire used on people from Santiago, Fogo, São Vicente
and Santo Antão: he concludes that Cape Verdean Crioulo is one language, with
variations in superficial structures such as phonetics. The main body of the work
consists of five different sections. The first two describe phonetics and phonology,
principally of Santiago. These are followed by comparative descriptions of the variants
of São Vicente and Santo Antão; of Santiago and Fogo; and of Santiago and São
Vicente.

189 **Estudos linguísticos: crioulos. Reedição de artigos publicados no** *Boletim*
da Sociedade de Geografia de Lisboa. (Linguistic studies: creoles.)
Re-edition of articles published in the *Bulletin of the Geographical*
Society of Lisbon.)
Edited by Jorge Morais-Barbosa. Lisbon: Academia Internacional da
Cultura Portuguesa, 1967. 447p. bibliog.

Morais-Barbosa provides an introduction, p. vii-xxiv, for this collection of early works
on Portuguese creole languages. F. Adolfo Coelho's 'Os dialectos românicos ou neo-
latinos na África, Ásia e América' (The Romance or neo-Latin dialects in Africa, Asia
and America), p. 1-234, 1880-86, demonstrates the Crioulo of Santiago in terms of
personal letters, notes on phonology and grammar, riddles and hypocorismas (p. 5-34).
Joaquim Vieira Botelho da Costa and Custódio José Duarte's 'O crioulo de Cabo
Verde' (The creole of Cape Verde), p. 235-328, 1886, is a fairly systematic description
of phonology and grammar, but related to norms of Portuguese grammar. Conjugation
tables are a useful lexicon of verbs. Appended is the Parable of the Prodigal Son in
Portuguese and the Crioulos of Santiago, Fogo, Brava, Santo Antão, São Nicolau and
Boa Vista. A. de Paul Brito's 'Dialectos crioulos-portugueses. Apontamentos para a
gramática do crioulo que se fala na ilha de Santiago de Cabo Verde' (Portuguese-
creole dialects. Pointers towards the grammar of the creole which is spoken on
Santiago, Cape Verde), p. 329-404, 1887, follows the model of Portuguese pedagogical
grammars, but includes many proverbs, phrases, vocabulary and verse in Crioulo.
E. Correia Lopes' 'Dialectos crioulos e etnografia crioula' (Creole dialects and creole
ethnography), 1947, is to be found on pages 405-30.

Language

190 **Miscelânea luso-africana: colectânea de estudos coligidos.** (Portuguese
African miscellany: a collection of essays.)
Edited by Marius F. Valkhoff. Lisbon: Junta de Investigações
Científicas do Ultramar, 1975. 319p.

Six of the fourteen articles in this collection refer to Cape Verdean Crioulo. 'A
comparative study of São-tomense and Cabo-verdiano creole' by Luiz Ferras and
Marius Valkhoff (p. 15-39) is a linguistic essay. 'A socio-linguistic enquiry into Cabo-
Verdiano creole' by Valkhoff (p. 41-58) gives results from a questionnaire (text
reproduced) into the language use and attitudes of forty-four Cape Verdean
respondents. 'Le monde créole et les îles du Cap Vert' (The creole world and the Cape
Verde Islands) by Valkhoff (p. 59-72) is a general essay on literature, culture and
religion. 'Cape Verde, Guinea-Bissau and São Tomé and Príncipe: the linguistic
situation' by Jorge Morais-Barbosa (p. 133-51) is a translation of the general and
comparative essay 'Cabo Verde, Guiné, e São Tomé e Príncipe: situação linguística' in
*Cabo Verde, Guiné, e São Tomé e Príncipe: curso de extensão universitária, ano lectivo
de 1965-1966* (q.v.), p. 149-64. 'Textos crioulos cabo-verdianos' (Texts in Cape
Verdean creole) by Sérgio Frusoni (p. 165-204) are nine poems and one short story by
this distinguished Crioulo poet. 'The creole dialect of the island of Brava' by Deirdre
Meintel (p. 205-56) is an excellent study. A description of phonology, grammar and
syntax is accompanied by discussion of etymology and socio-linguistic issues. Four
Crioulo texts with Portuguese and English translations are appended.

191 **The phonologies of Cape Verdean dialects of Portuguese.**
Mary Louise Nunes. *Boletim de Filologia*, vol. 21, nos 1-2 (1962-63),
p. 1-56. bibliog.

Nunes made tape recordings of the speech of four subjects, from Santo Antão, Boa
Vista, Brava and Fogo. She makes some interesting remarks on the difficulties of this
kind of fieldwork, particularly when the issues of social prestige are linked with
language use. Her subjects claimed not to know Crioulo, despite evidence to the
contrary. On the basis of this research she charts the phonologies of the variants of the
four islands. She concludes that she has found no phonological change that is
inconsistent with Portuguese or other Romance language systems.

192 **Pidgins and creoles.**
Loreto Todd. London: Routledge & Kegan Paul, 1974. 106p. 3 maps.
bibliog. (Language and Society Series).

Todd summarizes the principal schools of thought on the puzzling questions of the
origins and development of pidgin and creole languages. This is a straightforward and
readable – but never patronizing – volume. There are many specialized linguistic works
in this field: one of the more recent is *Pidgin and creole languages* by Suzanne
Romaine (Harlow, England; New York: Longman, 1988. 373p. bibliog.).

193 **A problemática da utilização das línguas nacionais: língua, nação,
identidade cultural.** (The problem of utilization of national languages:
language, nation, cultural identity.)
Dulce Almada Duarte. *Raízes*, nos 5-6 (1978), p. 35-80.

A politically orientated article which looks first at the use of Crioulo as a mark of Cape
Verdean post-colonial cultural identity. Duarte then asserts the full linguistic potential
of Crioulo. She notes that it has been successfully used – ironically, in the USA – as
the medium of instruction for maths, English and history. The suggestion is made that
Cape Verdean writers have a responsiblity to write in Crioulo, translating later to

Portuguese if they so wish. Crioulo also has a political role in the union between Guinea-Bissau and Cape Verde: it is an important point of contact between the two peoples. Duarte's main concern is that Crioulo should be used as the language of education, at the least for younger children for whom Portuguese is an utterly foreign language.

194 Romance creoles.
John N. Green. In: *The Romance languages*, edited by Martin Harris, Nigel Vincent. Beckenham, England; Sydney: Croom Helm, 1988, p. 420-73. bibliog.

Describing with clarity the essential concepts of creole language study, this chapter covers from language formation to present-day political implications. Linguistic study of various creoles with Portuguese, Spanish and French lexicons – including Cape Verdean Crioulo – leads him to conclude that there is enough evidence that these languages have sufficient structural similarities to be considered together as a group. He also concludes that these are 'Romance' languages in terms of their lexicons. He notes the very strong contemporary influence of education and mass media, which is causing a tendency for certain linguistic features of creoles to approximate more and more towards the European languages. Crioulo is used as an example of this trend.

195 Sobre a terminologia anatómica nos crioulos de Cabo Verde. (On the anatomical terminology of Cape Verdean creole languages.)
António de Almeida. *Anais. Junta de Investigações Coloniais*, vol. 4, no. 5 (1949), p. 5-17. bibliog.

Prepared for the use of medical staff, this is an extensive listing of body terms in Portuguese, Sotavento Crioulo and Barlavento Crioulo. A short essay considers the origins of the Crioulo terms.

196 A socio-historical approach to the problem of Portuguese creole in West Africa.
Germán de Granda. *International Journal of the Sociology of Language*, no. 7 (1976), p. 11-22. bibliog.

There is a theory that pidgin and creole languages with European-based lexicons all have their origins in Sabir, a maritime lingua franca of the medieval Mediterranean. Relexified with Portuguese to become a Portuguese pidgin it may have been the language of European expansion along the Atlantic coast of Africa. A study of the origins of Crioulo should not ignore works such as de Granda's, which deal with the social and linguistic background to the later development of Atlantic creole langugages.

Subsídios para um dicionário utilitário e glossário dos nomes vernáculos das plantas do arquipélago de Cabo Verde.
See item no. 75.

Comentários em torno do bilinguismo cabo-verdiano.
See item no. 351.

Religion

197 História da igreja de Cabo Verde. (History of the Cape Verdean church.)
Frederico Cerrone.   São Vicente, Cape Verde: Gráfica do Mindelo, 1983. 75p. bibliog.

This is a chronological history of the Roman Catholic Church in Cape Verde. Cerrone identifies four time periods. From 1460 to 1533 the Jesuits were present and active in evangelization work. The first churches and parishes were founded. In 1533 the Diocese of Ribeira Grande, Santiago was endowed, with responsibility for the Guinea coast as well as the archipelago. Cerrone describes the many problems faced by the bishopric between 1533 and 1866, principally the lack of religious personnel and the frequent pirate attacks on Ribeira Grande (now known as Cidade Velha). He notes the role of the Church in the slave trade. Mass baptism was given to slaves on their way to the Americas, but for those who were to stay in Cape Verde baptism could be chosen after six months of compulsory catechism. Between 1866 and 1940 the bishopric moved to Ribeira Brava, São Nicolau and the famous seminary-secondary school of São Nicolau was founded. This gained a reputation as a centre of educational excellence in West Africa. The separation of Church and state in 1911 had severe consequences for the Cape Verdean church and the seminary in particular, when public secondary education was moved to Mindelo. Cerrone's final section deals with the events of 1941-75, when the Salazarist state in Portugal supported the role of the Church. Cerrone calls this a 'renaissance'. A final section (p. 61-73) gives a brief outline of church history for each island.

198 A igreja de Cabo Verde e o desenvolvimento. (The Cape Verdean church and development.)
Paulino Livramento Évora.   [Praia]: Diocese de Cabo Verde, 1985. 20p.

Bishop Évora outlines the role of the Roman Catholic Church in Cape Verde in ameliorating the condition of man not only spiritually but economically and socially. This pastoral letter to the diocese of Cape Verde also mentions the work of Cáritas

Caboverdeana (Cape Verdean Charity), the Church's forum for social action. This organization was founded in 1976 and received formal government approval in 1978.

199 **Ilhas de Cabo Verde: origem do povo caboverdiano e da diocese de Santiago de Cabo Verde.** (The Cape Verde Islands: origins of the Cape Verdean people and the diocese of Santiago of Cape Verde.)
Bernardo P. Vaschetto. Boston, Massachusetts: Edição Farol, 1987. 670p. map. bibliog.

A general history of Cape Verde is followed by some interesting documents relating to the foundation of the Catholic Church in the islands during the period 1460 to 1700. A second section of the book covers the present-day work of the Church from 1973 to 1986.

200 **Jesuit documents on the Guinea of Cape Verde and the Cape Verde Islands 1585-1617 in English translation.**
P.E.H. Hair. *History in Africa*, vol. 16 (1989), p. 375-81.

Hair, from the University of Liverpool, UK, has been translating and annotating these documents, initially those sent by Avelino Teixeira da Mota and latterly those published by António Brásio in *Monumenta missionaria africana. África ocidental* (q.v.). Hair lists forty-eight documents which he has translated and will supply.

201 *Monumenta missionaria africana.* **África ocidental.** (*Monumenta missionaria africana*. West Africa.)
António Brásio. Lisbon: Agência-Geral do Ultramar, 1958-68. (2nd series, vols 1-4).

The second series of this truly monumental work covers the diocese of Cape Verde which stretched from the Senegal River down the Upper Guinea coast. The first series covered the diocese of São Tomé, which continued down the West African coast to the Cape of Good Hope. Although the diocese of Cape Verde was the first to be founded, Father Brásio points out that the diocese of São Tomé was the more important of the two and thus demanded his first attention. He has assembled, in chronological order, documents which contribute to the history of the Catholic Church's missionary activity. Most of these are letters, instructions and reports between Church authorities and on Church business, but not exclusively so. Some of the earlier documents are the reports of the early discoverers. Father Brásio has transcribed and lightly annotated the documents: introductory notes explain the system used. Volume 1 covers the years 1342-1499; volume 2 covers 1500-69; volume 3, 1570-1600; volume 4, 1600-22. Hair reports the publication of a fifth volume in 1979 (see *Jesuit documents on the Guinea of Cape Verde and the Cape Verde Islands 1585-1617 in English translation*). Each volume contains a subject, name and geographical index. Although many of these documents can be found published elsewhere, it is an invaluable aid to research to have them collated and presented in this way.

Religion

202 **Notes sur le catholicisme aux îles du Cap-vert.** (Notes on Catholicism in the Cape Verde Islands.)
Nelson Eurico Cabral. *Revue Française d'Études Politiques Africaines*, vol. 14, nos 165-66 (Sept.-Oct. 1979), p. 108-17.

The first half of this article is a brief history of the Roman Catholic Church in Cape Verde. Cabral's comments on the sexual activity of priests, who fathered prodigious numbers of children, are noteworthy. The second section deals with contemporary religious practices both within and without the Church.

203 **Notícia corográfica e cronológica do Bispado de Cabo Verde.**
(Geographical and chronological report of the bishopric of Cape Verde.)
Anon., edited by António Carreira. Praia: Instituto Caboverdiano do Livro, 1985. 116p. bibliog.

Carreira provides introduction, notes and comments for this edition of the 1784 text. The islands' geography and administration are described, but the anonymous author's principal orientation is towards their ecclesiastical history and organization. There is some interesting evidence of conflicts between civil and Church authorities and, sadly, of the frequency with which newly arrived clergymen and officials died of fever. Appended documents include a description of a disastrous voyage taken by the bishop D. João de Faro to the African mainland in 1741; biographies of seven of the bishops; lists of bishops and governors of Cape Verde.

204 **Religion and civilization in West Africa: a missionary survey of French, British, Spanish and Portuguese West Africa with Liberia.**
J.J. Cooksey, A. McLeish. London: World Dominion Press, 1931. 277p. map.

A brief chapter (p. 166-7) notes the successful evangelization work of the Church of the Nazarene on Brava, with its congregation of one hundred.

205 **Vangêle contód d'nôs móda.** (The gospel told in our way).
Sergio Frusoni, preface by Luís Romano. São Filipe, Cape Verde: Edição Terra Nova, 1979. 223p.

A posthumous edition of Frusoni's free adaption, in Crioulo, of Bartolomeo Rossetti's work in Roman dialect, 'Er vangelo secondi noantri'. Based on selected sections from the New Testament, the story of Christ is told in verse form. Black-and-white photographs of everyday Cape Verdean scenes emphasize this volume's message that Christianity is relevant in any land and in any language. Luís Romano's preface (p. 5-9) is an appreciation of Frusoni (1901-75), a talented Crioulo poet of Italian parentage. This is followed (p. 11) by 'a Christian group from Fogo' who describe the importance of hearing Christ's message in their own language.

206 **West African Christianity: the religious impact.**
Lamin Sanneh. London: C. Hurst, 1983. 286p. 2 maps. bibliog.

Sanneh takes an interesting approach to his subject. He concentrates on the role of Africans and the importance of African materials, rather than on that of the missionaries. His second chapter, 'The early pioneers: the church comes to West Africa, 1471-1703', p. 15-52, is of greatest relevance to Cape Verde (see p. 19-20 in particular). He notes that at one time it was hoped that the people of Cape Verde would do Christian outreach work in West Africa. This failed to happen.

Tabanca.
See item no. 424.

Society and Social Issues

Race and social structure

207 **Cabo Verde. (Aspectos sociais. Secas e fomes do século XX.)** (Cape Verde. [Social aspects. Droughts and famines of the 20th century].) António Carreira. Lisbon: Ulmeiro, 1984. 2nd ed. 207p. (Biblioteca Ulmeiro, no. 9).

This is a significantly expanded edition of the 1977 *Cabo Verde: classes sociais estrutura familiar, migrações* (Cape Verde: social classes, family structure, migrations) The work begins with some geographical and demographic data. These are followed by the disturbing chapter 'As secas e as fomes do século XX' (The droughts and famine of the 20th century), p. 17-134: this is an addition to the 1977 edition. After briefly describing the crises of 1580–83, 1610-11, 1809-11 and 1894-1900, Carreira covers that of 1901-4 in some detail, including distressing eye-witness accounts. He notes the role of locusts in the 1911-15 crisis, and World War I in those of 1916-18 and 1921-22 Disruption to shipping during World War II probably contributed to the famine of 1941-43, when a state of emergency was declared. He describes the administrative measures taken during the famine of 1947-48: feeding centres were set up, including one described as a 'concentration camp' on Ilhéu de Santa Maria (off the coast at Praia). Black-and-white photographs accompany the text. Subsequent chapters describe the legacy of the institution of slavery in social organization and family structures. The current status of emigrants, and the economic and social causes and consequences of emigration, are also covered in the final chapters.

208 **Cabo Verde e São Tomé e Príncipe: esquema de uma evolução conjunta.** (Cape Verde and São Tomé and Príncipe: outline of an evolution in common.) Francisco Tenreiro. Praia: Imprensa Nacional, Divisão de Propaganda, 1956. 16p.

The poet from São Tomé and Príncipe sets out his thoughts on the social development of the two countries. They were settled within twenty-five years of each other and, until the development of the large coffee and cacao plantations on São Tomé and

Príncipe in the first decades of the 19th century, there were many similarities between the two. He believes that at the time of writing São Tomé and Príncipe has a class system more markedly defined by race, and that Cape Verdean society has closer links with the Portuguese.

209 **The cultural dimension in the strategy for national liberation: the cultural bases of the unification between Cape Verde and Guinea-Bissau.**
Dulce [Almada] Duarte, translated from the Portuguese by José C. Curto. *Latin American Perspectives*, issue 41, vol. 11, no. 2 (Spring 1984), p. 55-66.

Amílcar Cabral's principle of unification is the keynote to this text. The historical processes which the author sees as leading to the formation of a homogeneous society in Cape Verde are outlined. Duarte suggests that there are deep-rooted cultural links between the peoples of these two nations which were obscured by the colonial policy of assimilation. The struggle for independence enabled many Cape Verdeans to discover their African identity. The November 1980 coup is, perhaps simplistically, referred to as an 'accidental event', and one which should not be allowed to slow the dynamic of 'cultural evolution'.

210 **Do funco ao sobrado ou o 'mundo' que o mulato criou.** (From the hut to the 'big house' or the 'world' which the *mulato* created.)
Gabriel Mariano. In: *Colóquios cabo-verdianos*. Lisbon: Junta de Investigações do Ultramar, 1959, p. 23-49. bibliog.

Mariano analyses race and culture in Cape Verdean society, which he contrasts with Bahia, Brazil, for its lack of overt racism. This is a celebration of creole culture, and the role of the *mulato* in transmitting that culture to all social classes.

211 **The Portuguese and the tropics.**
Gilberto Freyre. Lisbon: Executive Committee for the Commemoration of the Vth Centenary of the Death of Prince Henry the Navigator, 1961. 296p.

Although not containing any material specific to the archipelago, this is an example of Freyre's work which was both influential and provocative in Cape Verde. The venerable Brazilian sociologist articulates his theory of Luso-tropicality, lauding the hybrid vigour of a culture which he supposes to hardly vary whether in Portuguese Asia or Portuguese Africa or Brazil. See also *Um brasileiro em terras portuguêsas* (A Brazilian in Portuguese lands) (Rio de Janeiro: Livraria José Olympio Editôra, 1953. 438p.). This a collection of speeches made by Freyre on a trip around the Portuguese-speaking world, 1951-52. There is a long introduction on Luso-tropicality, and a brief speech entitled 'Em Cabo Verde' (In Cape Verde) (p. 221-2). Freyre remarks on the similarities between Cape Verde and northeast Brazil and describes the islands as a link between Portugal and Brazil.

212 **Race, culture and Portuguese colonialism in Cabo Verde.**
Deirdre Meintel. Syracuse, New York: Maxwell School of Citizenship and Public Affairs, Syracuse University, 1984. 201p. map. bibliog. (Foreign and Comparative Studies/African Series, no. 41).

An invaluable book, clearly written and thoroughly researched, which brings new material to light on some of the central issues of Cape Verdean culture and society. Chapters two to five describe the geographical and historical background. Drawing heavily on Portuguese-language sources, Meintel's accessible style makes these chapters a very useful English-language resource. Chapters six to eight deal more specifically with the issues of race and Meintel's own research. 'Race relations under colonialism: the post-slavery period' contains her findings from fieldwork in Brava and Fogo in 1972 on Cape Verdean racial terminology and the social implications of race. She discusses race in sexual relationships and marriage and the manifestations of racial hierarchy in ritual events such as local festivals. 'Colonizers and colonized: Cape Verdeans in the empire' looks at the ambiguous role of the Cape Verdean in the Portuguese colonial hierarchy and, most interestingly, the forms of cultural repression and resistance within Cape Verde. The use of Crioulo, for example, could take on political significance. She also looks at the cultural challenge posed by the *tabanca* (a mutual aid society with its own social structure) and the *rebelados* (rebels) who appeared to reject the state: see Julio Monteiro's *Os rebelados da ilha de Santiago* (The rebels of Santiago) (Praia: Centro de Estudos, 1974). A final chapter compares Cape Verdean, Brazilian and American race relations.

213 **Sobrados, lojas & funcos: contribuição para o estudo da evolução social da ilha do Fogo.** ('Big houses', shops and huts: contribution towards the study of the social evolution of Fogo Island.)
   Henrique Teixeira de Sousa. *Claridade*, no. 8 (May 1958), p. 2-8.
A study of the racial and social structure of Fogo, which notes the connections with the economic changes that affected the island as it moved away from a colonial plantation economy. Architecture reflects social status as do the roles taken by participants in the Fogo festivals known as *bandeiras*. See Teixeira de Sousa's earlier article 'A estrutura social do Fogo, em 1940' (The social structure of Fogo, in 1940) in *Claridade* no. 5 (Sept. 1947), p. 42-4, which makes special note of the social mobility of the *mestiço* in Fogo.

Código de família.
See item no. 254.

Women

214 **Femmes du Sahel: la désertification au quotidien.** (Women of the Sahel: desertification in everyday life.)
   Marie Monimart. Paris: Éditions Karthala: OCDE/Club du Sahel, 1989. 263p. map. bibliog.
From the difficulties of finding fuelwood for cooking to the fundamental social changes wrought by male emigration, women are disproportionately affected by drought and desertification. This is a study of their consequences and the development challenges for women. The women of Cape Verde share many of the experiences of women from the Sahelian mainland and this informative study enables comparisons to be made between the different nations. One of the areas on which it focuses is that of reafforestation. There is praise for the role of women in this work in Cape Verde: in Tarrafal, Santiago, for example, women have set up a business selling young trees to the forestry service. Women also make up a majority of the work-force involved in tree-planting and anti-erosion projects. She notes, however, that they are generally on lower grades, and hence lower salaries, than men. She also considers the work of the

Organização da Mulher de Cabo Verde (women's organization of Cape Verde): the OMCV promotes literacy programmes, child care, family planning and small-scale business initiatives. However, many rural women are alienated by the OMCV's political stance. Other aspects of government policy are noted. Family planning is a high priority: facilities, policy and problems with the Roman Catholic Church are described. Although the government affirms equality between the sexes and Cape Verde compares favourably in many respects, women are still considered as social inferiors.

215 **The logic of Cape Verdean female-headed households: social response to economic scarcity.**
Timothy J. Finan, Helen K. Henderson. *Urban Anthropology*, vol. 17, no. 1 (Spring 1988), p. 87-103. map. bibliog.

A fascinating piece of work, based on a study of rural Santiago, which illuminates several aspects of Cape Verde's economy and society. The poorest of all households are those twenty per cent of subsistence farms which are headed by unmarried women. The authors argue convincingly that this institution is the direct result of the lack of alternative economic opportunities. Access to irrigated land, public jobs and livestock ownership are compared for different types of household: unmarried women are least favoured in all instances. Men benefit disproportionately from off-farm employment: this is especially apparent in the form of emigration. Emigration has caused the sex ratio in rural Santiago to equal sixty-five men for every one hundred women. The article describes the pattern of family relationships and notes the existence of 'informal polygamy'. Children and family cooperation enable single women to survive: 'to manage one's life as an individual is as culturally unconvincing to a single woman as it is economically unwise'.

216 **Mujer.** (Woman.)
Praia: Organização da Mulher de Cabo Verde [OMCV], 1982-87. irreg.

A mixture of political material, OMCV business, culture, and advice on home economics, child care and health.

Un exemple d'évolution du statut de la sage-femme aux îles du Cap-Vert.
See item no. 218.

Juventude e adolescência, mulher e sociedade, psicopatias e desequilíbrios emocionais.
See item no. 221.

Health and medicine

217 **Estudo e combate de endemias na província portuguesa de Cabo Verde.**
(Study and combat of endemic diseases in the Portuguese province of
Cape Verde).
Manuel T.V. Meira. *Garcia de Orta*, vol. 9, no. 1 (1961), p. 99-107.
bibliog.

A brief description of the main diseases which affect the islands, the conditions which
stimulate them, studies undertaken and measures being carried out. Malaria has been
the most preoccupying illness, mainly affecting Santiago. The bibliography contains
over forty items.

218 **Un exemple d'évolution du statut de la sage-femme aux îles du Cap-Vert.**
(An example of the changing status of the midwife in the Cape Verde
Islands.)
Marguerite Depraetere. *Civilisations*, vol. 36, nos 1-2 (1986),
p. 251-7.

This is a study of the role of the midwife in the rural interior of Santiago. In the past
midwives were high-status members of the community and their services were
rewarded by the obligation of those they had delivered to offer them their labour.
Nowadays she is given money or agricultural produce from non-irrigated land. This
study also describes some of the midwives' other responsibilities. The disposal of the
placenta and umbilical cord is important, as is the preparation of the mother's food for
eight days subsequent to the birth. The midwife will use certain plants, especially
castor-oil, in foods and medicinal preparations for the mother. Many of these practices
emphasize the separation of the newly delivered mother from the rest of the
community, and from her husband in particular.

219 **The fever at Boa Vista in 1845-6, unconnected with the visit of the *Eclair***
to that island.
Gilbert King.   London: John Churchill, 1852. 110p.

This book is a contribution to the research into the causes of yellow fever. It is part of
a passionate debate, centring on this outbreak, as to whether the illness was contagious
or not. In 1845 the *H.M.S. Eclair* arrived in Sal-Rei, Boa Vista from the West African
coast and stayed for three weeks. Members of the crew became ill with yellow fever as
subsequently did members of the local population. One Dr McWilliam made a first
report, believing the disease to be contagious. Upon a further outbreak King – the
Inspector of Hospitals and Fleets – went to Boa Vista to investigate. He believed the
disease to have local origins. McWilliam's contribution to the dispute can be found in
his 'Remarks on Dr King's report', 1848 and 'Further observations', May 1852 (in
Medical Times and Gazette). Quite apart from this book's value as medical history, the
detail with which King conducts his investigation gives an insight into local life in a
style which at times resembles a detective novel.

220 **História da medicina em Cabo Verde.** (A history of medicine in Cape Verde.)
Henrique Lubrano de Santa-Rita Vieira.   Praia: Instituto Caboverdiano do Livro, 1989. 809p. bibliog. (Estudos e Ensaios).

With an apparently exhaustive use of the documents available from 1460 to 1975, Vieira traces the history of official medicine in the archipelago, making this volume of particular value for those interested in Portugal's colonial bureaucracy. It also covers the principal health problems of the 19th century – yellow fever, smallpox, measles, cholera, inadequate water supply to Praia and hunger. The bibliography of 135 items is a valuable resource.

221 **Juventude e adolescência, mulher e sociedade, psicopatias e desequilíbrios emocionais.** (Youth and adolescence, woman and society, mental illness and emotional disorders.)
Ireneu Gomes.   Praia: Instituto Caboverdiano do Livro, 1986. 37p. (Estudos e Ensaios).

This volume contains the text of three speeches on the theme of mental health made by the Cape Verdean Minister of Health. These are: 'O adolescente e a liberdade' (The adolescent and freedom), p. 9–17; 'Problemática social da mulher cabo-verdiana' (Social problems of the Cape Verdean woman), p. 19–29; 'Personalidades psicopáticas, neurose e crime' (Psychopathic personalities, neuroses and crime), p. 31–9. Gomes explains his subjects in general terms whilst relating them to societies – such as Cape Verde – in transition.

222 **A lepra na ilha do Fogo.** (Leprosy on Fogo Island.)
Henrique Teixeira de Sousa.   *Magma*, vol. 1, no. 1 (April 1988), p. 24-7.

Leprosy has long been present on Fogo. This an edited version of a 1952 report by the Delegacia de Saúde do Fogo (the Fogo Health Delegation). It first surveys the available 20th-century data on the number of cases, going on to describe the treatment and management of the disease.

223 **Nutrition et santé des enfants aux îles du Cap Vert.** (The nutrition and health of children in the Cape Verde Islands.)
Gaston Legrain, Miriam Cap.   *Environnement Africain*, vol. 4, nos 2-4 (1980), p. 111-30, 150, 188. 2 maps.

The authors attempt to find correlations between regional differences in infant health and such factors as population density, type of agriculture commonly practised, level of male emigration and access to health care. Statistics from the 1970s on infant mortality and nutrition are used. These are worse for rural areas in the interior of islands. Legrain and Cap conclude that infant health is better in areas of irrigated land and where households own their land. It is worse on unirrigated land, which tends to be the most remote from health centres, and more likely to have a high proportion of households headed by women. See 'The logic of Cape Verdean female-headed households: social response to economic scarcity', for a complementary study of the distribution of resources in rural areas.

224 **Serviços de saúde e assistência de Cabo Verde.** (Health and first-aid services in Cape Verde.)
António Tomaz Cabral. *Ultramar*, vol. 8, no. 30 (1967), p. 165-72.
A dry report on the structure of the health services and the location of facilities.

Sobre a terminologia anatómica nos crioulos de Cabo Verde.
See item no. 195.

Relief and aid

225 **Challenge and progress: the role of non-governmental aid in Cape Verde.**
Edited by Raymond A. Almeida. Praia: Instituto Caboverdiano de Solidariedade, 1983. 59p. 2 maps.
A brochure aimed at non-governmental aid organizations (NGOs), explaining the historical and geographical reasons for Cape Verde's need for aid. It also explains the role of the Instituto Caboverdiano de Solidariedade (the Cape Verdean Solidarity Institute) – itself a non-governmental organization – in coordinating aid projects, matching donors' interests with local projects. Many of the Instituto's achievements are documented, in such diverse fields as youth training, public transport and irrigation. Never underestimating the many problems which the islands face, this is nonetheless an encouraging perspective on the steps underway towards sustainable development. Special mention must be made of the black-and-white photographs which accompany the simultaneous English and Portuguese text. Unassuming portraits of the landscape and the men, women and chidren at work in it, they are a moving and representative tribute to this resilient nation.

226 **Development of national societies and co-operation: the viewpoint of the Red Cross of Cape Verde.**
Dario L. R. Dantas dos Reis. *International Review of the Red Cross*, no. 264 (May-June 1988), p. 213-18.
This article by the President of the Red Cross in Cape Verde describes the progress of his organization since 1980. Its principal activities are with the under-six age-group, providing food aid and nursery care. It is financed by a lottery and the sale of a 'Red Cross' stamp needed on some official documents.

227 **Plano de abastecimento de Cabo Verde em época de seca.** (Plan for the provisioning of Cape Verde in time of drought.)
A.N. Ramires de Oliveira, Júlio Monteiro, preface by H. Teixeira de Sousa, introduction by Luís de Albuquerque. Lisbon: Instituto de Investigação Científica Tropical, 1985. 331p. (Estudos, Ensaios e Documentos, no. 145).
Commissioned by order of the governor in 1959, this emergency contingency plan was produced in 1961. Although never put into operation, it is an interesting document in several respects. It aimed to fulfil Cape Verde's food requirements, synchronized with the agricultural calendar. It gives an idea of the administrative network operating in the islands together with the workings of government finances. It also provides localized information on population and food needs. H. Teixeira de Sousa's introduction graphically describes the effects of drought on the islands.

228 **Problemas de Cabo Verde: a situação mantém-se controlada.** (Problems of Cape Verde: the situation remains under control.)
António Lopes dos Santos. Lisbon: Agência-Geral do Ultramar, 1971. 93p.
Written during a serious drought, this is the governor's report to the legislative council. He speaks almost exclusively about the measures taken to alleviate the effects of drought, praising Marcello Caetano's Portuguese government for sending exactly the right amount of aid. Emigration to Portugal is being encouraged through several public agencies. The governor's priorities in dealing with the drought are to ensure that everyone receives an adequate level of nutrition, and that people should remain calm and daily life be undisrupted. He provides statistics to show the number of people benefiting from public assistance. This is in the form of food and vitamin distribution or public works programmes such as road-building. The cost of this to the Portuguese government is also shown. The III Plano de Fomento (development plan) is the framework for these programmes and it is described at some length. Central government legislation concerning Cape Verde is also outlined. The governor does not appear to be unaware of the gravity of the situation, but there is a depressing subtext to this report: the admitted increase in deaths from influenza and measles and the reality of malnourished children needing vitamin supplements. For a slightly earlier account of government measures to deal with this situation see *Progresso de Cabo Verde* (Progress in Cape Verde) by J.M. da Silva Cunha (Lisbon: Agência-Geral do Ultramar, 1969, 15p.).

Secas e fomes em Cabo Verde (achegas para o estudo das de 1845–1846 e de 1889-1890).
See item no. 135.

A igreja de Cabo Verde e o desenvolvimento.
See item no. 198.

Cabo Verde. (Aspectos sociais. Secas e fomes do século XX).
See item no. 207.

Politics and Government

General

229 **Aristides Pereira no interior de Santiago.** (Aristides Pereira in the
interior of Santiago.)
Praia: Edição Voz di Povo, 1978. 15p. map. (Edição Voz di Povo,
no. 2).

Between 11 and 18 July 1977 President Aristides Pereira went on a tour of the remote
rural and fishing communities of Santiago. This is a record of the journey with black-
and-white photographs and text extracts from the newspaper *Voz di Povo* (q.v.). It is
actually quite a good example of how government can work in Cape Verde:
photographs show a relaxed President and people discussing local projects. See also
Brava acolhe Presidente Aristides Pereira (Brava welcomes President Aristides Pereira)
(Praia: Edição Voz di Povo, 1978. 15p. [Edição Voz di Povo, no. 4]) for a record of
the President's visit to the various communities of this small island.

230 **Cape Verde: politics, economics and society.**
Colm Foy.   London: Pinter, 1988. 199p. map. bibliog.
(Marxist Regimes Series).

This is an excellent guide to the working of government in post-independence Cape
Verde and an extremely useful source of current data on politics, economics and
society. Foy gives a concise history of the ruling party – the Partido Africano da
Indepêndencia de Cabo Verde (PAICV) (African Party for the Independence of Cape
Verde) – noting the involvement of Cape Verdeans in the war in Guinea-Bissau and
the background and effects of the coup in Bissau in 1980 which led to the separation of
the Cape Verdean wing of the Partido Africano da Indepêndencia de Guiné e Cabo
Verde (PAIGC). This is probably the best description in English of the structure of the
PAICV and its involvement in society. Examples are given of its method of grass-roots
consultation. Potential weaknesses such as low urban turnout in recent elections and an
ageing party leadership are mentioned. Foy also manages to make sense of Cape
Verde's unusual economy. He is dealing with some extraordinary data – that, for
instance, agriculture occupies perhaps 90 per cent of the population in some way or

another, but accounts for less than 20 per cent of GDP (gross domestic product) and meets around 5 per cent of food needs. Even more surprisingly, famine is a thing of the past, and the balance of payments is usually positive. The economy relies, in fact, on revenues from the international airport on Sal (South Africa is a user), emigrants' remittances and varied sources of foreign aid. Also covered are industry, agricultural reform, health, education and foreign policy.

231 The Fortunate Isles: a study in African transformation.
Basil Davidson. London: Hutchinson, 1989. 221p. 2 maps. bibliog.

Davidson is well known in Cape Verde as a great friend to the nation, and this book will do nothing to change that opinion. A preliminary chapter on Cape Verde's history is far from being a dispassionate academic study. This intense personal involvement pays immense dividends in subsequent chapters dealing with events after the Second World War. Davidson's contacts as a journalist with the PAIGC in Guinea-Bissau during the struggle for independence have enabled him to gather valuable material on the Cape Verdean perspective on these events. Extracts from interviews with key-figures throw much-needed light on the resistance work of Cape Verdeans in Europe, Africa and Cape Verde. Equally valuable is Davidson's material on the confused period between the coup in Portugal on 25 April 1974 which overthrew the Caetano dictatorship, and Cape Verdean independence on 5 July 1975. In the final section, on the progress of the post-independence government towards its ideal of 'popular participation', Davidson gives the reader access to his impressions of government in action. There are, for example, accounts of a local meeting in rural Santo Antão discussing land reform with the PAICV official, and of a local court dealing with a case of drunkenness. This may not be the most tightly organized or rigorously indexed of reference works, but the value of its first-hand material cannot be doubted.

232 Guinée-Bissau, Cap-Vert: histoire et politique. (Guinea-Bissau, Cape Verde: history and politics.)
Patrick Chabal. *Le Mois en Afrique*, no. 190/191 (Oct./Nov. 1981), p. 119-39. bibliog.

This article summarizes the society, history and politics of Guinea-Bissau and Cape Verde. A final section discusses the causes and implications of the coup of 14 November 1980 in Guinea-Bissau, giving a contemporary perspective.

233 República de Cabo Verde: 5 anos de independência 1975-1980.
(Republic of Cape Verde: five years of independence 1975-80.)
Comissão do V Aniversário da Independência Nacional. Lisbon: Edições 70, 1980. 94p. map.

An official handbook to the republic, distributed by the Ministry of Foreign Affairs. Six chapters, with many black-and-white photographs, cover geography and population; the national symbols of flag, coat of arms and national anthem; history; the party and state institutions; the social and economic features of development; foreign policy and diplomatic relations.

234 **Sociedade, estado e partido político na República de Cabo Verde.**
(Society, state and political party in the Republic of Cape Verde.)
Leila M.G. Leite Hernandez. *Revista de Ciência Política*, vol. 31, no.
3 (July-Sept. 1988), p. 111-26.
In her opening discussion of Cape Verdean society Hernandez takes the interesting
approach of using a literary work – Teixeira de Sousa's *Ilhéu de contenda* (q.v.) – as
her informing text. This is in fact a very successful way of illustrating some of the
rigidities of colonial Cape Verdean rural society which have left their mark on present-
day culture. This colonial inheritance in public administration is the article's next
theme: transition is both a political and a cultural challenge for the PAICV. Finally,
Hernandez deals with the PAICV itself. A history of resistance to Portuguese rule is
traced back to protests in Santo Antão in 1886. Again, poets and writers are cited as
part of the islands' political history. The relationship of party and state is analysed, and
some of the problems in defining the state, the party and civil society are raised.
Essential to the functioning of this system are the organizations of popular
participation: their roles are described. This is a well-informed article which raises
some interesting questions about the Cape Verdean state.

Reforçar o partido e a democracia consolidar a independência.
See item no. 243.

PAIGC

235 **Os congressos da FRELIMO, do PAIGC, e do MPLA.** (The congresses
of the FRELIMO, the PAIGC and the MPLA.)
Luís Moita. Lisbon: Ulmeiro, 1979. 80p. (África em Luta, new series,
no. 1).
A comparative study of the three national parties of Mozambique (FRELIMO),
Guinea-Bissau/Cape Verde (PAIGC) and Angola (MPLA). Moita looks at constitutional structures, development strategies and attitudes to the struggle for independence.

236 **Manual político do PAIGC.** (PAIGC political handbook.)
Edited by Maria Isabel Pinto Ventura. [Lisbon]: Edições Maria da
Fonte, 1974. 2nd ed. 119p.
Intended to educate party members in the politics of the armed struggle, each chapter
is set out in the form of a question with an answer generally supplied from the words of
Amílcar Cabral. One of the questions which it is thought the party members might
wish answered is, not surprisingly, about how the PAIGC anticipates the liberation of
Cape Verde by military means. This is acknowledged to be difficult. Nevertheless,
Cabral adds, the advantage of difficult problems is that it forces people to think.

237 **Vencer a batalha da ideologia.** (Win the battle of ideology.)
Aristides Pereira.   Bissau: Edições PAIGC, 1980. 34p.

Pereira, in his capacity as general secretary of the PAIGC, made this report to the II
Sessão Ordinária do Conselho Superior da Luta (Second Ordinary Session of the
Higher Council of the Struggle) held in Bissau from 11 to 15 July 1980. It contains
reports and policy suggestions for the joint and parallel party institutions of Cape
Verde and Guinea-Bissau. With hindsight it is particularly interesting that Pereira
notes the lack of progress towards unity of the two countries. Bureaucracy and a lack
of motivation seem to be to blame.

PAICV

238 **O estado.** (The state.)
PAICV.   Praia: Edição do DIP do PAICV, 1984. 24p. (Documentos
do II Congresso).

The First Congress in 1981 had established that the joint party structures of the
PAIGC were untenable after the coup in Guinea-Bissau. The Second Congress of the
PAICV, held in 1983, confirmed the changes which had been made, and held new
elections to the Conselho Nacional (the National Council). A series of documents were
published to explain the new structures. *O estado* discusses the organization and role of
the state, the party's role in the state and the role of the masses.

239 **PAICV First Congress.**
Praia: PAICV; London: Mozambique, Angola and Guiné Information
Centre, 1981. 35p. (MAGIC State Papers and Party Proceedings. Series
III, no. 1).

These historic documents, in English translation, are from the special conference of
Cape Verdean PAIGC militants convened in January 1981 in response to the coup in
Guinea-Bissau on 14 November 1980. The conference transformed itself into a
congress and the Partido Africano da Independência de Cabo Verde (the African party
for the independence of Cape Verde) was formed. The documents include Aristides
Pereira's introductory speech giving his reasoned interpretation of events in Guinea-
Bissau. He discusses the ideological importance which unity between the two countries
had had. Free trade between the two countries and equal rights for their citizens had
been some of the positive aspects of the process towards unity. 'Cape Verdean
colonialism' had been one of the reasons given for the coup by its perpetrators: he
denies this, pointing out that there were very few Cape Verdeans in Guinea-Bissau,
and that claims that the constitution of Guinea-Bissau allowed a Cape Verdean to
become President were nonsense. Looking to the future, the party in Cape Verde must
act quickly to preserve continuity of government in Cape Verde and make the
necessary administrative changes. Other documents include the proclamation of the
PAICV, the general resolution of the First Congress of the PAICV and Pedro Pires'
closing speech (all of 20 January 1981). In a gracious valediction to unity, Pires thanks
the people of Guinea-Bissau for their help in winning Cape Verde its freedom.

240 **O partido.** (The party.)
PAICV. Praia: Edição do DIP do PAICV, 1984. 39p. (Documentos do II Congresso).

This document begins with a history of the PAICV and the PAIGC, going on to outline ideology, the training and role of party cadres and the PAICV's role in society as the leading political force. A final section deals with party development and consolidation – something considered very important after the disappointing events in Bissau in November 1980. Aristides Pereira, Cape Verde's president, felt that party discipline and ideology had been less than rigorous and that this helped allow the coup to occur.

241 **Partido Africano da Independência de Cabo Verde III Congresso (25-30 de Novembro de 1988).** (African Party for the Independence of Cape Verde [PAICV] III Congress [25-30 November 1988].)
[Praia]: Departamento de Acção Ideológica do CN, [1989]. 86p. (Documentos de Congresso).

The Third Congress's slogan is 'Num mundo em transformação, um partido para o futuro' (A changing world, a party for the future). This document contains the resolutions passed at the congress and the secretary-general's closing speech.

242 **Programa e estatutos do PAICV.** (Programme and statutes of the PAICV.)
PAICV. Praia: Edição do DIP do PAICV, [1983]. 68p.

This document sets out the statutes of the new party. These were confirmed at the Second Congress in June 1983.

243 **Reforçar o partido e a democracia consolidar a independência.** (Strengthening the party and democracy, consolidating independence.)
Aristides Pereira. Praia: Edição do DIP do PAICV, 1983. 144p.

This is the Conselho Nacional's report to the Second Congress of the PAICV, given by the Secretáry-General, Aristides Pereira. It is a wide-ranging document, covering the party, the state, economic and social development, organizations in Cape Verdean society and foreign relations. In fact, almost every feature of life in Cape Verde is given an informal annual report: agencies reviewed range from nature lovers to emigrants' support, from agrarian reform to sport to publishing.

244 **O trabalho ideológico do partido.** (The party's ideological work.)
PAICV. [Praia]: Edição do DIP do PAICV, 1983. 34p. (Documentos do II Congresso).

Communication and discussion are important to the working of the PAICV and this paper describes methods of diffusion of party ideology and ideological education. This is not just for party members, but also for the general population so as to make 'participative democracy' a reality.

245 **Unidade e Luta.** (Unity and Struggle.)
Praia: Conselho Nacional do PAICV, 1976- . periodicity varies.

In newspaper format, this was first the information organ of the Cape Verde branch of the PAIGC. It began a second series in August 1980, and a third in 1984. It contains political reporting and articles on the party's role in society. *Informação* (Information)

(Praia: Departamento de Acção Ideológica do Secretariado do Conselho Nacional do PAICV, 1987- . irreg.) is the internal party publication.

Sociedade, estado e partido político na República de Cabo Verde.
See item no. 234.

Tribuna.
See item no. 465.

Government and administration

246   **Assembleia Nacional Popular da República de Cabo Verde.** (The People's National Assembly of the Republic of Cape Verde.) Mindelo, Cape Verde: Edição da ANP, 1983. 112p.

Four documents concerned with the functioning of the Cape Verdean parliament are published here. The first (p. 7-71) is the Regimento da Assembleia Nacional Popular (rules of the People's National Assembly), 1982, which governs the powers and procedure of parliament. The next (p. 75-85) is the Estatuto dos deputados da República de Cabo Verde (statute on Cape Verdean deputies), 1982, which sets out who is eligible to become a deputy and what their powers, immunities and responsibilities are. Third (p. 89-103) is the Lei orgânica da Assembleia Nacional Popular (fundamental law of the People's National Assembly), 1982, which determines parliament's structures and administration. These are laws nos 6/II/82, 7/II/82 and 8/II/82 respectively. The last document (p. 107-12) is the Regulamento do Conselho Administrativo da Assembleia Nacional Popular (regulations of the Administrative Council of the People's National Assembly) which is the code by which the administrative structures work.

247   **FARP: 10 anos na defesa da nação.** (FARP: 10 years in the defence of the nation.)
[Praia]: Direcção Política das FARP e Milícias, [1985]. 41p.

Produced for the tenth anniversary celebrations of Cape Verde's independence, this is a brochure describing the history and work of the Forças Armadas Revolucionárias do Povo (the People's Revolutionary Armed Forces). The origins of the army are with the so-called 'Grupo de 1965' (the 1965 group) who were a small number of Cape Verdeans who decided to leave Cape Verde and join the PAIGC's armed struggle in Guinea-Bissau. The work goes on to describe the contemporary role of the army. National service is for all men aged between 18 and 25: this is described as not simply a means of raising manpower, but of training young people in the idea of serving their country. Training programmes in combat and political education are described, with sport and cultural programmes also noted. Officer selection, training and education are also covered. The armed forces provide manpower for projects in the community – in construction work, literacy programmes, and most importantly, in the reafforestation programme. They have planted around one million trees since independence. This volume clearly considers that the army's most important work is that of educating the young men who enter it, with political education a high priority.

248   **I e II sessões legislativas da 2ª Legislatura. Documentos.** (The first and
second legislative sessions of the Second Legislature. Documents.)
Assembleia Nacional Popular.   Praia: Edição da ANP, 1981. 44p.

Texts of selected speeches made in parliament are published here. Not quite a series as
such, but for further records of parliamentary activity see also *3ª sessão legislativa da II
Legislatura – 1982 (discursos parlamentares)* (The third legislative session of the second
Legislature – 1982 [parliamentary speeches]) (Mindelo, Cape Verde: [n.p.], 1982.
62p.) and *IV sessão legislativa da II Legislatura – 1982. Discursos parlamentares* (The
fourth legislative session of the second Legislature – 1982. Parliamentary speeches)
(Assembleia Nacional Popular da República de Cabo Verde. Praia: Edição da ANP,
1983. 70p.).

249   **Programa de governo 1986-90.** (The government programme 1986-90.)
Pedro de Verona Rodrigues Pires.   Praia: Edição do Gabinete do
Primeiro Ministro, 1986. 106p.

The Prime Minister, Pedro Pires, presents the government programme for the third
legislature. This covers generalities of the state, democracy and development;
administration; foreign relations; social policy; and economic policy. In this latter
section it is interesting to note the positive and encouraging attitude which is taken
towards private enterprise.

Developments in Angola, Cape Verde and São Tomé and Príncipe.
See item no. 152.

A constituição da República de Cabo Verde: un parlamentarismo sem modelo.
See item no. 251.

Boletim Oficial de Cabo Verde.
See item no. 460.

Constitution and Legal System

Constitution

250 **Constituição da República de Cabo Verde.** (Constitution of the Republic of Cape Verde.)
Praia: Grafedito, [n.d.]. 41p.

This is the constitution which embraces the 'institutional alterations' necessary after the coup in Guinea-Bissau in November 1980. The coup separated the two countries and prompted the formation of the PAICV. The revisions were made in February 1981 to a constitution which had originally been approved in September 1980.

251 **A constituição da República de Cabo Verde: un parlamentarismo sem modelo.** (The constitution of the Republic of Cape Verde: a parliamentary system without a model.)
Luís Mendonça. *Revista do Ministério da Justiça*, vol. 8, no. 21 (July-Dec. 1983), p. 93-116.

Mendonça compares the constitution to that of other developing nations and makes many references to Amílcar Cabral's political thinking. In confronting the contentious issue of democratic government in a one-party state this interesting article concludes that Cape Verde's constitution enshrines the role of the people through participation in mass organizations. It is hard to see how this system could be easily repeated in a more populous, less close-knit society.

252 **Les institutions organiques de 1975 du Cap Vert et de 1973 de la Guinée-Bissau.** (Fundamental institutions of Cape Verde, 1975, and Guinea-Bissau, 1973.)
André Durieux. Brussels: Académie Royale des Sciences d'Outre-Mer, 1980. 40p.

The first part of this work deals with the law on the political organization of Cape Verde which came into being, with independence, on 5 July 1975. Durieux summarizes the articles of this law, which deals with the role of the PAIGC, the institutions of parliament, presidency, ministerial government and judicial power. Pre-existing legislation is kept in force except where it contradicts national sovereignty, subsequent legislation or the principles and objectives of the PAIGC. This was not a constitution proper: Durieux comments, in fact, that it is an unusual law because it omits so much. He notes the omission of rulings on citizenship, on conditions for becoming a deputy and that little is said about rules for the PAIGC, or on the economic system. He comments on its relationship to a future constitution and constitutional association with Guinea-Bissau. The constitution of Guinea-Bissau of 24 November 1973 is discussed in a second section. He notes its commitment to unity between the two countries: working against unity is a punishable offence; Cape Verdeans are considered to be citizens of Guinea-Bissau. A final section includes comparisons between the two laws.

253 **Political and administrative statute of the province of Cape Verde.**
Ministry of the Overseas Provinces. Lisbon: Agência-Geral do Ultramar, [1963]. 41p.

This document is a fine example of Portuguese colonial hypocrisy. The second article states that Cape Verde is an autonomous region of the Republic of Portugal with its own internal juridical charcter. However, the system of government subsequently outlined belies any local autonomy. The Lisbon-appointed governor has immense power. The legislative assembly is a rubber-stamping body of twenty-one members. Eighteen of these are elected: six from the electoral roll, two by taxpayers of 1000 or more *escudos*, two by public administrative bodies, two by an employers' association, two by 'bodies representing the working class', two by bodies representing moral, social or cultural interests and two by private institutions. None of the members of the consultative body is elected.

Law

254 **Código de família.** (Family code.)
Ministério da Justiça. Praia: Edição do Gabinete de Estudos, Legislação e Documentação do Ministério da Justiça, 1981. 46p.

Decreto-Lei no. 58/81 encodes all aspects of marriage, parental obligations, adoption and guardianship. Overturning the 1966 civil code, it is widely considered to be a legislative landmark of the post-colonial era. For example, there is no legal discrimination against children born outside marriage, thus bringing Cape Verdean law into accord with the realities of Cape Verdean life.

255 **Colectânea de Jurisprudência.** (Collection of Jurisprudence.)
Praia: Ministério da Justiça, Direcção-Geral de Estudos, Legislação e Documentação, 1980- . annual.

Publishes decisions of the supreme court. Unfortunately it is somewhat adrift in its publishing schedule.

256 **Estatutos do IPAJ.** (Statutes of the Institute for Legal Support and
Assistance.)
Ministério da Justiça. Praia: Edição do Gabinete de Estudos,
Legislação e Documentação do Ministério da Justiça, [1982]. 34p.
The IPAJ (Instituto do Patrocínio e Assistência Judiciários) was founded in 1978 and
these are its revised statutes. The document gives the reader an idea of the aims and
functions of the lawyers of Cape Verde. The IPAJ members work both privately and as
a free legal aid service.

257 **Extracto da intervenção proferida pela Dra. Vera Duarte no seminário
nacional 'Juventude e desenvolvimento' sobre a tema 'direitos e
responsibilidades dos jovens'.** (Extract from Vera Duarte's contribution
on the theme of 'rights and responsibilities of young people' to the
national seminar on 'Youth and development'.)
Vera Duarte. *Revista do Ministério da Justiça*, vol. 8, no. 20 (Jan.-
June 1983), p. 155-62.
Duarte outlines the legal status of children with regard to the Código de Menores
(code for minors), 1982, Decreto-Lei no. 89/82. She also covers the legal aspects of
children and families, and juvenile delinquency.

258 **Legislação penal.** (Penal legislation.)
Ministério da Justiça. Praia: Edição do Gabinete de Estudos,
Legislação e Documentação do Ministério da Justiça, 1979. 20p.
An interesting collection of laws published in the three years following independence.
Although varied in content, they give an impression of the priorities and problems of
the new government. Decreto-Lei no. 37/75 punishes the spreading of rumours which
threaten public order and are counter-revolutionary. Decreto-Lei no. 32/77 establishes
a pricing system for essential goods and services: these will either have a fixed price, a
controlled price or a price subject to a determined profit margin. Portaria no. 59/77
punishes speculation in essential goods. Decreto no. 1/78 notes that Cape Verde is
heavily reliant on imported food, which is becoming increasingly expensive, partly
because of the number of middlemen involved in its distribution. This edict defines
which middlemen are permissible. Decreto-Lei no. 40/78 deals with an integral part of
Cape Verdean life, the distilling of sugar-cane rum. The cost of licences and the tax on
sugar-cane cultivation are brought up to date. Decreto-Lei no. 78/78 increases the
penalties for receiving stolen goods.

259 **Lei da nacionalidade e regulamento.** (Law and regulations concerning
nationality.)
Ministério da Justiça. Praia: Edição do Gabinete de Estudos,
Legislação e Documentação do Ministério da Justiça, 1979. 25p.
Two documents are published here, the law of nationality of 1976 (Decreto-Lei
no. 71/76) and the accompanying regulations setting out the necessary paperwork
(Decreto no. 197/76). Nationality is an issue complicated in Cape Verde by the rights
of citizens of Guinea-Bissau and by the needs of the large numbers of Cape Verdeans
who live and raise families abroad. This legislation accommodates both.

260 **L'organisation judicaire dans les colonies portugaises.** (The judicial
system of the Portuguese colonies.)
A. de Almada Negreiros. Brussels: Institut Colonial International,
1908. 31p.

The first part of this work deals with the judicial system from 1495 to 1894. This period
covers the rule of the captains whose judicial powers were later given to the *ouvidôres*
(judges) who acted as if they were in Portugal; the many abuses of judicial power such
as participating in smuggling; and the frequent use of exile to the colonies as a
punishment. Details of developments and legislation relevant to Cape Verde are listed
on pages 11-12. The second part covers the decree of 20 February 1894. This brought
all colonial judicial matters together in one document. Cape Verde and Guinea-Bissau
became part of the judicial district of Lisbon.

261 **Reformar contra os dias antigos.** (Reforming against the past.)
Luís Mendonça. *Revista do Ministério da Justiça*, vol. 7, nos 17-19
(Jan.-Dec. 1982), p. 157-63.

Mendonça discusses the rather limited role of customary law in Cape Verde and
praises the post-independence legislation which synthesizes the written and the
unwritten codes of the past. He describes the new law as a Cape Verdean 'common
law'. For further material on customary law see 'Direito escrito, direito costumeiro. A
formação de um novo direito' (Written law, customary law. The formation of a new
law), Ministério da Justiça, *Revista do Ministério da Justiça*, vol. 4, no. 7 (1979), p. 49-
58; and 'Comunicação apresentada pelo Ministro da Justiça de Cabo Verde ao
seminário internacional sobre direito costumeiro' (Paper presented by the Cape
Verdean Minister of Justice to an international seminar on customary law) by David
Hopffer Almada, *Revista do Ministério da Justiça*, vol. 9, no. 22 (Jan.-June 1984),
p. 169-80.

262 **Revista do Ministério da Justiça.** (Review of the Ministry of Justice.)
Praia: Edição do Gabinete de Estudos, Legislação e Documentação do
Ministério da Justiça, 1975/1976- . periodicity varies.

This is a well-produced and scholarly journal, published three times a year for the
period 1978-79 and twice a year between 1980 and 1984, with some problems in
maintaining a regular publishing schedule. Founded by the Minister of Justice, David
Hopffer Almada, its aim is to increase knowledge about the law and to reflect the
changes being brought about by post-colonial government. Staple features are texts of
new legislation, jurisprudence from decisions of the Conselho Nacional de Justiça (the
National Council of Justice), official dispatches, tribunal sentences, comparative law
(usually dealing with law from the other Portuguese-speaking African nations) and
articles concerning various aspects of justice and the judicial system in Cape Verde.

263 **II encontro dos Ministros da Justiça de Angola, Cabo Verde, Guiné-
Bissau, Moçambique e São Tomé e Príncipe.** (The second meeting of the
Ministers of Justice of Angola, Cape Verde, Guinea-Bissau,
Mozambique and São Tomé and Príncipe.)
Revista do Ministério da Justiça, vol. 9, no. 23 (1985), p. 1-98.

This is a special issue of the *Revista do Ministério da Justiça*, covering the proceedings
of the meeting held in Praia in November 1983. The first session covers changing the
colonial court into a people's court: Cape Verde's paper appears on pages 41-7. The
second session concerns the balance between the role of the judge and that of
jurisprudence as the source of law: Cape Verde's paper appears on pages 84-94 and

notes the importance of jurisprudence in Cape Verde's legal system. The third session discusses the mechanisms of legal control inside and outside the courts: the various institutions involved in the legal system in Cape Verde are outlined on pages 124-32. Finally the role of lawyers and legal aid is dealt with: in Cape Verde, this means the IPAJ (p. 155-66). This is an interesting opportunity to compare the papers of the five nations. Unfortunately, the 'I encontro dos Ministros da Justiça de Angola, Cabo Verde, Guiné-Bissau, Moçambique e São Tomé e Príncipe' (The first meeting of the Ministers of Justice of Angola, Cape Verde, Guinea-Bissau, Mozambique and São Tomé and Príncipe) which was published in another special issue of the *Revista do Ministério da Justiça* (vol. 4, no. 7, 1979, 58p.), contains only papers from Cape Verde. These concerned the building of new states and new legal systems (p. 9-21), building popular justice (p. 23-48), and forming a new law from the heritage of written law and customary law (p. 49-58).

Legislação publicada de 1975 a 1985.
See item no. 314.

Prison

264   **Tarrafal: o pântano da morte.** (Tarrafal: the swamp of death.)
     Cândido Fernandes Plácido de Oliveira, introduction by José
     Magalhães Godinho.   Lisbon: Editorial República, 1974. 152p.
     (Colecção Documentos).

Between 1936 and 1974 Tarrafal, Santiago, was the site of an infamous prison, run by the PIDE [Portuguese secret police], where many of the opponents of colonial rule and the dictatorship in Portugal were sent. Godinho's introduction gives some biographical details about de Oliveira. He was a sports journalist and an anti-fascist who spent the years from 1936 to 1943 in Tarrafal. This book is a distressing account of his experiences there and a memorial to the many who died. His first chapter passionately denies that Tarrafal is merely a penal colony: it is, rather, a concentration camp where prisoners are held long after their sentences have been completed or, indeed, without ever having been sentenced. Some Cape Verdeans were also imprisoned in Tarrafal. De Oliveira comments on how Cape Verdeans in general are exploited by the Portuguese. He gives a description of the prison buildings and the prison régime: both are designed to ensure isolation. Cruelly, a wall was built for the sole purpose of preventing the prisoners from ever seeing out of the camp to the sea. Malaria, combined with a lack of medical care and quinine, took a dreadful toll of prisoners: de Oliveira estimates that fifteen per cent of prisoners between 1936 and 1943 died of malaria. Tuberculosis was another killer. The final chapter, 'Frigideira: a câmara de cimento' (Saucepan: the cement chamber) gives a horrific account of the punishment cells where temperatures reached 40-60°C and prisoners were intentionally exposed to mosquitoes.

265 **Tratamento institucional com as pessoas privadas de liberdade e sua reincorporação no seio da sociedade.** (Institutional treatment for persons deprived of their freedom, and their reintegration into society.)
Revista do Ministério da Justiça, vol. 4, nos 8-9 (Jan.-Aug. 1979), p. 151-8.

Cape Verde's very poor prison facilities are described. There is only one prison, the Cadeia Civil de São Vicente (the São Vicente civil prison), and it is underfunded. Re-education is an important aim of the prison service, and although conditions are difficult, workshops, sport and literacy programmes do take place. A humane view is taken of the causes of crime, with poverty and unemployment cited and the particular problems of mentally ill and juvenile offenders noted. This humanity is also shown in the frequent amnesties which the president grants to prisoners, although lack of facilities may be another motive.

Foreign Relations

General

266 **Blockfreie Aussenpolitik eines afrikanischen Kleinstaates: das Beispiel Kap Verde.** (Non-aligned foreign policy in small African states: the case of Cape Verde.)
Peter Meyns. Hamburg, Germany: Institut für Afrika-Kunde, 1990.
151p. 2 maps. bibliog. (Arbeiten aus dem Institut für Afrika-Kunde, no. 63).

Post-independence Cape Verde's foreign policy of non-alignment is examined in this useful volume. Meyns first gives the relevant context to this policy by outlining Cape Verde's history and socio-economic structure. Challenges common to Third World island states are also discussed. Some of the particular problems of Cape Verde's foreign relations are looked at in detail. These include the importance of Cape Verdean emigrant communities, reliance on foreign aid, the failure of the proposed union with Guinea-Bissau and the continuing controversy over the granting of landing rights on Sal to South African Airways. The importance of PALOP (the organization of the five Portuguese-speaking African nations) is highlighted. Finally the recent programme of 'extroversion' – the entry of Cape Verde into the global economy – is examined. Meyns final conclusions are that, despite obvious handicaps, Cape Verde has 'a self-determined and active foreign policy', greatly facilitated by its 'strict non-alignment'. A lengthy English-language summary, p. 147-51, and a good bibliography, p. 137-45, contribute to the value of this study.

267 **Brazilian relations with Portuguese Africa in the context of the elusive 'Luso-Brazilian community'.**
Wayne A. Selcher. *Journal of Interamerican Studies and World Affairs*, vol. 18, no. 1 (Feb. 1976), p. 25-58. bibliog.

In the early 1970s Brazil was trying to balance a foreign policy which both supported the African non-aligned nations and yet also maintained a good relationship with Portugal. As part of the relationship with Lisbon, Selcher explains, Brazil hoped to be able to use Cape Verde as a support base for her South Atlantic fleet. Although respectably quick to recognize Guinea-Bissau's independence, Brazil remained non-committal in her attitude to Cape Verde. See also Selcher's *The Afro-Asian dimension of Brazilian foreign policy, 1956-1972* (Gainesville, Florida: University Presses of Florida, 1974. 252p. bibliog.) on Brazil's ambiguous attitude to the Portuguese colonies. José Honório Rodrigues' *Brazil and Africa* (translated by Richard A. Mazzara and Sam Hileman. Los Angeles; Berkeley, California: University of California Press, 1965. 382p.) covers a much greater time-span (1500-1960) and includes some interesting historical material on the early exchanges of people and foodstuffs between Brazil and Africa, a process in which Cape Verde played a notable role.

268 **Cabo Verde: imagens de dez anos de diplomacia 1975-1985.** (Cape Verde: pictures from ten years of diplomacy 1975-85.)
[Praia]: Edição Ministério dos Negócios Estrangeiros, 1985. 56p. map.

Cape Verde's foreign policy of non-alignment is affirmed in this brochure of photographs and text. The African regional organizations of which Cape Verde is a member – the OAU (Organization for African Unity), ECOWAS (Economic Community of West African States), CONCP (Conferência das Organizações Nacionalistas das Colónias Portuguesas) and CILSS (the Permanent Interstate Committee for Drought Control in the Sahel) – are outlined, as are the many other international relations which Cape Verde maintains, including its active membership of the United Nations Organization (UN). Cooperation for development and protection for Cape Verdean emigrants abroad are the other foreign policy essentials.

269 **Cabo Verde: opção por uma política de paz.** (Cape Verde: option for a policy of peace.)
Renato Cardoso. Praia: Instituto Caboverdiano do Livro, 1986. 109p. bibliog. (Colecção Estudos e Ensaios).

Cardoso, in his capacity as adviser to the Prime Minister, presented this paper at a seminar on Portuguese-speaking Africa, Portugal and the USA (May 1985). It outlines Cape Verdean foreign policy, with particular reference to Cape Verde's role in the negotiations on the future of Angola. Policies on cooperation and development, African unity and the Lomé Convention are also addressed.

270 **Discursos de Sua Excelência Senhor Aristides Maria Pereira Presidente da República de Cabo Verde proferidos no estrangeiro, no ano de 1983.** (Speeches given abroad in 1983 by His Excellency Aristides Maria Pereira, President of the Republic of Cape Verde.)
Praia: Grafedito, 1984. 69p.

The text of keynote speeches made at the seventh summit conference of non-aligned nations, the thirty-eighth session of the General Assembly of the UN, the fifth conference of the Club du Sahel, the twenty-second session of the general conference of UNESCO (UN Educational, Scientific and Cultural Organization) and the fourth conference of the heads of state of the five Portuguese-speaking African nations.

271 **Visita do Presidente João Figueiredo à Nigéria, Guiné Bissau, Senegal, Argélia e Cabo Verde Novembro 1983.** (The visit of President João Figueiredo to Nigeria, Guinea-Bissau, Senegal, Algeria and Cape Verde in November 1983.)
Brasília: Presidência da República, Gabinete Civil, Secretaria de Imprensa e Divulgação, 1984. 152p.

On his way home after visiting various countries of West and North Africa, the Brazilian president stopped off at Sal, Cape Verde for a few hours. The texts of speeches made by Figueiredo and President Pereira of Cape Verde are reproduced here (p. 133-52). Figueiredo remarks on the strong historical and cultural links between the two nations and notes the many official contacts between them. The contribution which the Cape Verdean emigrant workers make to Brazilian society is acknowledged. The two leaders issued a 22-point joint communiqué (p. 139-44), confirming their friendly relationship and expressing concern about events in Southern Africa and Central America.

Integration, development and equity: economic integration in West Africa.
See item no. 289.

With Guinea-Bissau

272 **The coup in Guinea-Bissau: chronology.**
People's Power in Mozambique, Angola and Guinea-Bissau, no. 17 (Spring 1981), p. 16-22.

Events from 14 November 1980 to 15 January 1981 are set out as reported in *Voz di Povo* (17 January 1981). This account seems to emphasize Guinean complaints about the relationship with Cape Verde. Cape Verdeans are blamed for delays in the supply of food: this is denied. UPANG (Patriotic Anti-colonialist Union of Guinea-Bissau) is quoted as praising the coup as 'the end of the burden of the most bloodthirsty and heinous age-old foreign domination': they are presumed to be referring to Cape Verde. PAIGC reactions in Cape Verde to the coup are given, as are those of other nations. Barry Munslow's article 'The coup in Guinea-Bissau and the Cape Verdian response' (*Communist Affairs*, vol. 1, no. 1 [1982], p. 55-60. bibliog.) is useful as a gloss on the relevant aspects of *PAICV First Congress* (q.v.).

273 **A questão da unidade no pensamento de Amílcar Cabral.** (The question of unity in Amílcar Cabral's thinking.)
Sérgio Ribeiro, prefaces by Vasco Cabral, Alfredo Moura. Lisbon: Tricontinental Editora, 1983. 55p. (Colecção Terceiro Mundo).

Apart from the addition of prefaces by Vasco Cabral and Alfredo Moura, this is otherwise the same work that Ribeiro presented in *Continuar Cabral: simpósio internacional Amílcar Cabral 17 a 20 de Janeiro de 1983* (q.v.). It is a useful interpretation of Cabral's thoughts on African unity and unity between Cape Verde and Guinea-Bissau, as well as a discussion of the historical links between the two nations. Its main interest, however, lies in Ribeiro's thoughts about more contemporary relations – and divergences – between the two countries. He notes that in 1980

97

40 per cent of Cape Verde's trade was with Portugal and only 1 per cent with Guinea-Bissau. Nevertheless there are some logical products for them to trade, such as salt and construction materials from Cape Verde for agricultural produce from Guinea-Bissau. He suggests that Cape Verde should try to direct its economy towards Africa via a privileged link with Guinea-Bissau. He fears that without some kind of unity Guinea-Bissau will be swallowed into the French sphere of influence of Senegal and Guinea-Conakry.

274 **'Unidade e luta': the struggle for unity between Guinea-Bissau and Cape Verde.**
Colm Foy. *People's Power in Mozambique, Angola and Guinea-Bissau*, no. 15 (Winter 1979), p. 10-27.
The colonial administration and historical links of the two countries are outlined: between 1640 and 1834 they were ruled jointly under the governor of Cape Verde; from 1834 to 1879 Guinea-Bissau was a subprefecture of Cape Verde; from 1879 to independence they were administered separately. The future prospects for unity are discussed. At the time of writing there were some coordinated development plans between the two nations, although Foy sees their great physical, social and economic differences. He concludes that, 'They are after all, 600 miles apart and travel over such distances is unthinkable for the vast majority of the population, so the only commitment to unity anyone can have is going to be on a relatively high ideological level'.

The cultural dimension in the strategy for national liberation: the cultural bases of the unification between Cape Verde and Guinea-Bissau.
See item no. 209.

Guinée-Bissau, Cap-Vert: histoire et politique.
See item no. 232.

Vencer a batalha da ideologia.
See item no. 237.

PAICV First Congress.
See item no. 239.

Les institutions organiques de 1975 du Cap Vert et de 1973 de la Guinée-Bissau.
See item no. 252.

International aid

275 **Agreement on the accession of the Republic of Cape Verde to the ACP-EEC Convention of Lomé.**
London: HMSO, 1977. 7p. (European Communities, no. 30 [1977]).
A text of the agreement made in Brussels, 28 March 1977, admitting Cape Verde to the Lomé Convention. This is an important source of aid for Cape Verde. For more information on the background and prospects of the third Lomé Convention see the collection of papers edited by Robert Boardman, Timothy M. Shaw, Panayotis

Soldatos, *Europe, Africa and Lomé III* (Lanham, Maryland; London: University Press of America, 1985. 158p.).

276 **Aid in Africa.**
Guy Arnold. London: Kogan Page; New York: Nichols, 1979. 240p. bibliog.

A general guide to who gives aid to whom and their reasons and methods for so doing. The wider political and economic issues of aid dependency are discussed: Arnold concludes that 'the poor get poorer'. *Inter alia* information can be found on some of Cape Verde's donor relationships with Canada, the European Economic Community (EEC), the USSR, Saudi Arabia, Sweden and West Germany.

277 **Aspectos financeiros da cooperação entre Portugal e os PALOP à luz da adesão portuguesa à CEE.** (Financial aspects of the cooperation between Portugal and the Portuguese-speaking African nations in the light of Portuguese accession to the EEC.)
Jochen Oppenheimer. *Estudos de Economia*, vol. 6, no. 3 (April-June 1986), p. 321–34.

Portugal's bilateral role is likely to be replaced by the EEC's multilateral one. Tables show the amounts of Portuguese aid to her former African colonies for the years 1980-84. These figures demonstrate Cape Verde's favoured position. See also *Portugal – países africanas – CEE cooperação e integração* (Portugal – African nations – EEC cooperation and integration), edited by Eduardo de Sousa Ferreira and Paula Fernandes dos Santos (Lisbon: Gradiva; CEDEP, 1985. 174p.), which is the report of a workshop on the effects on Portugal's accession to the EEC. A section on relations between Portuguese-speaking African nations, the EEC and Portugal (p. 101-67) contains some details of the type and sources of aid received by Cape Verde.

278 **Cape Verde: a very poor country strives to improve its lot.**
The Courier, no. 107 (Jan.-Feb. 1988), p. 15-31. map.

The Courier is an European Community journal concerned with the Africa-Caribbean-Pacific (ACP) nations who are signatories to the Lomé Conventions. This issue's 'country report' features Cape Verde. Ministers and public officials are interviewed about issues which affect development and foreign cooperation. For example, the system of food aid and distribution – largely carried out through the stores of the government public supply company, EMPA – is explained. Programmes for the development of agriculture, light industry, the CABNAVE shipyard (Mindelo) and the international airport at Sal are discussed. The airport is an important factor in Cape Verde's foreign relations: in 1979 the OAU classed the islands as a frontline state because of their dependence on South African royalties. US sanctions against South African flights have seriously affected revenue. Aristides Pereira and Pedro Pires give substantial interviews. Finally Martino Meloni, the EEC delegate in Cape Verde, specifies the areas of cooperation between the EEC and Cape Verde. These have focused on food aid, electricity generation, water supply and reafforestation. *The Courier* (no. 65 [Jan.-Feb. 1981], p. 17-29) published a similar report entitled 'Cape Verde: the Sahel in the sea'.

Foreign Relations. International aid

279 **The Club du Sahel: an experiment in international co-operation.**
Anne de Lattre, Arthur M. Fell. Paris: Organization for Economic
Cooperation and Development, 1984. 112p. map. bibliog.

The Club du Sahel, set up in 1976, is a joint organization of the Organization for
Economic Cooperation and Development (OECD) and the Permanent Interstate
Committee for Drought Control in the Sahel (the CILSS). Cape Verde became a
member of CILSS in 1975, joining Burkina Faso, Chad, Gambia, Mali, Mauritania,
Niger and Senegal. The original role of the Club du Sahel was the coordination of
drought aid to CILSS countries. It has since become involved in stimulating research,
planning and action for the long-term development of the Sahel. This volume reports
on the work of the Club du Sahel and considers its value as a new form of international
development cooperation. The bibliography (p. 99-112) contains material published by
CILSS and the Club du Sahel, arranged by subject.

280 **Crisis in the Sahel: a case study in development cooperation.**
Noel V. Lateef, preface by Michael Reisman. Boulder, Colorado:
Westview Press, 1980. 287p. (Westview Special Studies in Social,
Political and Economic Development).

Lateef describes current development policies in the Sahel and examines the
international programme for the region following the 1968-74 drought. Particular
attention is given to the USA's role in the Sahel Development Programme. Cape
Verde is included as part of the Sahel, but is not treated specifically.

Challenge and progress: the role of non-governmental aid in Cape Verde.
See item no. 225.

Economy

General

281 **Algumas notas sobre a expansão monetária e a monetarização da economia Cabo-Verdiana (1950-1973).** (Notes concerning monetary expansion and monetarization of the Cape Verdean economy [1950-73].)
João Estêvão. *Estudos de Economia*, vol. 6, no. 3 (April-June 1986), p. 279-91. bibliog.

A brief survey of the historical background to Cape Verde's almost permanent currency crisis leads into a detailed review of the period in question. From 1950 to 1970 the Banco Nacional Ultramarino played an important role in the eight-fold increase in the money supply although the credit which it supplied notoriously did not go to investment in agriculture or industry. External sources such as Portuguese state expenditure and emigrants' remittances were also of significance. This has all contributed to the enlargement of monetary 'space'. Estêvão divides the Cape Verdean economy into three zones: the monetarized urban zones of Praia, Mindelo and Sal; the semi-monetarized mercantile sector; and a sector of the agricultural community which is little penetrated by money, being self-sufficient farmers and using reciprocal labour. Gradually, the distinctions between these zones are being eroded. There is a summary in English.

282 **Alguns aspectos das relações financeiras e económicas interterritoriais.** (Some aspects of the financial and economic relationships between the territories).
J. Freitas Mota. *Boletim Trimestral Banco Nacional Ultramarino*, no. 98 (April-June 1974), p. 3-51; no. 99 (July-Sept. 1974), p. 3-31.

Part one reports on the economic situation of the then Portuguese colonies, giving information on balance of payments, reserves, debt, imports, exports, private business. Part two discusses the economic, financial and legal implications of decolonization.

283 **Bibliografia Sobre a Economia Portuguesa.** (Bibliography on the Portuguese Economy.)
Compiled by Amaro D. Guerreiro. Lisbon: Instituto Nacional de Estatística, Publicações do Centro de Estudos Económicos, 1948/1949- . annual.

Up until 1974 this bibliography contains material on all the colonies. As it is arranged by country, material on Cape Verde is easy to find. Country sections are further subdivided by subject: items are frequently listed under more than one subject heading. A vast number of periodical and newspaper articles, as well as monographs, have been indexed. The first volume, covering 1948-49, was published in 1958.

284 **Cabo Verde – um território condenado?** (Cape Verde – a doomed territory?)
Alfredo de Sousa. Lisbon: Instituto Superior de Ciências Sociais e Política Ultramarina, 1963. 10p.

A gloomy factual survey of the Cape Verdean economic situation which points out the significant imbalance between the funds supplied by the 1959 II Plano de Fomento (development plan) and the amount of capital needed to stimulate production. He also draws attention to the increasing population: he believes that a reduction in the birth rate and continuing emigration are necessary. In similar pessimistic vein see Pedro de Sousa Lobo's 'Vida económica de Cabo Verde' (Cape Verde's economic life) in *Ultramar*, vol. 4, no. 4 (1964), p. 75-92.

285 **Considerações sobre alguns problemas fundamentais de Cabo Verde.** (Thoughts on some of Cape Verde's fundamental problems.)
José Bacellar Bebiano. Lisbon: Junta de Investigações do Ultramar, 1959. 42p. bibliog.

Bebiano describes the contemporary economic conditions and outlines some of the problem areas. He is critical of the government's management of the economy, pointing out lack of continuity and funding for development projects. Sectors of the economy with potential for growth are described. Also published in: *Colóquios cabo-verdianos* (q.v.), p. 141-82.

286 **The co-operative movement in the Cape Verde Islands: a survey.**
Richard Morgan, Shallin Chaudry. *Yearbook of Agricultural Co-operation* (1983), p. 193-207. bibliog.

A comprehensive survey of cooperatives and their role in Cape Verde's post-independence development programme. Popular participation is an important concept in this programme, and gradual and voluntary expansion of the cooperative sector should assist in ending share-cropping, increasing land under irrigation and facilitate access to agricultural extension services and literacy programmes. Although cooperativism is new to Cape Verde, there is a traditon of *junta-mão* (mutual aid, labour exchange) to build upon. During the confused period between the 25 April 1974 coup in Portugal and Cape Verdean independence on 5 July 1975 many Portuguese shopkeepers left the islands: in response the PAIGC organized a semi-clandestine distribution network. Eight consumer cooperatives survive in Santiago from this period. At the same time some agricultural cooperatives were founded on seized, deserted or relinquished irrigated properties. The role and legal status of the national coordinating body – the Instituto Nacional das Cooperativas (National Institute of Cooperatives) – is described. Its main function is as a conduit, converting donor aid into low-interest loans. The present state of the movement is outlined. Most cooperatives are in the agricultural sector, but industrial cooperatives are becoming more important, reflecting increasing urban demand from Praia and Mindelo. Consumer cooperatives are gradually assuming importance in smaller settlements. Fishing, however, has been a difficult sector in which to establish cooperatives.

287 **The effects of Portugal's accession to the European Community on the exports of the ACP countries.**
Matthew McQueen, Robert Read. *Estudos de Economia*, vol. 6, no. 3 (April-June 1986). p. 369-84.

The accession of Portugal, Greece and Spain to the EEC is predicted to provide competition for ACP exports to Europe. This is relevant to Cape Verde if Portugal tries to protect its fish-canning industry. Cape Verde exports canned tuna to the EEC, but only uncanned fish to Portugal. Cape Verde's other exports addressed in this article are bananas and cattle hides.

288 **Estrutura económica de Cabo Verde.** (Economic structure of Cape Verde.)
S. Martins Pinho. *Boletim Trimestral, Banco Nacional Ultramarino*, no. 92 (Oct.-Dec. 1972), p. 3-28. map.

Pinho provides facts, figures, tables and graphs on gross national product (GNP), agricultural production, industrial activity, construction, electricity, transport, telecommunications, tourism, internal trade, imports, exports, balance of payments, public finance and banking.

289 **Integration, development and equity: economic integration in West Africa.**
Peter Robson. London: George Allen & Unwin, 1983. 181p. map. bibliog.

Introductory chapters cover the theory and practicalities of development and integration. These are followed by studies of the various regional groupings. Of relevance to Cape Verde is the chapter 'The Economic Community of West African States', p. 86-123. ECOWAS was formed in 1975 and has sixteen member countries. Robson discusses its objectives, procedures and the different economies of its members. He also covers the benefits and problems of trade liberalization and fiscal harmonization. See also the collection of essays in *Trade & development in Economic Community of West African States (ECOWAS)*, edited by Adeyinka Orimalade and R.E. Ubogu (New Delhi: Vikas, 1984. 589p.).

290 **Investir em Cabo Verde: uma oportunidade para Portugal.** (Investing in Cape Verde: a new opportunity for Portugal.)
Ernesto Ferreira da Silva. *Expresso* (21 Oct. 1989), p. C14.

This article explains the new opportunities for investment in Cape Verde in the light of the policy of 'extroversão' (extraversion). See also *Blockfreie Aussenpolitik eines afrikanischen Kleinstaates: das Beispiel Kap Verde* for further detail on Cape Verde's external economic policy.

291 **The Least Developed Countries.**
United Nations Conference on Trade and Development Secretariat.
New York: United Nations, 1984- . annual.
An annual report on economic trends amongst the least developed countries (LDCs),
which contains essays, news on development issues for each country and statistical data
for the LDCs as a group.

292 **Programa de colónia de Cabo Verde.** (Programme for the colony of
Cape Verde.)
Mário Alfama Ferro, Alexandre de Almeida, Machado Saldanha.
Lisbon: Ministério das Colónias, Primeira Conferência Económica do
Império Colonial Português, 1936. 111p.
The colony's economic programme is set out, covering commercial policy, credit,
agriculture and infrastructure. A similar work of this era is Machado Saldanha's *A
evolução e o apetrechamento económico de Cabo Verde. Conferência* (The economic
development and equipment of Cape Verde. A lecture) (Porto, Portugal: Edições da
1ª Exposição Colonial Portuguesa, 1934. 19p.).

293 **As transformações económicas ocorridas em Cabo Verde: notas para um
debate.** (Economic transformations in Cape Verde: notes for a debate.)
Alves da Rocha. *Revista Internacional de Estudos Africanos*, nos 8-9
(Jan.-Dec. 1988), p. 193-217. bibliog.
This article analyses Cape Verde's unusual economic development. Unlike the other
Portuguese-speaking African nations and despite the severe problems of the Sahelian
climate, Cape Verde has in recent years shown sustained economic growth. The author
comments on the effects of the II Plano Nacional de Desenvolvimento 1986-1990 (the
Second National Development Plan 1986-90), but the most important factors are an
intelligent use of food aid and external investment by emigrant Cape Verdeans. Tables
published here give figures for GNP, investments, prices, and balance of payments.
There is a summary in English.

Cape Verde: politics, economics and society.
See item no. 230.

Development

294 **Cape Verde: survival without self-sufficiency.**
Deirdre Meintel. In: *African islands and enclaves*, edited by Robin
Cohen. Beverly Hills, California; New Delhi; London: Sage, 1983
(Sage Series on African Modernization and Development, vol. 7),
p. 145-64. bibliog.
A lengthy introductory section describes and explains the historical reasons for Cape
Verde's underdevelopment by the Portuguese. The value of Cape Verdean migrant
labour within the Portuguese empire is seen as a powerful disincentive for investment

in the islands' own economic future. Meintel goes on to summarize the areas of the economy which the post-independence government aims to develop. Priority has to be given to increasing fresh water supplies for human consumption and agriculture. However, it is recognized that under no conditions could agriculture supply more than thirty per cent of food needs. Fishing probably offers greater economic potential. The all-important policy on foreign aid is given close attention: Cape Verde tries to retain political independence, is non-aligned and encourages multilateral as well as bilateral agreements. Internal social and political aspects of development are also described. Given that Cape Verde can never be self-sufficient in food, Meintel considers that its progress towards development has been relatively successful. See also *Desenvolvimento e pesquisa no longo prazo em Cabo Verde* (Long-term development and research in Cape Verde) by Armando Trigo Abreu and Horácio Soares (Lisbon: Instituto Gulbenkian de Ciência, 1983. 300p.).

295 **Lutar pelo desenvolvimento económico e social.** (Struggle for economic and social development.)
PAICV. [Praia]: Edição do DIP do PAICV, 1983. 28p. (Documentos do II Congresso).

The economic context is set, followed by the party's modest and realistic political and social objectives. A third section outlines the strategy for development. It is interesting to note the importance given to halting the rural exodus. It is suggested here that this process threatens the traditonal Cape Verdean way of life, and could lead to the virtual depopulation of certain islands.

296 **Mass mobilization for national reconstruction in the Cape Verde Islands.**
Basil Davidson. *Economic Geography*, vol. 53, no. 4 (Oct. 1977), p. 393-6.

An impressionistic rather than scholarly comparison of colonial and post-independence government policies toward drought management and development. During the 1968-75 drought Davidson describes the Portuguese government as shamed into providing relief funds as charity or payment for public works. The new government is encouraging foreign aid and local initiatives. See also *L'Afrique étranglée* (Africa strangled) by René Dumont and Marie-France Mottin (Paris: Éditions du Seuil, 1980. 264p. bibliog.) and the chapter, 'Au Cap-Vert, lutte implacable contre la désertification' (The implacable struggle against desertification in Cape Verde), p. 226-33, for further detail on the post-independence struggle for more irrigated land, and, quite simply, for more water.

297 **Primeiro plano nacional de desenvolvimento 1982/85. Volume 1.**
Relatório geral. (The first national developmment plan 1982-85. Volume 1. General report.)
Secretaria de Estado da Cooperação e Planeamento, introduction by José Brito. Praia: The author, 1983. 144p.

José Brito's cautious introduction to this report notes that the lack of any planning background, reliable statistics and regional studies may make this development plan difficult to implement. The plan itself refrains from setting unrealistic goals. It first describes the current socio-economic situation before setting out a sector-by-sector analysis of projects. Appendices give the budget and personnel implications of the projects.

298 **States, microstates and islands.**
Edited by Edward Dommen, Philippe Hein. Beckenham, England: Croom Helm, 1985. 216p. bibliog.
Although this collection of essays on the cultural, economic, environmental and political viability of microstates does not specifically refer to Cape Verde, the general development ideas which are discussed are very relevant.

Cabo Verde: dez anos de desenvolvimento.
See item no. 3.

Challenge and progress: the role of non-governmental aid in Cape Verde.
See item no. 225.

Cape Verde: a very poor country strives to improve its lot.
See item no. 278.

Desenvolvimento rural.
See item no. 309.

Economic history

299 **Estudos de economia caboverdiana.** (Essays on the Cape Verdean economy.)
António Carreira. Lisbon: Imprensa Nacional, 1982. 342p. bibliog.
It is a common view that Cape Verde was so long uninhabited for the good reason that it offered no incentive to human habitation: the climate is unreliable and there are no obvious natural resources. Carreira here sets out to prove that – contrary to received opinion – Cape Verde was not necessarily an economic impossibility. He studies, in three separate essays, the production and export of *urzela* (*Rocella tinctoria*, a dye-yielding lichen), sugar cane and *purgueira* (*Jatropha curcas*, a plant with oil-yielding seeds) in as great detail as the records allow. The monopoly companies such as the Companhia Geral do Grão Pará e Maranhão (1758-78) were closely involved in these activities. Through painstakingly compiled statistics Carreira shows the volume and value of these export products. That they brought little benefit to the local population and were permitted to decline is as much due to colonial neglect and unfavourable trade policies as an inherent lack of economic viability. The book contains in its numerous appendices the text of many original documents, including a fascinating letter of complaint from the *urzeleiros* (the gatherers of *urzela* from the rock faces) against the harsh conditions of their work and the merchants who cheated them.

300 **Subsídios para a história da moeda em Cabo Verde (1460-1940).**
(Contributions towards the history of money in Cape Verde [1460-1940].)
Alvaro Lereno. Lisbon: Agência Geral das Colónias, 1942. 254p.
A well-documented work on one of the troublesome aspects of the Cape Verdean economy during this period. From the beginning, Cape Verde was plagued by the disappearance of money. This was a great hindrance to trade, and numerous petitions

(reproduced here) were sent to Lisbon asking for the value of the coinage to be raised to compensate for its scarcity. Counterfeit coins were also a problem, and there was always a quantity of foreign currency circulating. *Panos* (woven cotton cloths) were used as currency for several centuries: Lereno lists some of the different styles and values. In 1911 a universal *escudo* was created for Portugal and the colonies, but in 1920 the Cape Verdean government prohibited its export, even between the islands, above a limited amount. Paper notes were introduced with the creation of the Banco Nacional Ultramarino in 1864 whose first branch in Cape Verde was founded in Praia in 1865. The banking and monetary system is described.

As companhias pombalinas.

See item no. 117.

A navegação de longo curso e o comércio nas ilhas de Cabo Verde no século XIX.

See item no. 303.

Transport

301 Black men of the sea.
Michael Cohn, Michael K.H. Platzer, preface by Peter Stanford.
New York: Dodd, Mead, 1978. 158p. bibliog.
Two chapters are of interest. 'Whalers' (p. 82-90) is a brief survey of the history of whaling, a history which involves many Cape Verdeans. Cape Verde was a popular stopping-place for whalers on long voyages who took on supplies and crew. Cape Verdeans were happy to accept the low wages, and the possibility of entering the US without immigration control. They came to make up larger and larger proportions of US whaling crews, eventually becoming officers, captains and owners. 'The Cape Verdean packet trade' (p. 91-104) describes the intrepid voyages made by the often elderly boats owned by American Cape Verdeans. Passengers and goods were carried between New England and the archipelago from the last years of the 19th century until the 1960s. Based on interviews with surviving crew members, the terrible things that happened at sea – on journeys that could last over two months – are recalled, and ships such as the *Ernestina* are remembered with affection. For more information on whaling see also Carl Haywood's article, 'American contacts with Africa: a bibliography of the papers of the American whalemen' in *African Studies Bulletin*, vol. 10, no. 3 (Dec. 1967), p. 82-95.

302 Listen! the wind.
Anne Morrow Lindbergh, foreword by Charles A. Lindbergh.
London: Chatto & Windus, 1938. 274p. 4 maps.
In 1933 Anne and Charles Lindbergh carried out a survey flight of possible transatlantic airline routes. The book is an account of the expedition which included several days in Praia where there was already a little-used French installation.

303 **A navegação de longo curso e o comércio nas ilhas de Cabo Verde no século XIX.** (Long-distance shipping and commerce in the Cape Verde Islands in the 19th century.)
António Carreira. *Raízes.* nos 7-16 (July 1978–Dec. 1980), p. 8-32.
Focusing on the period between 1812 and 1837 Carreira notes the effects of the Napoleonic wars and the restrictions on the slave trade on shipping calling at Cape Verde. He has compiled figures for numbers of ships and their nationality, destination and origin. The principal business was in slaves, live animals and whaling.

304 **Notícias TACV.** (TACV News.)
[Praia]: Direcção-Geral do TACV, [1987]- . monthly.
A monthly newsletter keeeping passengers informed about new developments in the national airline, Transportes Aereos de Cabo Verde (TACV). For a special feature celebrating thirty years of operation see Luis Carvalho's article 'TACV: trinta anos de vida e 150,000 passageiros em 1988' (TACV: thirty years of existence and 150,000 passengers in 1988) in *Tribuna* (20 Jan. 1989), p. 6-7. Basic information on the airports of Sal and Praia can be found in *Airports international directory* by Malcolm Ginsberg and Amanda Bratt (Sutton, England: IPC Transport Press, 1981. 727p.).

305 **Novas esperanças para o Porto Grande.** (New hopes for Porto Grande.)
Humberto Morais, interviewed by Tozé Barbosa. *Notícias*, vol. 1, no. 8 (July 1988), p. 23.
The Secretary of State for the merchant navy answers questions on the future development prospects for the superb natural harbour of Porto Grande, Mindelo.

306 **Relatório da viagem da corveta *Mindello* de Lisboa a Loanda pela Maderia, S. Thiago e S. Thomé.** (Report of the voyage of the corvette *Mindello* from Lisbon to Luanda via Madeira, Santiago and São Tomé.)
Augusto Castilho.   Lisbon: Imprensa Nacional, 1892. 77p. 3 maps.
Castilho was a captain in the Portuguese Navy, and this report is of his ship's journey (1891-92) to join the West African–South American naval division. One of his orders was to ensure maximum mileage for minimum coal consumption: this is a subject in which he takes an almost obsessional interest in recording and tabulating. He is almost as meticulous in keeping his normal logbook, making this a historic record of naval shipping and shipping conditions in general in the East Atlantic.

307 **Viagem a Cabo Verde.** (Journey to Cape Verde.)
Vasco Callixto.   Lisbon: [n.p.], 1974. 147p. map.
This would be a very ordinary travelogue of no particular merit if it were not for Callixto's boyish obsession with facts and figures about transport. There is information here about air and sea links, and the quality and length of road surface. Callixto travelled around the islands by local authority jeep, and in many places this is still the most practical mode of transport.

Atlantic Islands: Azores, Madeira, Canary and Cape Verde Islands.
See item no. 86.

Roteiro do archipelago de Cabo Verde.
See item no. 89.

Agriculture

General

308 **A agricultura do arquipélago de Cabo Verde. Cartas agrícolas.**
Problemas agrários. (The agriculture of the Cape Verde archipelago.
Agricultural maps. Agrarian problems.)
J.A. Teixeira, L.A. Grandvaux Barbosa. Lisbon: Junta de
Investigações do Ultramar, 1958. 178p. [maps]. (Memórias da Junta de
Investigações do Ultramar, no. 2).
A comprehensive survey of the agriculture of the islands.

309 **Desenvolvimento rural.** (Rural development.)
Homero Ferrinho. Praia: Instituto Caboverdiano do Livro, 1987.
266p. bibliog. (Estudos e Ensaios).
Successful and sustainable development in Cape Verde's rural regions is probably the
key to the islands' future. This work covers theoretical and practical aspects of the
subject. A first section deals with the issues of the political values and ideas associated
with development and ideals of human equality and respect. It also discusses factors
which affect and facilitate development. A second section describes the rural
environment, covering such things as population, sociology, technology and ecology. A
final section takes a practical approach, suggesting methods of planning and
technology, and describing how agents can work successfully. A key concept is that of
active participation by the local population.

310 **The evolution of Cape Verde's agriculture.**
Emilio F. Moran. *African Economic History*, no. 11 (1982), p. 63-86.
map.
Moran traces many of Cape Verde's agricultural problems back to the beginning of
Portuguese colonization, which he shows to have been totally inappropriate in its
systems of landholding and crop management when applied to the delicate
environment of these Sahelian islands. Focusing on the islands of Santiago, Fogo and

Santo Antão, he examines the system of land tenure and ownership from the 15th century to the present day, explaining how unequal distribution of land and the system of share-cropping reduce incentives to improve the land. He also notes the role which taxation could play in altering this situation. He makes a study of the environmental conditions which affect agriculture. The islands have a Sahelian climate, but are much more densely populated than the other countries of the Sahel. Traditional Sahelian pastoral nomadism would not support the population, and the islands do not provide an extensive land mass for internal migration as an alternative to famine. The Portuguese introduced inappropriate crops to the islands. Irrigated land was used for tropical cash crops, and corn introduced as the staple crop. Moran points out that corn has a water requirement twice that of sorghum or millet. He suggests that corn had a high 'European' status, whereas sorghum and millet were associated with Africa. Thereafter climate rather than policy was blamed for crop failure. Whilst Cape Verde continues to receive food aid Moran thinks that the difficult task of changing a dietary staple will not be attempted.

311 **Família e trabalho numa comunidade camponesa de Cabo Verde.**
(Family and labour in a peasant community in Cape Verde.)
A. Trigo de Abreu. *Revista Internacional de Estudos Africanos*, no. 3 (Jan.-Dec. 1985), p. 85-106.

Research was carried out amongst a community of ninety peasant families in northwest Santiago. The labour demands of maize cultivation are described and the time needed to cultivate one hectare of corn is calculated. There is a 'rigid agricultural calendar' dictated by climate, which is very labour intensive at certain periods of the year. The labour supply methods are outlined and tables show which types of family make use of which of the various types of labour supply. Immediate family and other kinship relations are universally used. There are also two types of labour reciprocity schemes: *djuda* (literally, help) is a casual lending of labour; *junta-mão* (literally, joined hands) is the exchange of specified amounts of labour at defined times. They are all essential to ensuring the flexibility of labour supply. There is a summary in English.

312 **The farm system under duress: agricultural adaptations on the Cape Verde Islands.**
Timothy J. Finan. *Human Organization*, vol. 47, no. 2 (1988), p. 109-18. bibliog.

Finan studies the agriculture practised by a sample of 237 rural households in Santiago using the Farming Systems Research and Extension approach. This aims to promote technological change within the socio-economic context of the rural household. A clear distinction is made between irrigated market-orientated farming systems and non-irrigated subsistence farming, both of which are described. Irrigation is the principal technological response to drought and the sources and allocation of water for irrigated land are outlined. Households which have access only to non-irrigated land have made social responses to drought. This is most clear in the use of reciprocal labour, described by Finan as the 'sharing of scarcity'; he refers to A. Trigo de Abreu's 'Família e trabalho numa comunidade camponesa de Cabo Verde' (q.v.). Systems of land tenure are described. Some interesting points are made about the system of share-cropping which has often been thought to be a purely exploitative practice. Nevertheless, the post-independence government has found it very difficult to eradicate. It appears that share-cropping is part of the rural community's strategy to distribute resources in a non-monetarized economy: the land of elderly people is often share-cropped by younger relatives. Finally, the sharing of farm products is discussed. This is usually associated with non-irrigated farms and can act as unofficial social security. It is another example of the importance of community action for survival in arid zones.

313 **The food crisis and the socialist state in Lusophone Africa.**
Rosemary E. Galli. *African Studies Review*, vol. 30, no. 1 (March 1987), p. 19-44.

Galli casts a critical glance at the agricultural policies of the former Portuguese colonies. Cape Verde is praised for its recent investments in soil conservation and irrigation projects, and some of the initiatives taken to increase the tenure rights of agricultural workers. However, there is criticism of the state's control of irrigated land, either directly or through cooperatives. This is seen as an extension of the colonial system whereby the best lands were controlled from the top, and export crops, rather than local staple foods, grown.

314 **Legislação publicada de 1975 a 1985.** (Legislation published from 1975 to 1985.)
[Praia]: Ministério do Desenvolvimento Rural e Pescas, 1986. 251p. map.

The ten years' worth of legislation published here by the Ministry of Rural Development and Fisheries is a valuable record of the ministry's work, although it does not include material on fisheries and water. The legislation is divided into four sections: internal ministry organization; agriculture, forestry and livestock; agrarian reform; and the smaller organizations which work under the umbrella of the ministry. This final section is very informative on the many cooperatives and development initiatives taking place at the local level.

315 **Perspectivas agrícolas de São Nicolau.** (Agricultural prospects for São Nicolau.)
Mateus Nunes. *Garcia de Orta*, vol. 9, no. 2 (1961), p. 389-92.

São Nicolau is an island whose people are heavily dependent on agriculture. It has also been one of the worst affected by drought. In this very gloomy report Nunes doubts that agriculture will ever be able to support the population. Soil erosion, which he describes, is the main problem. In recent years, of course, areas of the island have greatly benefited from irrigation projects financed by foreign aid, for instance the French BURGEAP project at Fajã: see, for example, J.-C. Andreini, L. Bourguet 'Les barrrages souterrains. Mise en oeuvre au Cap Vert. Conditions d'application au Sahel' (Underground dams. Their construction in Cape Verde. Conditions for their application in the Sahel) in *Hydrogéologie: Géologie de l'Ingénieur* (no. 4 [1984], p. 393-9).

316 **A reforma das estruturas agrárias de Cabo Verde.** (The reform of Cape Verde's agrarian structures.)
João Pereira Silva. Praia: Gabinete da Reforma Agrária, Ministério do Desenvolvimento Rural, [n.d.]. 63p. bibliog.

As part of the preparation for major land reforms, the Minister of Rural Development produced this introduction to the draft legislation of 1979. He refers to the legislation currently in force and describes the changes which have taken place in land ownership since independence. The draft legislation (which is reproduced in the second half of the volume) sets out to abolish share-cropping and rent payment in the form of labour. It also aims to regularize 'squatters's rights' in certain cases whilst safeguarding absentee landlords' rights in other instances. In reality, the practice of share-cropping has been difficult to eradicate.

Agricultural products

317 Agroforestry in the West African Sahel.
Advisory Committee on the Sahel, Board on Science and Technology for International Development, Office of International Affairs, National Research Council, USA. Washington DC: National Academy Press, 1983. 86p. 2 maps. bibliog.
Although not referring specifically to Cape Verde, this study of tree management concerns the types of trees being planted in Cape Verde, notably varieties of drought-resistant acacia.

318 Banana diseases in the Cape Verde Archipelago.
A.R. Noronha. *Garcia de Orta*, vol. 17, no. 2 (1969). p. 187-94. bibliog.
Bananas are the islands' most important export crop. This article reports on the results of fieldwork into the causes of disease.

319 Cabo Verde: duas tentativas para a sua valorização agro-pecuária.
(Cape Verde: two attempts to increase its agricultural and pastoral value.)
M. dos Santos Pereira. In: *Cabo Verde, Guiné, São Tomé e Príncipe: curso de extensão universitária, ano lectivo de 1965-1966.* Lisbon: Instituto Superior de Ciências Sociais e Política Ultramarina, Universidade Técnica de Lisboa, 1966, p. 959-1006. 8 maps.
The first suggested programme is for the protection of vegetable cover and prevention of soil erosion. This would involve ending the cutting of trees and bushes, ceasing to use ecologically marginal land and ending 'excessive' animal ownership. The second programme is to introduce sheep to replace the destructive goats. Sheep are more valuable than goats, so fewer would be needed. This appears to be a well-researched proposal.

320 The Cape Verde region (1499 to 1549): the key to coconut culture in the western hemisphere?
H. C. Harries. *Turrialba*, vol. 27, no. 3 (July-Sept. 1977), p. 227-31. map. bibliog.
Harries speculates on the possible origins of Atlantic seaboard coconut palms. He suggests that they may all have come from Mozambique via Cape Verde or the Cape Verde peninsula of Senegal. This kind of knowledge is very important in understanding the coconut population's resistance to disease.

321 **Estudos sobre a fertilidade dos solos de Cabo Verde (ilha de Santiago).
IV – Deficiências na nutrição mineral da bananeira.** (Studies of soil
fertility in Cape Verde [Santiago Island]. IV – Deficiencies in mineral
nutrition for banana trees.)
M. Mayer Gonçalves, A. P. Silva Cardoso, C. Oliveira e Silva. *Garcia
de Orta, Série de Estudos Agronómicos*, vol. 7, nos 1-2 (1980), p. 1-8.
map. bibliog.

The short notes which correspond to parts I–III are 'Nutritional deficiencies of bananas
in Santiago Island – Cape Verde'; 'Banana nutrition studies in Santiago Island – Cape
Verde: $3^2(N,K)$ x $2(Zn)$ fertilizer trials' and 'Banana nutrition studies in Santiago
Island – Cape Verde: $3^2(N,K)$ fertilizer trials', published in *International Banana
Nutrition Newsletter*, nos 1, 2 and 3 (1979, 1980 and 1981) respectively. Widespread
deficiencies of nitrogen and, to a lesser extent, potassium and zinc have been noted in
soils where bananas are grown. Fertilizer trials in five different banana–producing
regions of Santiago (marked on the map provided) suggest the possibility of increasing
the annual production of bananas to up to seventy-five tonnes per hectare. The
bibliography contains several references to works on the soil fertility of Santiago
produced by the Missão de Estudos Agronómicos do Ultramar (Overseas Agronomic
Study Group). There is a summary in English.

322 **As lagartas polífagas – *Heliothis armigera* (Hübner) e *H. peltigera*
(Schiff) – no arquipélago de Cabo Verde.** (Polyphagous caterpillars –
Heliothis armigera [Hübner] and *H. peltigera* [Schiff] – in the Cape
Verde Archipelago.)
A. Coutinho Saraiva. *Garcia de Orta*, vol. 11, no. 3 (1963), p. 593-9.
bibliog.

Saraiva discusses methods of pest control with regard to maize and tomatoes. See also
his article 'A grande lagarta perfurado das gramíneas – *Sesmia botanephaga* Tams &
Bowden – no arquipélago de Cabo Verde' (The corn-borer caterpillar – *Sesmia
botanephaga* Tams & Bowden – in the Cape Verde archipelago) (*Garcia de Orta*, vol
11, no. 2 [1963], p. 355-70. bibliog.). These maize pests affect crops on Maio and
Santiago, but it is not economically viable to spend money on pesticide.

323 *Milho zaburro* **and** *milho maçaroca* **in Guinea and in the islands of Cabo
Verde.**
A. Teixeira da Mota, António Carreira. *Africa* (London), vol. 36,
no. 1 (Jan. 1966), p. 73-84.

A carefully documented contribution to the debate on the history of the introduction
of maize to West Africa. Through a study of early texts and the linguistic evidence of
Kriul (the creole of Guinea-Bissau) the authors make a convincing case for the
introduction of maize from post-Columbian America. They are critical of the thesis of
M.D.W. Jeffreys' '*Milho zaburro* = *milho de Guinee* = maize' (*Garcia de Orta*, vol.
11, no. 2 (1963), p. 213-26. bibliog.) that maize had already reached West Africa,
brought by the Arabs, prior to the arrival of Europeans. The article provides some
evidence on the early development of agriculture in Cape Verde and the time-scale in
which the cultivation of maize replaced that of sorghum and *Pennisetum*. A slightly
revised version of the article is published in Portuguese under the title 'O milho
zaburro e o milho maçaroca na Guiné e ilhas de Cabo Verde' in *Revista de História
Económica e Social* (no. 17 [Jan.-June 1986], p. 5-20). See also 'The evolution of Cape
Verde's agriculture'.

324 **Moléstias do cafeeiro em Cabo Verde.** (Diseases of coffee bushes in Cape Verde.)
A.R. Noronha, M. Celeste Ramos. *Garcia de Orta*, vol. 17, no. 2 (1969), p. 209-14.

The authors report on fungal diseases found on coffee bushes on Fogo, Santiago and Santo Antão, islands where there is some commercial cultivation taking place. There is a summary in English.

Fishing

325 **État, marché et pêcheurs marins artisanaux en Afrique francophone et lusophone.** (State, market and small-scale marine fishermen in French-and Portuguese-speaking Africa.)
Jean-Philippe Platteau. *Afrique Contemporaine*, no. 154 (1990), p. 3-34.

The government of Cape Verde has recognized the potential for development of small-scale fishing and has encouraged voluntary expansion in this sector. This article discusses the sources of potential obstacles to growth, taking the key factors to be the role of the state and access to markets, technology and resources. Although Platteau is covering a large number of African states, there is a surprisingly large amount of information about Cape Verde. Some of the problems facing small-scale fishing development are outlined. The islands are physically isolated from the technical developments taking place in more advanced nations; tuna fishing can be vulnerable to industrial fishing; the fishing communities are isolated from their markets. Fishermen's wives have to travel long distances inland to sell or barter the catch – as anyone who has had to share the back of a crowded truck with a large and dead tuna fish will confirm. Market conditions are such that it is said that the less Cape Verdean fishermen catch, the richer they are. On the positive side of the balance, Platteau seems to approve of the government's fishing policy; foreign aid, in particular from the Netherlands, is forthcoming; agencies are happy to assist fishermen with loans for development as they make it a point of honour to repay their debts.

326 **Le *Gérard Tréca* aux îles du Cap-Vert.** (The *Gérard Tréca* in the Cape Verde Islands.)
E. Postel. *Garcia de Orta*, vol. 2, no. 3 (1954), p. 311-18. map. bibliog.

In 1952 the research vessel the *Gérard Tréca* undertook a survey of the concentration of thonides (tuna) in Cape Verdean waters. This report describes the fish caught and concludes that Cape Verde has some previously unappreciated fishing grounds south and west of Fogo.

327 **Proceedings of the symposium on the living resources of the Atlantic continental shelf between the Straits of Gibraltar and Cape Verde.**
Marine Biology and Environment Branch, Fishery Resources and Exploitation Division, FAO. Rome: FAO, 1969. 74p. (Fisheries Report, no. 68).

The report of the symposium proceedings includes abstracts of papers presented, focusing on assessment of fishery stocks and the need for their conservation. See abstract no. 26 'New contribution to the study of copepods of the Cape Verde Archipelago' by Inácia de Paiva (p. 41) and abstract no. 27 'On the *Siphonophora calcycophora* of the Cape Verde Islands' by Teresa S. Neto (p. 41): both papers refer to plankton. Abstract no. 62, 'Biology and distribution of the main commercial fishes, and peculiarities of their fishing by trawl on the shelf from Cape Spartel to Cape Verde' by L. Domanevsky (p. 54) is principally concerned with mackerel.

328 **A propósito de prospecções piscatórias nos mares de Cabo Verde e da Guiné.** (On fishery prospecting in the seas of Cape Verde and Guinea-Bissau.)
F. Frade. *Garcia de Orta*, vol. 2, no. 3 (1954), p. 319-28. map.

Frade summarizes the results of a survey of the fishing potential of these waters, and makes suggestions for their exploitation. He also reports on a study of sexual maturity in tuna.

329 **Rapport national sur les statistiques de pêche du Cap-Vert.** (National report on fishing statistics for Cape Verde).
H.S.R. Vieira. In: *Fishery Committee for the Eastern Central Atlantic, Report of the Second Session of the Working Party on Fishery Statistics. Dakar, Senegal, 8-10 February 1982.* Rome: FAO, 1982 (Fisheries Report, no. 265), p. 19-25.

This is a short report on the state and problems of statistical research into artisanal and industrial fishing in Cape Verde. There are ten tables showing details of method and location of fishing activity and the weight and type of fish caught.

330 **Reflexões sobre a pesca em Cabo Verde.** (Reflections on fishing in Cape Verde.)
Praia: Secretaria de Estado das Pescas, 1986. 499p. map.

This edition, published with the assistance of the FAO (United Nations Food and Agriculture Organization), contains the texts of papers presented at the first national conference on fishing held in 1985. Papers cover artisanal fishing; industrial fishing; the state of research into fishery resources; the work of the government agencies involved in fishing and fish processing; the organizations which assist fishing communities; the government programmes which provide vocational training, business support and social security for people involved in fishing; international commerce; and the role of women in fishing communities.

331 **The tuna fisheries of Cape Verde and Senegal.**
Marine Fisheries Review, vol. 43, no. 10 (Oct. 1981), p. 26-9. map.

Tuna is the single most important species caught in Cape Verde: it is also the single most important domestically produced export. This is a concise and factual report on the industry and the government agencies involved. The fleet is described: it is largely

Fishing

pole-and-line vessels which return to port daily and carry no ice. There are three larger ships which the government owns through INTERPESCA. FAO and Arab assistance are thought to be providing more vessels. Coldstore facilities, and associated Dutch cooperation, are described. In 1978 a 200-mile Exclusive Economic Zone (EEZ) was declared. The government is cautious about granting licences, and tends to do so only on condition that licensees help develop Cape Verdean fishing and tranship part of their catch via Mindelo. The article concludes that 'The government's decision to promote the industry's development may eventually make Cape Verde's tuna fishery one of the most important in Africa'.

Labour

332 Angola – Cape Verde – Guinea – Mozambique – San Tomé and Príncipe – Timor: rural labour code.
[Geneva]: International Labour Office, 1962. 87p. (Legislative Series, 1962, Portugal 1).

The rural labour code was of particular relevance to Cape Verde in its clauses dealing with emigration and contracted employment: many Cape Verdeans were contracted to work on the plantations of São Tomé and Príncipe.

333 Information sur le marché de l'emploi dans les pays de l'Afrique sahélienne. (Information on the labour market in the Sahelian African countries.)
Geneva: Bureau International du Travail, 1981. 117p.

This is a preliminary report into labour force planning and assessment of labour needs in Sahelian countries which was carried out by the UN and DANIDA (the Danish international development agency). Cape Verde conforms to many of the Sahelian labour force characteristics which are established by this study, in particular migration, women's importance in agriculture and poor government structures to study the problems. In discussing the prospects for development the report notes Cape Verde's lack of these planning structures. A report from the Cape Verdean government cites the problem of underemployment, and the priority given to absorbing potential unemployment in the agricultural sector. Several works relevant to Cape Verde are mentioned in a bibliographical annex to the main body of the work. See also *Human resources and development in Guinea-Bissau and Cape Verde* by R. Duncan, R. Galli and R. Comfort (Washington DC: AID, 1981).

334 **Programa e estatutos.** (Programme and statutes.)
União Nacional dos Trabalhadores de Cabo Verde – Central Sindical.
[Praia]: Edição do DIPC/UNTC-CS, [n.d.]. 43p.

Several years elapsed after independence before the structures and functioning of the trade union movement were defined. This document sets out the programme for the União Nacional dos Trabalhadores de Cabo Verde – Central Sindical (National Union of Cape Verdean Workers – Trade Union Federation [UNTC-CS]) and its role in society. This is followed by the UNTC-CS rules. See Colm Foy, *Cape Verde: politics, economic and society*, p. 98-104, on the relationship between the PAICV and the UNCT-CS.

Labour in Portuguese West Africa.
See item no. 179.

Família e trabalho numa comunidade camponesa de Cabo Verde.
See item no. 311.

Statistics

335 **African socio-economic indicators, 1986.**
Statistics Division. Addis Ababa: United Nations Economic
Commission for Africa, 1989. 79p. map.

Thirty-five different sets of statistical information are divided between economic indicators, and social and demographic indicators. Most are set out country by country within geographical region, although a minority deal with Africa as a whole. Useful technical notes preface the main body of the work.

336 **Anuário Estatístico: Colónia de Cabo Verde.** (Statistical Yearbook: Colony of Cape Verde.)
Praia: Serviços de Estatística da Colónia de Cabo Verde. annual. 1933-52.

These collections of statistical tables give substantial documentation of demographic, economic, administrative and social aspects of life in Cape Verde. See also *Anuário Estatístico do Império Colonial* (Statistical Yearbook for the Colonial Empire) (Lisbon: Instituto Nacional de Estatística, annual, 1944-68) which covers all the Portuguese colonies. Portuguese statistical sources can be rather confusing as they often underwent changes of title and author: a useful reference is the *Catálogo das publicações* (Catalogue of publications [93p.]) produced by the Instituto Nacional de Estatística in 1976.

337 **Boletim Trimestral de Estatística.** (Quarterly Statistical Bulletin.)
Praia: Direcção-Geral de Estatística, 1949- . quarterly.

Through all the vagaries of colonial statistical publications, this bulletin has been a remarkably consistent and resilient publication. It covers amongst other things demography, domestic production and consumption, foreign trade, prices, banking and finance, and communications. In 1987 a transitional bulletin was produced to absorb the Direcção-Geral de Estatística's *Boletim Trimestral do Comércio Externo* (Quarterly Bulletin of Foreign Trade), first published in 1949, which documents imports and exports.

Statistics

338 **Elementos para apreciação da evolução socio-económica em Cabo Verde (1980-1987).** (Elements for understanding socio-economic change in Cape Verde [1980-87].)
Praia: Direcção Geral de Planeamento, Ministério do Plano e da Cooperação, 1989. 60p.
Five sections show statistics relevant to understanding socio-economic developments in Cape Verde. The section covering population gives statistics showing demographic change for the years 1980-87 and projections for the decade 1990–2000. Next, the supply of basic needs is covered, with regard to education, health, water supply and food. Economic change is shown for a wide range of economic indicators. Then, manufacturing costs are compared with Senegal and Mauritius in terms of such things as electricity, water and manpower. A final section compares indicators with other ECOWAS countries, showing how favourably Cape Verde compares to other West African nations in terms of infant mortality, per capita income and other indicators of socio-economic development.

339 **Selected statistics on regional member countries / Statistiques choisies sur les pays membres régionaux.**
Statistics Division, Planning and Research Department. [Abidjan]: African Development Bank, 1987. 77p.
Fifty-four tables, generally for the period 1975-85, cover social and economic indicators for the African nations. This is particularly helpful when comparing performances for different nations. Thus it can be established that, for example, life expectancy in Cape Verde, at 64 years, is beaten only by those of the Seychelles and Mauritius.

340 **Statistics Africa: sources for social, economic and market research.**
-    Joan M. Harvey.   Beckenham, England: CBD Research, 1978. 2nd ed. 374p.
Items 366-75 refer to statistical sources for Cape Verde (p. 79-81). Addresses are supplied. There are indexes of organizations, titles and subjects.

1° recenseamento geral da população e habitação 1980.
See item no. 171.

Education

341 **O cabo-verdiano, um portador de cultura. Sugestões de correcção de educação e ensino em Cabo Verde.** (The Cape Verdean, a courier of culture. Corrective suggestions for education and teaching in Cape Verde.)
Nuno Miranda. In: *Colóquios cabo-verdianos*. Lisbon: Junta de Investigações do Ultramar, 1959, p. 51-80.
Miranda calls for a relevant education to be provided in Cape Verde, and criticizes education which is divorced from its surroundings.

342 **Colóquio sobre educação e ciências humanas na África de língua portuguesa 20-22 de Janeiro de 1975.** (Conference on education and human sciences in Portuguese-speaking Africa, 20-22 January 1975.) Lisbon: Fundação Calouste Gulbenkian, 1979. 386p. bibliogs.
Many distinguished figures, including Philip D. Curtin, Avelino Teixeira da Mota, Orlando Ribeiro and René Pélissier, atttended this conference on the future for education and research in Portuguese-speaking Africa. The working papers are mostly on general themes, although the question of higher education facilities for Cape Verde and Guinea-Bissau is mentioned by Orlando Ribeiro. Information can also be found on relevant research organizations in Portugal. The volume concludes by publishing 'Bibliografia da Junta de Investigações Científicas do Ultramar sobre ciências humanas e sociais' (Bibliography of the Board of Overseas Scientific Research on the human and social sciences) (p. 327-76). Up to 1975, this covers history, social sciences in general, physical and social anthropology, human geography, demography, language, literature and religion. Also published by the Fundação Calouste Gulbenkian is *A educação na República de Cabo Verde. Análise sectorial. Volume 1* (Education in the Republic of Cape Verde. Analysis by sector. Volume 1), 1987.

Education

343   **A Educação em Cabo Verde.** (Education in Cape Verde.)
Praia: Imprensa Nacional. 1977- . quarterly.
Produced by the Ministério da Educação e Cultura (Ministry of Education and
Culture), the journal is intended to keep teachers and other education professionals in
contact with each other. It contains pedagogic material and information relevant to
Cape Verde's education system.

344   **O ensino em Cabo Verde.** (Education in Cape Verde.)
Antero de Barros. *Ultramar*, vol. 5, no. 2 (1964), p. 67-81.
Details on the history, administration, law and contemporary facilities (including
vocational training) of education in the islands. See also 'A escola em Cabo Verde'
(The school in Cape Verde) by A. Amara Lopes (*Ultramar*, vol. 5, no. 2 [1964], p. 44-
56) for a general discourse on problems of education in Africa, and the extent to which
these affect Cape Verde.

345   **Para uma universidade da Guiné-Bissau/Cabo Verde.** (For a university
of Guinea-Bissau/Cape Verde.)
João Manuel Varela. *África: Literatura, Arte e Cultura*, vol. 1, no. 1
(July 1978), p. 57-64.
Varela, a neurologist, presents a plan for a university of the two nations, based in
Bissau. He envisages an initial six faculties, with a specialized brain institute to serve
the entire continent. These ideas, in particular that of the institute, are expanded in
'As faculdades de medicina na revolução africana' (Medical faculties in the African
revolution) (*Raízes*, nos 7-16 [July 1978–Dec. 1980], p. 71-85). A sobering reply to
these ambitions is provided by Armando Soares in 'Notas críticas sobre o "projecto"
de João Manuel Varela' (Critical notes on João Manuel Varela's 'project') (*África:
Literatura, Arte e Cultura*, vol. 1, no. 4 [April-June 1979], p. 446-50). Soares suggests
that vocational education and improved middle and further education are more
appropriate to Cape Verde's needs and resources. He also notes the good access which
Cape Verdeans have to overseas universities.

346   **Reforma do sistema do ensino: reflexão e situação do processo.** (Reform
of the education system: reflections and report on the process.)
Ministério da Educação. *Voz di Povo* (20 July 1988), p. 6-8.
A concise report on the structures and aims of the ongoing reform of Cape Verdean
education, covering primary and secondary schooling and teacher training. See also
Cape Verde: politics, economics and society.

Literature

History and criticism

347 **África: Literatura, Arte e Cultura.** (Africa: Literature, Art and Culture.)
Lisbon: África, Literatura, Arte e Cultura, 1978- . periodicity varies.
Edited by Manuel Ferreira, this journal deals principally with the five Portuguese-speaking African countries. It publishes poetry, short stories, extracts from novels, and literary and cultural criticism from distinguished contributors. It is an excellent source for book reviews of recent Cape Verdean literary publications.

348 **America in Cape Verdean poetry before independence.**
Fernando J.B. Martinho. *Research in African Literatures*, vol. 13, no. 3 (Autumn 1982), p. 400-12.
Martinho studies the extent to which migration to the United States has been reflected in the Cape Verdean poetry since *Claridade* (q.v.). He makes an inventory of references to the United States, which is not exclusive and does not include material from the oral tradition. Nevertheless, this is a valid area of study. His concluding paragraph makes a very interesting comment upon the differing responses of Cape Verdean poets to those of other Portuguese-speaking African nations. The latter tend to identify with African-American experiences of slavery, struggle and more recent victories for civil rights. For the Cape Verdeans however, America is simply the distant land of 'fascination and disenchantment'.

349 **Bibliografia das literaturas africanas de expressão portuguesa.**
(Bibliography of literature from Portuguese-speaking Africa.)
Gerald Moser, Manuel Ferreira. Lisbon: Imprensa Nacional, 1983. 405p.
This is the essential reference work on literature from Portuguese-speaking Africa, a product of immense research by these two experts. Introductions are in Portuguese and English, entries in Portuguese. Layout – including facsimiles of covers and photographs of writers – is clear and accessible. Entries are arranged by country within four

categories: oral literature (Cape Verde p. 39-41); 'art literature' (Cape Verde p. 125 63); literary history and criticism (Cape Verde p. 267-78); literary periodicals (Cape Verde p. 305-8). There is one index by author and title and one biographical index Works published up to 1979 are included.

350 **Claridade: Revista de Arte e Letras.** (Clarity: A Review of Art and Literature.)
Prefaces by Baltasar Lopes, Manuel Lopes, Manuel Ferreira. Linda-a-Velha, Portugal: África, Literatura, Arte e Cultura, 1986. (Colecção para a História das Literaturas Africanas de Expressão Portuguesa).
Claridade, a magazine published between 1936 and 1963 in nine issues, was a cultural landmark in its own right. This facsimile collection with a comprehensive introduction by Manuel Ferreira must be indispensable to anyone interested in Cape Verdean literature and culture. *Claridade* provided the first regular forum for a serious consideration – if not, as is sometimes claimed, the discovery – of a Cape Verdean identity. The modernist movements in Portugal and Brazil and the regionalist writer of the Brazilian Northeast were clearly an influence. Focused on Jorge Barbosa Baltasar Lopes and Manuel Lopes, the *claridoso* group of writers and poets publishe articles on sociology, creole culture and oral literature, as well as short stories and poetry. Notable contributors were Pedro Corsino Azevedo, Corsino Fortes, Arnald França, Gabriel Mariano, Nuno Miranda, Félix Monteiro and Osório de Oliveira Given the transience of many Cape Verdean magazines – often now impossible to trac – this immaculately presented edition is of immense value.

351 **Comentários em torno do bilinguismo cabo-verdiano.** (Comments on Cape Verdean bilingualism.)
Manuel Ferreira. In: *Colóquios cabo-verdianos.* Lisbon: Junta de Investigações do Ultramar, 1959, p. 51-80. bibliog.
In a discussion which has evolved little over the years Ferreira defends the literary us of Crioulo, but is equally aware of some of the advantages of using Portuguese. Th principle advantage of the latter is the infinitely greater audience which can b reached. He avoids being prescriptive, simply noting that Cape Verdean writers hav two languages at their disposal.

352 **Um conceito de literatura Cabo-Verdiana independente.** (A view of an independent Cape Verdean literature.)
Nuno de Miranda. *Estudos Portugueses e Africanos*, vol. 12, no. 2 (July-Dec. 1988), p. 65-8.
A discussion of the new directions that Cape Verdean literature may take onc political imperatives have lessened. Nuno de Miranda, perhaps controversially, see this as an opportunity for greater authorial freedom.

353 **Critical perspectives on Lusophone literature from Africa.**
Edited by Donald Burness. Washington DC: Three Continents Press, 1981. 307p. bibliog.
A collection of papers and essays from various sources, several of which refer to Cap Verdean literature. These are 'Cape Verde and São Tomé-Príncipe: a search for ethni identity', p. 119-41, Richard A. Preto-Rodas; 'Cape Verdean poetry and the PAIGC' p. 143-57, Russell G. Hamilton; 'Baltazar Lopes: Cape Verdean pioneer', p. 158-72 Norman Araújo; 'The review entitled *Claridade*', p. 173-95, Norman Araújo; 'Ne

direction in Cape Verdean literature? The first numbers of *Raízes*', p. 198-202, Norman Araújo; 'Consciencialização na literatura caboverdiana' (Consciousness raising in Cape Verdean literature), p. 241-63, Onésimo Silveira; '*Claridade* ou a redescoberta das raízes' (*Claridade* or the rediscovery of roots), p. 289-94, Manuel Ferreira; '*Certeza* ou a aleluia deslumbrante dos dezoito anos' (*Certeza* or the dazzling halleluja of eighteen-year-olds), p. 295-9, Manuel Ferreira.

354 **Elementos para uma bibliografia da literatura e cultura portuguesa ultramarina contempôranea: poesia, ficção, memoralismo, ensaio.**
(Elements for a bibliography of contemporary Portuguese overseas literature: poetry, fiction, memoirs and essays.)
Amândio César, Mário António. Lisbon: Agência-Geral do Ultramar, 1968. 177p.
A back-up resource: entries for Cape Verde appear on pages 13-27 and are arranged alphabetically by author. There is no index.

355 **Essays in Portuguese-African literature.**
Gerald M. Moser. University Park, Pennsylvania: Pennsylvania State University, 1969. 88p. map. (Pennsylvania State University Studies, no. 26).
Although containing little material specifically devoted to Cape Verde, it is nonetheless of interest to see developments at the time of writing in Portuguese-speaking Africa as a whole. Moser notes that Cape Verdean writers are distinct from the others in many respects: he suggests, for example, that the élite are not alienated from Cape Verde in the way that the African élite are alienated from Africa.

356 **Estudos sobre literaturas das nações africanas de língua portuguesa.**
(Studies on the literatures of the Portuguese-speaking African nations.)
Alfredo Margarido. Lisbon: A Regra do Jogo, 1980. 558p.
A collection of essays and reviews previously published in various journals, sometimes under a pseudonym. Essays on Cape Verdean literature, dating from 1960 to 1978, are grouped together on pages 403-66. As well as identifying general themes, there are works of criticism on the poetry of Nuno Miranda, António Pedro and Amílcar Cabral, on Manuel Lopes' novel *Os flagelados do vento leste* (q.v.), on Baltasar Lopes' novel *Chiquinho* (q.v.) and on the formation of Crioulo.

357 **Fire: six writers from Angola, Mozambique and Cape Verde.**
Donald Burness. Washington DC: Three Continents Press, 1977. 148p. map.
A chapter is devoted to 'Baltasar Lopes and the *morna* of Cape Verde' (p. 75-95). A biography of the man who chose to work at the Gil Eanes secondary school in Mindelo rather than teach at the University of Lisbon is followed by an essay on his literary work. An afterword to the volume as a whole is provided by Manuel Ferreira, who mentions Cape Verde's African heritage and cultural independence.

Literature. History and criticism

358 **Flight and fidelity in Cape Verdean poetry before independence: the revolutionary phase.**
Norman Araújo. *Research in African Literatures*, vol. 13, no. 3 (Autumn 1982), p. 383-99.

Araújo looks at the theme of evasionism and anti-evasionism – the commitment to acknowledging what might be termed 'political realities' in poetry – between the years 1961 and 1975.

359 **Littérature et revues littéraires au Cap-Vert. Histoire et perspective.**
(Literature and literary reviews in Cape Verde. History and outlook.)
Pierrette Chalendar, Gérard Chalendar. *Le Mois en Afrique*, vol. 17, nos 198-99 (May-June 1982), p. 142-53.

A concise summary of the general trends of Cape Verdean literature which also includes some interesting notes on its evolution during the first years after independence.

360 **Les littératures africaines de langue portugaise: à la recherche de l'identité individuelle et nationale.** (African literatures in the Portuguese language: in search of individual and national identity.)
Edited by the Fundação Calouste Gulbenkian. Paris: Fondation Calouste Gulbenkian Centre Culturel Portugais, 1985. 570p. bibliogs.

Papers presented at an international conference held in Paris from 28 November to 1 December 1984 are reproduced in this volume. Contributions are in Portuguese or French. Grouped together on pages 447-552 are a seemingly disproportionate number of papers devoted to Cape Verdean literature: David Brookshaw on *Chiquinho* (q.v.) and *Claridade* (q.v.), p. 185-92; Donald Burness on *Contra mar e vento* (q.v.), p. 193-8; Nelson Eurico Cabral on racial, political, social and emotional significance of surname usage in Cape Verdean literature, p. 199-206; Benilde Justo Lacorte Caniato on Manuel Ferreira's *Hora di bai* (q.v.), p. 207-13; Alberto Duarte de Carvalho on aggression in Cape Verdean poetry, p. 215-24; Pierrette and Gérard Chalendar on the work of Luís Romano, p. 25-32; João António Estêvão on Teixeira de Sousa's *Ilhéu de contenda* (q.v.) and research in political economy, p. 233-70; Manuel Ferreira on the myth of the Hesperides in Cape Verdean poetry, p. 241-50; Ameth Kebe on *Chuva braba* (q.v.), by Manuel Lopes, p. 251-6; Felisberto Vieira Lopes (the poet Kaoberdiano Dambara) on the study of Cape Verdean literature, p. 257-61; Leão Lopes on Cape Verdean culture, p. 263-7; Gregory McNab on the short stories of Virgílio Pires, p. 269-75; Luzia Garcia do Nascimento on *Voz de prisão* (q.v.), p. 277-82; José Carlos Seabra Pereira on the *Almanach Luso-Africano* (q.v.), p. 283-9; Pierre Rivas on insularity in Cape Verdean poetry, p. 291-4; Maria Elsa Rodrigues dos Santos on Jorge Barbosa's poetry, p. 295-302; Henrique Teixeira de Sousa on the Church and literature in Cape Verde, p. 303-8; T.T. Tiofe on the last fifty years of Cape Verdean poetry, p. 309-15. There are also twelve papers on 'general problems' (p. 447-552) given by Benjamin Abdala Junior, Patrick Chabal, Eduardo de Sousa Ferreira, Albert Gerard, Russell G. Hamilton, Luís Kandjimbo, Eugénio Lisboa, Alfredo Margarido, Fernando J.B. Martinho, João Alves das Neves, Helena Riausova and Salvato Trigo.

361 **As máscaras poéticas de Jorge Barbosa e a mundividência cabo-verdiana.** (The poetic masks of Jorge Barbosa and the divided Cape Verdean world.)
Maria Elsa Rodrigues dos Santos, preface by Manuel Ferreira.
Lisbon: Editorial Caminho, 1989. 247p. map. bibliog.

A work of literary criticism which gives a portrait of the poet Jorge Barbosa (1902-71) within the context of wider Cape Verdean literary life. An appendix contains correspondence from the 1930s and 1940s between Barbosa and fellow-writer Manuel Lopes (1907-).

362 **Negritude as a theme in the poetry of the Portuguese-speaking world.**
Richard A. Preto-Rodas. Gainesville, Florida: University of Florida Press, 1970. 85p. (University of Florida Humanities Monograph no. 31).

Preto-Rodas intends that this study 'will trace the gradual rise of racial consciousness as shown by non-white poets and its flowering into one or more facets of contemporary Negritude'. A preliminary chapter explains the concept of negritude as a literary theme. See the third chapter, 'Cape Verde and São Tomé-Príncipe: a search for ethnic identity' (p. 32-54) for an introduction to what Preto-Rodas makes seem an interesting and worthwhile area of study in Cape Verdean written literature. An appendix of philological observations notes linguistic similarities between the Portuguese spoken in Brazil, Cape Verde and Angola.

363 **Notas sobre poesia e ficção cabo-verdianas.** (Notes on Cape Verdean poetry and fiction.)
Arnaldo França. Praia: Centro de Informação e Turismo, 1962. 23p.

First published in *Cabo Verde: Boletim de Propaganda e Informação* (new series, no. 1/157 [Oct. 1962]), França concludes a survey of Cape Verdean literary trends by questioning the benefits of the continuing 'paternal' influence of the generation of *Claridade* (q.v.).

364 **Reflexões sobre a literatura cabo-verdiana ou a literatura nos meios pequenos.** (Reflections on Cape Verdean literature or the literature of small milieux.)
Manuel Lopes. In: *Colóquios cabo-verdianos.* Lisbon: Junta de Investigações do Ultramar, 1959, p. 1-22.

Lopes looks at Mindelo society and its cultural environment and considers the town's influence on 20th-century writers. He also gives a general discourse on Cape Verdean literature.

365 **Voices from an empire: a history of Afro-Portuguese literature.**
Russell G. Hamilton. Minneapolis, Minnesota: University of Minnesota Press, 1975. 450p. map. bibliog. (Minnesota Monographs in the Humanities, vol. 8).

This is indubitably the first English-language source of literary criticism which the interested reader should consult. It combines breadth of vision with critical attention to detail. The introduction (p. 3-22) covers the basic concepts of an 'Afro-Portuguese literature' – Luso-tropicality, negritude, the role of Portugal and Brazil. The written literature of Cape Verde is covered in a section of its own (p. 233-357) made up of four chapters. The first chapter describes the social and cultural environment. This is followed by a detailed examination of *Claridade* (q.v.), and its precursors and successors in the world of literary publishing in Cape Verde. Next, a chapter covers poetry from the *claridoso* movement, through evasionism, Africanism and up to the political poetry of the early 1970s. There are three detailed studies of the *claridoso* poets Jorge Barbosa, Osvaldo Alcântara and Manuel Lopes. Finally, a chapter deals with narrative, an increasingly important literary form. The relative influences of Brazilian Northeast regionalism, Brazilian modernism and Portuguese neo-realism are considered and detailed study made of the works of Manuel Lopes, Baltasar Lopes, António Aurélio Gonçalves, Teobaldo Virgínio, Teixeira de Sousa, Luís Romano and Manuel Ferreira.

366 **Wanasema: conversations with African writers.**
Edited by Donald Burness.   Athens, Ohio: Ohio University Press,
1985. 95p. (Monographs in International Studies, Africa Series, no. 46).
Donald Burness interviewed Manuel Lopes in Lisbon in May 1983. An edited version of this interview is published on pages 81-9. He discusses *Claridade* (q.v.), which he says 'expressed the life of Cape Verde without foreign importation'. He also talks about Crioulo as a written language. He is not terribly enthusiastic about this but concedes that it 'has certain advantages over Portuguese'. The most astonishing feature of this interview is the vehemence of Lopes' dislike for the PAICV 'dictatorship' and his unusual claim that, 'Cape Verde is certainly more akin to Madeira than to Africa or any other country'.

Anthologies

367 **Antologia temática de poesia africana.** (Thematic anthology of African poetry.)
Mário de Andrade.   Lisbon: Livraria Sá da Costa Editora, 1976, 1979.
2 vols.
Twentieth-century poetry from all five of the Portuguese-speaking African nations has been selected by the Angolan anti-colonialist, Mário de Andrade (1928-90). Material is arranged in general chronological order and with an awareness of geographical area, but thematic relevance is highlighted. De Andrade's conviction is that the experience of colonialism and the struggle for liberation informs the poetry of these nations. Volume one, subtitled 'Na noite grávida de punhais' (In the night pregnant with daggers), covers the years from the 1930s to the end of the 1950s. The Cape Verdean poets Jorge Barbosa, Manuel Lopes, Pedro Corsino Azevedo, Osvaldo Alcântara, António Nunes, Aguinaldo Fonseca, Ovídio Martins, Gabriel Mariano, Onésimo Silveira, Mário Fonseca and Kaoberdiano Dambará are represented under the thematic headings 'Insularidade' (Insularity), 'Africanidade' (Africanness), 'Protesto' (Protest) and 'Prelúdio à libertação' (Prelude to liberation). Volume two, 'O canto armado' (The armed song) contains material from 1961 onwards. The Cape Verdeans in this volume are Abílio Duarte, Kaoberdiano Dambará, Ovídio Martins, Corsino Fortes, Tacalhe, Kwame Kondé, Osvaldo Osório, Sukre D'Sal and Emanuel Braga Tavares, appearing under the headings 'Salazar espantado' (Salazar suprised), 'Vem independência flor' (The flower of independence comes) and 'Kabral ka morrê' (Cabral hasn't died). Each volume has a preface by de Andrade and biographical notes on the poets.

368 **Aulil.**
Hugo Rodrigues, Alberto Gomes, Madalena Tavares, Pedro Vieira,
José Cabral. São Vicente, Cape Verde: Gráfica do Mindelo, 1987,
123p.
A collection of short stories and poems by five residents of Sal. Their biographies (at
the back of the volume) demonstrate very clearly the island's dependence on the
international airport. In fact, the very first item is a poem by Hugo Rodrigues called
'Aeroporto' (Airport). Although not every work is about Sal, it is a rare opportunity to
find out about life on this small island. Incidentally, 'Aulil' is an Arab place-name,
which is thought to refer to a source of salt on the West African coast (see *Corpus of
early Arabic sources for West African history*).

369 **Contos portugueses do ultramar: volume 1.** (Portuguese short stories
from overseas: volume 1.)
Edited by Amândio César. Porto, Portugal: Portucalense, 1969. 379p.
(Colecção Ultramar, no. 2).
The first volume of this anthology of contemporary short stories covers Cape Verde,
Guinea-Bissau and São Tomé and Príncipe. Gathered together on pages 19-153 are
samples of the work of some of Cape Verde's finest writers – António Aurélio
Gonçalves, Baltasar Lopes, Gabriel Mariano, Jorge de Sena, Manuel Ferreira, Manuel
Lopes, Ovídio Martins, Teixeira de Sousa and Teobaldo Virgínio.

370 **Contravento: antologia bilingue de poesia caboverdiana.** (Headwind: a
bilingual anthology of Cape Verdean poetry.)
Edited and translated by Luís Romano. Taunton, Massachusetts:
Atlantis, 1982. 329p.
Works from over thirty major and minor Cape Verdean poets of the 20th century are
presented in Crioulo and Portuguese.

371 **A horse of white clouds: poems from Lusophone Africa.**
Selected and translated by Donald Burness, foreword by Chinua
Achebe. Athens, Ohio: Ohio University Center for International
Studies, 1989. 193p. (Monographs in International Studies, Africa
Series, no. 55).
Eighteen poems from Cape Verde, by Jorge Barbosa, Manuel Lopes, Osvaldo
Alcântara, Yolanda Morazzo, Gabriel Mariano, Ovídio Martins, Onésimo Silveira,
Corsino Fortes, Arménio Vieira, João Rodrigues, Luís Silva and Ana Júlia are
presented in their original Portuguese, facing Burness's translations. Burness has
chosen to translate freely rather than literally: the results are more than acceptable.
Unfortunately there are a number of irritating spelling errors in the original texts, and
a poem by Amílcar Cabral about Cape Verde, 'Naus sem rumo / Ships without
moorings' appears with the poems from Guinea-Bissau. Another recent work of
English-language translations of Cape Verdean literature is *Across the Atlantic* by
Maria Moreira Ellen (North Dartmouth, Massachusetts: Center for the Portuguese-
speaking World, Southeastern Massachusetts University, 1989). Included are works of
prose and poetry by Baltasar Lopes, H. Teixeira de Sousa, Orlanda Amarílis, Manuel
Ferreira and João Lopes Filho.

Literature. Anthologies

372 **Jogos florais 12 de Setembro 1976.** (Games of flowers 12
    September 1976.)
    Introduction by Ovídio Martins.   Praia: Instituto Caboverdiano do
    Livro, [n.d.]. 121p.

A collection of prize-winning poems by the Cape Verdean poets Arménio Vieira,
Oswaldo Osório, Jorge Carlos Fonseca, Armando Lima, Vera Duarte, Pedro Gregório
Lopes, Vasco Oliveira Martins, Pedro Delgado, João Rodrigues, Marino Verdeano
Raimundo, João de Deus Lopes da Silva.

373 **No reino de Caliban. 1° volume: Cabo Verde e Guiné-Bissau.** (In
    Caliban's kingdom. Volume one: Cape Verde and Guinea-Bissau.)
    Manuel Ferreira.   Lisbon: Seara Nova, 1975. 328p.

It is tempting to suggest that this anthology, a work of great scholarship, is the most
important publishing event for Cape Verdean literature since *Claridade* (q.v.). Work
from almost forty Cape Verdean poets is gathered together, arranged by poet within
broadly chronological literary movements. These are often associated with one of the
several short-lived literary reviews, and each section is introduced by a brief, but
thoroughly researched, essay. There are biographical and publishing notes for each
poet. Poetry in Crioulo is in a separate section. Manuel Ferreira's essay 'Uma aventura
desconhecida' (An unknown adventure), p. 16-63, introduces the volume. It is a
masterly survey of the themes and influences of Portuguese-speaking African
literature. The Cape Verdean poets in this volume are António Pedro, Jorge Barbosa,
Manuel Lopes, Osvaldo Alcântara, Pedro Corsino Azevedo, António Nunes, Arnaldo
França, Guilherme Rocheteau, Nuno Miranda, Tomaz Martins, Aguinaldo Fonseca,
Gabriel Mariano, Ovídio Martins, Onésimo Silveira, Terêncio Anahory, Yolanda
Morazzo, Corsino Fortes, Arménio Vieira, Jorge Miranda Alfama, Mário Fonseca,
Oswaldo Osório, Rolando Vera-Cruz, Armando Lima Junior, Dante Mariano,
Sukrato, Tacalhe, António Mendes Cardoso, Daniel Filipe, João Vário, Luís Romano,
Teobaldo Virgínio, Jorge Pedro, Virgílio Pires, Eugénio Tavares, Pedro Cardoso,
Sérgio Frusoni, Jorge Pedro Barbosa and Artur Vieira. Guinea-Bissau is represented
by António Baticã Ferreira, p. 319-28.

374 **Panorama de la poésie du Cap-Vert.** (Panorama of the poetry of Cape
    Verde.)
    J. Castro Segovia.   [Kinshasa]: Université Nationale du Zaire, 1980.
    140p.

Acknowledging his debt to Manuel Ferreira, Segovia has translated into French a
substantial number of the poems included in Ferreira's anthology *No reino de Caliban.
1° volume: Cabo Verde e Guiné-Bissau* (q.v.). The volume also includes short essays
and biographical notes.

375 **Poesia de Cabo Verde.** (Poetry from Cape Verde.)
    José Osório de Oliveira.   Lisbon: Agência Geral das Colónias, 1944.
    [n.p.].

A selective anthology of poems from Jorge Barbosa, Manuel Lopes, Osvaldo
Alcântara, Pedro Corsino Azevedo and Nuno Miranda which follows an essay by de
Oliveira. Although from Portugal, de Oliveira was a great admirer of Cape Verdean
literature and was associated with *Claridade* (q.v.).

Prose

376   **Cais de pedra.** (Quay of stone.)
Nuno de Miranda. Praia: Instituto Caboverdiano do Livro, 1989. 313p.
A novel evoking the atmosphere of São Vicente in the 1940s. Miranda (1924-) has also published a collection of short stories entitled *Gente da ilha* (Island people) (Lisbon: Agência-Geral do Ultramar, 1961. 91p.).

377   **Chiquinho.**
Baltasar Lopes da Silva, preface by Alberto Carvalho.   Linda-a-Velha, Portugal: África, Literatura, Arte e Cultura, 1984. 5th ed. 299p.
Baltasar Lopes (1907-89) was an influential Cape Verdean writer and scholar, also publishing poetry under the pseudonym Osvaldo Alcântara. *Chiquinho* was first published by the *Claridade* magazine and publishing venture in São Vicente, Cape Verde in 1947. This edition is a facsimile of the first, including a reproduction of Manuel Filipe's cover design. Usually considered to be the first Cape Verdean novel (but see *O escravo*), before it finally reached publication chapters had appeared as short stories in issues of *Claridade* – 'Bibia' (vol. 1, March 1936) and 'Infância' (vol. 3, March 1937). *Chiquinho* (the name is a Cape Verdean diminutive of 'Francisco') epitomizes the *claridoso* determination to examine their own culture and environment. Its tripartite structure takes its narrator from boyhood to the verge of adulthood. 'Infância' (childhood) takes place in rural Caleijão, São Nicolau and is memorable for its description of creole culture. 'São Vicente' covers high school and dawning frustration with the colonial neglect of the islands. 'As Aguas' (The rains) is Chiquinho's return to drought-stricken São Nicolau as a teacher. Carvalho's preface indicates the influences which affected this and other *claridoso* works. Brazilian literary developments, of regionalism and modernism, were indubitably of great importance. The Brazilian Northeast is similar to Cape Verde, in both climate and social structure. *Chiquinho* might profitably be compared with the novels from this region of José Lins do Rego. Baltasar Lopes has also published a collection of short stories *Os trabalhos e os dias* (The labours and the days) (Praia: Instituto Caboverdiano do Livro, 1987, prefaces by Manuel Ferreira and Arménio Vieira. 83p.). See also the short story *A caderneta / The booklet*, translated by Vicente Rendall Leite (Praia: Instituto Caboverdiano do Livro, 1987. 19p.).

378   **Distância.** (Distance.)
Teobaldo Virgínio, preface by Luís de Sttau Monteiro.   Lisbon: Edições Ática, 1973. 153p.
A pleasant piece of prose which begins with the narrator's childhood in the countryside of Santo Antão, full of descriptions of the creole culture. The necessity of earning a living leads the narrator to the maritime life, first at the quayside of Ponta do Sol, Santo Antão and then to Sal, Mindelo and Brava. Virgínio (1924-) has also written the novel *Vida crioulo* (Creole life) (Lisbon: Livraria Bertrand, 1967. 188p.) and a collection of poems, *Viagens para lá da fronteira* (Journeys beyond the border) (Lisbon: Casa de Cabo Verde, 1973. 92p.).

379 **Drama de uma família caboverdiana.** (Drama of a Cape Verdean
    family.)
    Martinho de Mello Andrade, prefaces by Daniel Bacelar, Luís
    Romano. Mindelo, Cape Verde: The author, 1985. 75p. map.

Although there are some other minor poems and writings in this volume it is th
'Drama de uma família caboverdiana' (1957) which is of most interest. Andrade is
self-taught man, which may explain the naive but striking simplicity of this short stor
about the terrible famine in São Nicolau, 1941-42.

380 **O escravo.** (The slave.)
    José Evaristo d'Almeida, preface by Manuel da Veiga. Praia:
    Instituto Caboverdiano do Livro, 1989. 2nd ed. 157p.

Little seems to be known of Almeida: he was born in Portugal in the 19th century
spent a considerable length of time in Cape Verde and died in Guinea-Bissau in th
20th century. This, his only novel, was first published in Lisbon in 1856. It is set i
Santiago and gives a complex treatment of the issues of slavery and race. The herc
João, is a black slave in love with the unattainable *mestiça*, Maria. A melodramati
plot unfolds: this culminates in the fatal wounding of João, but he dies happy i
Maria's arms. Another interesting character is the hero's mother Júlia, who in he
hatred for slavery makes a pact with the devil. The re-edition of this work is
significant contribution to the study of Cape Verdean literature, and is well served b
Veiga's preface.

381 **Estória, estória. . . contos cabo-verdianos.** (Story, story. . . Cape
    Verdean tales.)
    João Lopes Filho, preface by Maria Manuela Paiva. Lisbon: Ulmeiro
    1983. 2nd ed. 123p. (Biblioteca Literária Ulmeiro, no. 1).

Nine short stories whose subject matter is firmly rooted in the experiences of rur:
Fajã, São Nicolau. Tales of slavery, emigration and memories of childhood ar
inseparable from descriptions of landscape and season. Language is enriched with th
Crioulo of São Nicolau, and the centrality of oral culture to the life of the rur:
community is reflected in its inclusion in the text. A glossary and translation of certai
phrases are helpfully appended by Lopes Filho (1922-).

382 **Famintos.** (The famished.)
    Luís Romano, prefaces by Helena Riausova, Pierette Chalendar,
    Gérard Chalendar. Lisbon: Ulmeiro, 1983. 369p. (Biblioteca Literári
    Ulmeiro, no. 3).

Romano (1922-) wrote this startling novel of Cape Verdean famine in the 1940s, bu
could not publish it within the Portuguese empire. It was smuggled through Africa t
Brazil where it was published in 1962 and promptly censored. It has a surreal an
ghastly quality, as befits its subject matter. A number of works of criticism have bee
stimulated by *Famintos*: see, for example, Ndoba Gasana's 'Littérature du Cap-Ver
(Cape Verdean literature) in *Présence Africaine*, no. 126 (1983), p. 99-111, as well a
the excellent prefaces to this edition.

383 **Os flagelados do vento leste.** (The scourged of the east wind.)
Manuel Lopes, preface by Luís Romano. São Paulo, Brazil: Editora
Ática, 1979. 271p. (Autores Africanos, no. 2).

First published in 1960 and described by Romano as a work of 'Cape Verdean realism',
this is a novel of the fierce ties between the Cape Verdean and the land. Set in rural
Santo Antão it describes in tragic detail the final triumph of drought over José da
Cruz's will to remain on his land. It is an ambitious novel – and none the worse for
that: one of the most striking scenes is the capricious battle between the winds in the
heavens above, which ultimately determines the fate of the people below. This edition
contains a helpful glossary of Crioulo terms used in the text. Lopes' first novel, *Chuva
braba* (Wild rain) (Lisbon: Edições 70, 1985. 166p.), was first published in 1956. This
too expressed the close relationship between man and the forces of the natural world,
although with rather greater optimism than the later novel. As well as novels, Lopes
has written poetry and several short stories: the most notable of these is 'Um galo que
cantou na baía' (A cock which crowed in the bay) which first appeared in *Claridade*
(q.v.), (no. 2 [August 1936], p. 2-3, 9).

384 **Ilhéu de contenda.** (Island of conflict.)
Henrique Teixeira de Sousa. Lisbon: Editorial O Século, 1978. 381p.
(Colecção Palmeira).

In this novel Teixeira de Sousa (1919-) uses his careful and concise prose style to
dissect the 20th-century colonial society of his native island, Fogo. Class, politics and
sex are all important issues. Several commentators have considered this novel an
accurate enough social document to refer to it in studies of Cape Verdean politics and
economy: see *Sociedade, estado e partido político na República de Cabo Verde* and
João António Estêvão's essay 'Literatura caboverdiana e investigação em economia
política: o exemplo de *Ilhéu de contenda* de Teixeira de Sousa' (Cape Verdean
literature and research into political economy: the example of *Ilhéu de contenda* by
Teixeira de Sousa) in *Les littératures africaines de langue portugaise: à la recherche de
l'identité individuelle et nationale* (q.v.), p. 233-40. His other works of fiction include
the novels *Capitão de mar e terra* (Captain of land and sea) (Mem Martins, Portugal:
Publicações Europa-América, 1984. 390p.) and *Xaguate* (Mem Martins, Portugal:
Publicações Europa-América, 1987. 354p.). This latter novel deals with the effects of
an emigrant returning to Fogo. He has also published a collection of short stories,
Contra mar e vento (Against sea and wind) (Lisbon: Prelo, 1972. 192p.).

385 **A casa dos mastros.** (The house of masts.)
Orlanda Amarílis, preface by Pires Laranjeira. Linda-a-Velha,
Portugal: África, Literatura, Arte e Cultura, 1989. 131p. (Colecção
Africana).

Amarílis (1924-) produces well-structured, well-written short stories. Her latest
collection of short stories is again distinguished by the strength of her portraits of
female characters – a comparative rarity in Cape Verdean literature. Her earlier works
include *Ilhéu dos pássaros* (Island of the birds) (Lisbon: Plátano Editora, 1982. 132p.)
and *Cais-do-Sodré té Salamansa* (From the Cais-do-Sodré to Salamansa) (Coimbra,
Portugal: Centelha, 1974. 124p.). She is particularly drawn to the subject of the Cape
Verdean diaspora and the bonds which link the scattered community. Her work is also
distinguished by the use of Crioulo in dialogue.

386   **O jardim dos rubros cardeais: 'flashes' de uma viagem.** (The garden of red cardinal birds: 'flashes' of a journey.)
João Rodrigues.   São Vicente, Cape Verde: Gráfica do Mindelo, 1986. 61p.

Rodrigues (1931-) has written a literary travelogue which gives particularly vivid descriptions of Brava. Traditional *mornas* are inserted into the text. His other works of fiction include the short stories collected together in *Caminhos agrestes* (Rural paths) (Praia: Instituto Caboverdiano do Livro, 1984. 45p.) and the short and nostalgic novel of Mindelo childhood, *Casas e casinhotos* (Houses and hovels) (São Vicente, Cape Verde: Gráfica do Mindelo, 1981, preface by Luís Romano. 109p.). Rodrigues has a pleasant and deceptively simple style of writing.

387   **. . .Levedando a ilha.** (. . .Leavening the island.)
Maria Margarida Mascarenhas.   Praia: Instituto Caboverdiano do Livro, 1988. 82p.

Although resident in Lisbon, Mascarenhas (1938-) has been active in many Cape Verdean literary ventures. This volume contains her collected short stories.

388   **Noite de vento.** (Windy night.)
António Aurélio Gonçalves, preface by Arnaldo França.   [Praia]: Instituto Caboverdiano do Livro, 1985. 211p.

Gonçalves (1901-84) contributed short stories and criticism to *Claridade* (q.v.). Nine of his short stories are collected together in this volume: 'Noite de vento' (Windy night) 'Pródiga' (Prodigal); 'O enterro de nhâ Candinha Sena' (The burial of Mrs Candinha Sena); 'Virgens loucas' (Crazy virgins); 'História do tempo antigo' (Story of the older days); 'A consulta' (The consultation); 'Biluca'; 'Burguezinha' (The little bourgeois) 'Miragem' (Mirage). Largely set in Mindelo, and unusual in treating women characters with serious interest, these stories are usually described as works of naturalism and realism. França's preface gives biographical and publishing notes.

389   **Quem é quem.** (Who's who.)
Maria José.   Praia: Instituto Caboverdiano do Livro, 1988. 109p.

A rare example of Cape Verdean writing for the theatre, this is a play in three acts. It draws heavily on traditional Cape Verdean culture: it uses, for example, one of the characters to tell a story from the Ti Lobu (Uncle Wolf) cycle. There are even footnotes to explain Crioulo words and usages. In effect this Crioulo culture is the theme of the play: in the final scene the young hero Zé says, 'Descobri que sou um crioulo' (I've discovered that I'm a creole).

390   **O testamento do Sr. Napumoceno da Silva Araújo.** (Sr Napumoceno da Silva Araújo's will.)
Germano Almeida.   Mindelo, Cape Verde: Ilhéu Editora, 1989. 184p.

An entertaining novel about the eccentric – and dead – hero of the title. It is also a portrait of small-town Mindelo.

391 **Vida e morte de João Cabafume.** (Life and death of João Cabafume.)
Gabriel Mariano, preface by Maria Cristina Pacheco. Lisbon: Vega,
[n.d.]. 149p.

Mariano (1928-) will probably always be best known as the author of the poem
'Capitão Ambrósio' (in *No reino de Caliban* [q.v.], p. 176-8) in which the captain leads
the people under the 'bandeira negra da fome' (black banner of hunger). Mariano is,
however, also a talented prose writer as these nine short stories testify. This work was
first published in 1976.

392 **Voz de prisão.** (Prison voice.)
Manuel Ferreira, forewords by Maria Lucia Lepecki, Joaquim
Namorado. Lisbon: Plátano Editora. [n.d.]. 3rd ed. 110p.

Although Ferreira (1917-) is Portuguese his work, both literary and academic,
expresses his commitment to Cape Verde. He is involved in initiatives to publish work
from Portuguese speaking Africa and is co-director of the Institute of African Studies
at the University of Lisbon. His works of fiction are primarily concerned with Cape
Verde. *Voz de prisão* (first published in 1971) is probably his most interesting book. It
is a short, dense novel which meshes together the experiences of the pre-independence
Cape Verdean diaspora. Set in a comfortable Lisbon flat, conversation links stories
from Cape Verde, America, Angola and Portugal. Survival in alien worlds is
celebrated, but the figure of Nelson/Victor is a reminder of the imperative of political
activity and its attendant dangers. Perhaps the most remarkable feature of the novel is
its use of both Crioulo and Portuguese, highlighting the political implications of
language in a colonial situation. It is also one solution to the dilemma which faces the
Cape Verdean writer of whether to use Portuguese or the mother-tongue Crioulo.
Ferreira's other works of fiction include the novel *Hora di bai* (Hour of leaving)
(Lisbon: Plátano Editora, 1972. 3rd ed. 265p.), and the collections of short stories
Morabeza (Amiability) (Lisbon: Edição Ulisseia, [1965]. 2nd ed. 125p. preface by José
Cardoso Pires), *Terra trazida* (Carried land) (Lisbon: Plátano Editora, 1972. 221p.)
and *Grei* (People) (Lisbon: Plátano Editora, 1984. 3rd ed. 90p.).

Poetry

393 **Algas e corais.** (Seaweed and coral.)
Pedro Monteiro Cardoso. Vila Nova de Famalicão, Portugal: The
author, 1928. 100p.

Cardoso (1890-1942) is one of the more interesting pre-*Claridade* poets. The first
section of *Algas e corais* is not on the whole particularly remarkable, being competent
poetry that would have been acceptable in Portugal. There is, however, an occasional
glimpse of the problematic issues of a Cape Verdean identity. A separately numbered
section of twenty-five pages contains verses in Crioulo and translations into Crioulo of
Brazilian songs. Another of Cardoso's publications is *Hespéridas* (Vila Nova de
Famalicão, Portugal: The author, 1930, 64p.), a collection of poems written around
1905. This consists of two groups of poems, 'Ciclo mítico' (Mythical cycle) and 'Ciclo
histórico' (Historical cycle). The mythical cycle is a fanciful working of the legend of a
fabulously wealthy kingdom which disappeared beneath the Atlantic: this may be

Cardoso's response to the question of Cape Verde's origins as a culture and a people. The historical cycle begins with the Portuguese discovery of the islands and although patriotic to Portugal in outward expression it is Cape Verdean in theme, describing famine, drought and emigration, and working Crioulo *mornas* (songs) into the text of some of the poems.

394 **Caboverdeamadamente construção meu amor.** (The building of my love is Cape Verdean.)
Oswaldo Osório, foreword by Sukre D'Sal.   Lisbon: Publicações Nova Aurora, 1975. 46p. (Literatura Nova, no. 3).

Subtitled 'poems of the struggle', this collection of poems by Osório (1937-) is divided into two parts. The first are clandestine poems from 1967-73, the second are from after 1974. His most recent collection of over twenty poems is the mellower *Clar(a)idade assombrada* (Clarity and age astonished) (Praia: Instituto Caboverdiano do Livro 1987. 82p.). His writing is always informed by a deep understanding of the Cape Verdean poetic heritage.

395 **Cântico da manhã futura.** (Hymn for the coming morning.)
Osvaldo Alcântara, foreword by Amaro Alexandre da Luz.   Praia: Banco de Cabo Verde, 1986. 126p.

Osvaldo Alcântara, one of the outstanding *claridoso* poets, is the pseudonym under which Baltasar Lopes (1907-89) wrote his poetry. This is the first time that a significant proportion of the poems have been published together. Until now they were widely scattered in many and diverse publications (see *Bibliografia das literaturas africanas d expressão portuguesa*). Whilst not a 'political' poet, he has never been blind to the realities of life in Cape Verde, nor failed to express *caboverdianidade*. Two work deserve special mention. One is the eight poems gathered together under the title 'Romanceiro de S. Tomé' (São Tomé song-cycle) which unsensationally finds a parallel between the sufferings of Christ and those of the Cape Verdeans sent to work in th plantations of São Tomé. The other is the 'Itinerário de Pasárgada' (The Pasárgada journey) group of five poems, which is one of the best examples of 'evasionism' – tha expression of longing for some mythical land beyond the seas – in Cape Verdea poetry.

396 **Canto a Cabo Verde.** (Song for Cape Verde).
David Hopffer Almada.   Praia: Instituto Caboverdiano do Livro, 1988. 67p.

This work is in two parts: 'Canto da longa noite' (Song of the long night), his poem from 1968-74; 'Canto da nova esperança' (Song of new hope) which covers 1975-8 Almada uses Crioulo in some of his texts. He is, of course, better known as a membe of the government.

397 **Duas línguas, dois amigos – uma saudade, two languages, two friends – memory.**
Jorge Barbosa, translated from the Portuguese by Vicente Rendall Leite.   Praia: Instituto Caboverdiano do Livro, 1986. 91p.

Sometimes less than idiomatic English translations of seventeen of Barbosa's bette known poems are published alongside the original works in Portuguese.

98 **Emergência da poesia em Amílcar Cabral: 30 poemas.** (Emergence of poetry in Amílcar Cabral: thirty poems.)
Oswaldo Osório.   Praia: Grafedito, [1984]. 81p.   (Colecção Dragoeiro, Estudos e Documentos).

. selection of thirty poems by the young Amílcar Cabral, dating from the 1940s to the arly 1950s are gathered together. Osório adds some interesting notes on the future AIGC founder and leader's poetic works. He reports on the exciting discovery of a •llection of Cabral's poems in Mindelo, and attempts to establish a chronology for the nown works. He also gives a biographical context to the poetry. See also 'The poet mílcar Cabral' by Gerald Moser (*Research in African Literatures*, vol. 9, no. 2 [Fall)78], p. 176-97) for literary criticism. Patrick Chabal's 'Littérature et libération ationale: le cas d'Amílcar Cabral' (Literature and national liberation: the case of .mílcar Cabral) (in: *Les littératures africaines de langue portugaise: à la recherche de identité individuelle et nationale* (q.v.), p. 457-91) is a scrupulously researched essay, hich concludes that Cabral's 'gifts as a writer were fundamentally political', and :marks that Cabral himself had no literary pretensions. Twelve poems from 1945-46 :e annexed to this essay.

)9 **Grito.** (Shout.)
Viriato Gonçalves, preface by John B. Leite.   [Boston, Massachusetts]: [The author], [1987]. 103p.

. collection of uncompromising poems on Cape Verdean issues – 'A chuva não vem' (he rains don't come) and 'Morri de fome' (I died of hunger), for example. Some are ritten in Crioulo.

)0 **Jorge Barbosa: poesias I.** (Jorge Barbosa: poems I.)
Jorge Barbosa, introduction by Manuel Veiga.   Praia: Instituto Caboverdiano do Livro, 1989. 194p.

)rge Barbosa (1902-71) was one of the leading lights of the *claridoso* movement. His rst volume of poetry *Arquipélago* (1935) was, in fact, the first Claridade publication, receding the launch of the magazine of the same name by a year. This is the first)lume of a project to publish Barbosa's collected works and it contains the three •llections *Arquipélago* (Archipelago) (São Vicente, Cape Verde: Edições Claridade,)35. 43p.), *Ambiente* (Ambient) (Praia: Minerva de Cabo Verde, 1941. 49p.) and *aderno de um ilhéu* (An island notebook) (Lisbon: Agência-Geral do Ultramar ivisão de Publicações e Biblioteca, 1956. 98p.). Manuel Veiga provides an erudite itroductory essay 'Signos e símbolos em Jorge Barbosa: uma tentativa de análise :miológica' (p. 7-54) (Signs and symbols in Jorge Barbosa: an attempt to give a :miological analysis).

)1 **Pão e fonema.** (Bread and phoneme.)
Corsino Fortes, afterword by Mesquelita Lima.   Lisbon: Sá da Costa, 1980. 2nd ed. 97p.

)rtes (1933-) was born in São Vicente and for many years was Cape Verde's nbassador in Angola. He is considered by many to be Cape Verde's greatest and iost innovative poet. *Pão e fonema*, first published in complete form in 1974, is his :st-known work. It is a version of that critical Holy Grail, the Cape Verdean epic. A rologue and three cantos are made up of individual poems. This structure holds •gether a progression through the almost surreal expression of the intimate ties :tween Cape Verdeans and the land, the nightmare of emigration, and its potential •r political education and a changed homecoming. Lima points out that in Fortes' use

139

Literature. Poetry

of both Portuguese and Crioulo it is the Portuguese which is made to feel the impact o Crioulo. This breaks with earlier conventions whereby Crioulo was merely present as a 'guest' in the Portuguese language. The post-independence sequel to this work i, *Árvore e tambor* (Tree and drum) (preface by Ana Mafalda Leite, Lisbon: Publicaçõe Dom Quixote; Instituto Caboverdiano do Livro, 1986. 130p.).

402 **Pérolas do sertão.** (Pearls from the backland.)
João Rodrigues. São Vicente, Cape Verde: Gráfica do Mindelo, 1986. 18p.

Images of music evoke nostalgia for Cape Verde in this poem dedicated to the pain o emigration.

403 **Poemas de longe.** (Poems from far away.)
António Nunes, prefaces by Manuel Ferreira, H. Teixeira de Sousa, Jaime de Figueiredo. Praia: Instituto Caboverdiano do Livro, 1988. 2nd ed. 54p.

A facsimile of the first edition of 1945, with the addition of Manuel Ferreira' biographical notes, H. Teixeira de Sousa's reminiscences and a critical essay by Jaime de Figueiredo. Nunes' (1917-51) poetry shows the strong influence of the movemen associated with the literary periodicals *Claridade* (q.v.) and *Certeza* (Certainty (Mindelo, Cape Verde: Sociedade de Tipografia e Publicidade, 1944. 2 issues).

404 **Poemas 1971-1979.** (Poems 1971-79.)
Arménio Vieira. Lisbon: África Editora, 1981. 105p. (Colecção Cântico Geral).

An anthology of the work of this inventive, witty and committed poet. It has bee gathered from diverse sources, with approximately one-third of the poems no previously published.

405 **40 poemas escolhidos.** (Forty selected poems.)
Nuno de Miranda, introduction by Leandro Tocantins. Lisbon: Agência-Geral do Ultramar, 1974. 101p. (Colecção Unidade, Poesia).

This is a collection of slightly revised poems from Miranda's two earlier volumes, *Cai de ver partir* (Quay of watching leaving) (Lisbon: Orion, 1960) and *Cancioneiro da ilh* (Island songbook) (Braga, Portugal: Edição Pax, 1964). Nuno de Miranda (1924-) is figure who looms large in Cape Verdean cultural life, and these poems show the influence of his close associations with the literary periodicals *Claridade* (q.v.) an *Certeza*.

406 **Terra gritante.** (Screaming land.)
Luís Tolentino, preface by Luís Romano. Praia: Grafedito, [n.d.]. 32p (Colecção Dragoeiro, no. 3).

Tolentino (1949-) was sent in 1973 to the São Nicolau concentration camp in Angol for political actvities against the Portuguese colonial state. Both his imprisonment and his political opinions have made a profound mark on this collection of poems, writter between 1971 and 1975 and published at some time after 1983. The title poem was in fact seized by the PIDE (the Portuguese security police).

140

407 **Universo da ilha.** (Island universe.)
Vasco Martins. Praia: Instituto Caboverdiano do Livro, 1986. [n.p.].
(Colecção Poesia, no. 3).

Luísa Figueira's line illustrations are as much part of this interesting publishing experiment as Martins' ten poems. Each of the untitled poems is printed on the outside of a separate sheet of stiff, folded paper. This opens out to reveal the poem in a facsimile of what is probably the author's handwriting. Facing is Figueira's fantastical visual interpretation. The poems are abstract ruminations on real and metaphysical islands. The illustrations repeat the theme with strange blendings of men and rocks.

408 **Versos da juventude.** (Verses of youth.)
Januário Leite, preface by João Filipe Gonçalves. Queluz, Portugal: Edições Paúl, [n.d.]. 111p.

Leite (1856-1930) from Santo Antão demonstrates in this posthumous edition the influence of Portuguese sentimental verse on an early generation of Cape Verdean poets.

Written literature in Crioulo

409 **Kau Berde sen mančonča. . .posia na kiriolu badiu.** (Cape Verde. . .poetry in the Crioulo of Santiago.)
Henrique Lopes Mateus. Faro, Portugal: The author, 1981. 38p.

An energetic stream of poetry in Crioulo, which probably benefits from being heard in performance. It demonstrates many of the features of oral poetry: it uses repetition, rhyme, lots of exclamation marks and has an immediacy of setting, using actual dates and names of people and places. It is about everyday life in Santiago – food, women, crops, poverty, friends – and dispenses advice on these subjects. Very entertaining: 'Dia dimingu pa ken ki e rubeladu / nen gresa nen misa ka ai ta badu / sabru ka Somada dentu'l merkadu / menbra ai ta spiadu ti kunkistadu' (On Sunday the rebellious / go neither to church nor to Mass / but to the market at Assomada / to watch the girls, then win them).

410 **Natal y kontus.** (Christmas and stories.)
Tomé Varela da Silva. Praia: Instituto Caboverdiano do Livro, 1988. 163p.

Another contribution by da Silva (1950-) towards the establishment of Crioulo as a literary language, this is a collection of twenty-five stories of Cape Verde which are more or less related to the theme of Christmas. He has also published a volume of poems in Crioulo entitled *Kardisantus* ([Praia]: Instituto Caboverdiano do Livro; Carlos Veiga, 1987. 45p.): the title refers to a type of thistle.

411 **Negrume (lzimparín).** (Twilight.)
Luís Romano, prefaces by Edgar Barbosa, Nilo Pereira. Rio de
Janeiro: Editora Leitura, 1973. 222p.
This is a collection of short stories and poems written in Crioulo and accompanied by
Portuguese translations. An introduction (p. 11-14) discusses the use of Crioulo as the
medium of expression for Cape Verdean literature. Romano also takes the opportunity
to apologize for the sentimentality of this interesting volume.

412 **Oju d'agu.** (Spring of water.)
Manuel Veiga. Praia: Instituto Caboverdiano do Livro, 1987. 229p.
A Crioulo novel, which consciously reflects Cape Verde's heritage of oral literature in
its use of verse within the narrative.

413 **Vinti šintidu letrádu na Kriolu.** (Twenty feelings written in Crioulo).
Káká Barbosa, forewords by Manuel Veiga, Oswaldo Osório. Praia:
Instituto Kabuverdiana di Livru, 1984. 65p.
Káká is the *nome de casa* of Carlos Alberto Lopes Barbosa (1947-). This volume is an
example of recent interest among Cape Verdean writers in working with the resources
of the oral tradition and, of course, the Crioulo language. The twenty poems here are
divided into two sections. The first 'Son di nôs erança' (Sound of our heritage) shows
the influence of Barbosa's childhood in the interior of Santiago in its use of the rhythm
and themes of *finasons* (improvised verse). The poems of 'Son di ravoluçon' (Sound of
revolution) are innovative in language use and textual layout. Incidentally something
rather odd seems to have happened to this edition in the printing process: facing pages
contain versions of the text which are identical in everything except details of
orthography. Unless this is an avante-garde statement of some description, it is a
graphic demonstration of the difficulties of establishing Crioulo as a written language.

Vangêle contód d'nôs móda.
See item no. 205.

Contravento: antologia bilingue de poesia caboverdiana.
See item no. 370.

Mornas: cantigas crioulas.
See item no. 428.

Culture and the Arts

General

414 A aventura crioula. (The creole adventure.)
Manuel Ferreira, preface by Baltasar Lopes. Lisbon: Plátano Editora,
1985. 3rd ed. 386p. bibliog.

A revised version of the first edition of 1967, this is a wide-ranging and thoroughly researched study of Cape Verdean culture. Ferreira begins by questioning some of the assumptions made about Cape Verde by commentators such as Gilberto Freyre. The existence of a Cape Verdean culture seems not to have been visible to many. This is not the case with regard to the debates about racial origin: Ferreira summarizes the arguments. His text is illustrated by examples from various aspects of Cape Verdean culture, whether music, language or cuisine. He goes on to examine the cultural implications of Crioulo: he considers the issues of bilingualism, the history of Crioulo studies and its use in written literature. His next chapters discuss the *morna* (Crioulo song form), oral narratives and written literature. Many of the commentators to whom Ferreira refers are rather preoccupied with establishing cultural origins, either in Africa or Europe. The value of Ferreira's own comments are in their comprehension of the thematic and functional integration of Cape Verdean cultural expression with Cape Verdean realities: he sees Cape Verdean culture in its own terms. The appended bibliography of literary and cultural materials, p. 337-71, is immensely valuable. It is divided between Cape Verdean and non-Cape Verdean authors.

415 As aves em algumas superstições indígenas da Guiné e de Cabo-Verde.
(Birds in some native superstitions from Guinea and Cape Verde.)
António de Almeida. *Portugal em Africa*, 2nd series, no. 1 (1944),
p. 31-9; 2nd series, no. 2 (1944), p. 90-8. bibliog.

An anecdotal rather than a thorough and academic survey and de Almeida admits to a lack of material. Nevertheless there is information here on customs and beliefs associated with owls, vultures, seagulls, crows, swallows and domestic fowl. He supplies some unappetizing remedies from Fogo; for instance, the use of a black cock's blood to cure anthrax or a mixture of seagull grease and cow dung as a remedy for rheumatism.

Culture and the Arts. General

416 **Bandeiras da ilha do Fogo: o senhor e o escravo divertem-se.** (The *bandeiras* of Fogo Island: the master and the slave enjoy themselves.) Félix Monteiro. *Claridade*, no. 8 (May 1958), p. 9-22.

The *bandeiras* are popular festivals from Fogo, ostensibly celebrating patron saints. The *bandeira* is a banner representing a saint. Monteiro discusses possible origins for the festival, concluding that both Africans and Europeans contributed to its evolution. He describes the *bandeiras* in some detail. The preparation of food is very important: in effect this would have been the private festival for the slaves or servants, with music and dancing. The pestling of corn by the women announces the beginning of the festivities. The slaughtering of an animal for meat is seen by Monteiro to have elements of a ritualistic sacrifice. He goes on to describe the 'aristocratic' aspects of the *bandeira*, when the saint's banner used to be carried into church on horseback. A mass is held and a procession leads down to the beach, where horse racing takes place. An interview with two former riders, José de Guilhermina and Alino de Môro, is published in *Magma*, vol. 1, no. 1 (April 1988), p. 28-9, under the title 'Cavalos e cavaleiros da ilha do Fogo' (Horses and horse riders of Fogo Island). For an account of a recent *bandeira*, see *Race, culture and Portuguese colonialism in Cabo Verde*.

417 **Cabo Verde: apontamentos etnográficos.** (Cape Verde: ethnographic notes.) João Lopes Filho, foreword Luís Romano. Lisbon: [n.p.], 1976. 54p. bibliog.

The first essay in this volume is 'Contribuição para o estudo da habitação rural em Santiago de Cabo Verde' (Contribution to the study of rural housing in Santiago, Cape Verde) (p. 13-40). This discusses the African origins of the traditional round houses known as *funcos*: these are now much less common than rectangular houses. The layout, building materials, roofing, building use and location are described for both types. The second essay is 'Berimbau e cimbó: dois instrumentos musicais em vias de desaparecimento no arquipélago de Cabo Verde' (*Berimbau* and *cimbó*: two musical instruments on the verge of disappearing from the archipelago of Cape Verde) (p. 45-54). The *berimbau* is described from sources referring to Angola, South Africa and Brazil: descriptions from Niger and Senegal are used for the *cimbó*. The use of the instruments in the rural interior of Santiago is described: they have disappeared from all the other islands.

418 **Cabo Verde – elo antropológico entre a África e o Brasil?** (Cape Verde: an anthropological link between Africa and Brazil?) Luíz Romano. *Cabo Verde: Boletim Documental e de Cultura*, vol. 15, nos 19-21 (April-June 1964), p. 27-39.

Romano describes aspects of the traditional culture of Santo Antão, his island of origin, managing to put a wide range of information into relatively few pages. From his childhood he recalls superstitions – of the evil eye, of ghosts who played the *berimbau* (a musical instrument of African origin, similar to a jew's harp), and, of course, the bogeymen *gongon*, *cachorrôna* and *canelinha*. He notes the traditional festivals of Santo Antão, including the *fetal* which celebrates the distillation of the first drops of the island's renowned sugar-cane rum. Practices associated with birth – such as the *guarda-cabeça* (literally, 'protect the head') which takes place seven days after the birth of a baby – and sexual relations are also covered. Twenty days after the birth the *queima da bufareira* (burning an oily-seed bearing plant) takes place when parents can resume sexual relations: through an analysis of Brazilian, Cape Verdean and Kimbundu expressions for female genitalia Romano believes he can find evidence of cultural common ground. Although confessing that the article does not really develop the theme of the 'anthropological link', the author believes that Brazilians will find much in it that is familiar.

419 **Cabo Verde – renascença de uma civilização no Atlântico médio.** (Cape Verde – renaissance of a civilization in mid-Atlantic.)
Luís Romano. Lisbon: Edição da Revista Ocidente, 1970. 2nd ed. 210p. bibliog.

A near encyclopaedia of the folk traditions and oral literature of Santo Antão. Chapters give examples, descriptions and commentaries for such things as lovers' language; children's games and rhymes; songs for accompanying the bulls turning the sugar-cane presses; songs for guarding newly sown fields from crows; songs for oarsmen; spells to cast out evil spirits; songs for the Porto Novo festival of the Holy Apostles; songs for the Christmas and New Year season; love letters; proverbs; terminology for fetishes and taboos; musical instruments; implements of chastisement; a glossary of traditional medicine; literary texts in Crioulo; oral narratives of Tio Pedro (Uncle Peter) and Tio Lobo (Uncle Wolf) in Crioulo with Portuguese translations; the lyrics and music of *mornas*; songs for brides; riddles; glossary of culinary terms; the plastic arts. There is also an extensive and valuable glossary on pages 161-205, which gives terms in the Crioulo of Santo Antão, the equivalent Portuguese lexical item and literal meaning in Portuguese.

420 **Compreensão de Cabo Verde.** (Understanding Cape Verde.)
Nuno de Miranda. Lisbon: Junta de Investigações do Ultramar, 1963. 80p. bibliog.

An unusual, but pleasing, introduction to Cape Verdean culture conducted in large part through an anthology of literary texts. The importance of the totemically Cape Verdean phenomenon of *Claridade* is noted, but the book in the main studies external influences which have made their mark on Cape Verdean culture. It covers the African influences on food and its preparation, on wedding and funeral ceremonies, on *tabanca* (mutual aid societies), *batuque* (a traditional form of music, dance and song) and the game of *ouri*. It also acknowledges the indubitable Portuguese influence on language, dress and urban architecture, and the English who introduced the game of cricket.

421 **Contribuição para o estudo da cultura cabo-verdiano.** (Contribution towards the study of Cape Verdean culture.)
João Lopes Filho. Lisbon: Ulmeiro, 1983. 57p. (Biblioteca Ulmeiro no. 15).

A discussion of the need to preserve Cape Verde's cultural heritage and the role of culture at the present day. The chapter 'Cultura cabo-verdiana' (Cape Verdean culture) (p. 23-36) is the most interesting part of the book. It describes in theoretical terms the experience of colonialism and colonial cultural policy in Cape Verde. See also *Defesa do património sócio-cultural de Cabo Verde*.

422 **Folclore caboverdiano.** (Cape Verdean folklore.)
Pedro Monteiro Cardoso, introduction by Luíz Silva, prefaces by Alfredo Margarido, J.B. Amâncio Gracias. Paris: Solidariedade Caboverdiana, 1983. [2nd ed.]. 120p. map. bibliog.

With the addition of the contributions of Luíz Silva and Alfredo Margarido, this is a facsimile of the first edition of 1933 (Porto, Portugal: Edição Maranus). Silva has written a well-informed essay on emigrants and Cape Verdean language and culture,

Culture and the Arts. General

p. vii-xxix. Margarido's preface, 'A perspectiva histórico-cultural de Pedro Monteir
Cardoso' (Pedro Monteiro Cardoso's historical and cultural perspective), p. xxx
lxxxiii, is a substantial biography of the author. It is also a salutory corrective to th
view that before *Claridade* (q.v.). Cape Verde had no independent literary identit
Cardoso's own interest in Cape Verdean culture is demonstrated by the text whic
follows. This collection of items includes essays and notes on Cape Verdean cultu
and literary material in Crioulo. A short essay, p. 33-51, on Cape Verde and Braz
finds similarities in language and culture between the two countries. Further notes c
Crioulo follow. There are also examples of *mornas* and other verse in Crioulo. The
include *batuque* and *finaçom* (improvised songs).

423 **Introdução ao estudo das danças de Cabo Verde.** (Introduction to the
study of the dances of Cape Verde.)
Tomaz Ribas. *Garcia de Orta*, vol. 9, no. 1 (1961), p. 115-21. bibliog
There is a substantial amount of background introduction to wade through befo
reaching the material on dances. Sadly there is very little on technicalities or context
performance, Ribas being more concerned to establish a hierarchy of extern
influences. So, the *torno* is the most 'African', the *morna* is the most 'European' an
the *coladeira*, *taca* and *landum* are hybrids. Like most observers of Cape Verdea
dances he feels free to comment on their 'sensuality'. See also his article 'A qualidac
espectacular das danças de Cabo Verde' (The element of spectacle in Cape Verdea
dances) (*Cabo Verde: Boletim Documental e de Cultura*, vol. 15, nos 19-21 [April-Jur
1964], p. 1-3).

424 **Tabanca.** (Mutual aid association).
Félix Montiero. *Claridade*, no. 6 (July 1948), p. 14-18; no. 7 (Dec.
1949), p. 19-26.
In an interesting study of this important feature of Cape Verdean culture, Monteir
focuses on the *tabanca* of Achada Grande, Praia. The *tabanca* is a mutual a
association which has its own distinctive festivals. It has its own social structur
including a king, queen, 'court' functionaries and young girls called the *filhas de san*
(daughters of the saint). Alongside the funeral rites for its members, the *tabanca*
most visible activity is the celebration of its patron saint. In this case it is St Joh
Monteiro describes some of the ceremonies including the use of the 'sacred' drums an
the importance of the dancing of the *filhas de santo*. Part of the ceremony takes plac
in church. Even during years of terrible famine it is imperative that the celebratio
take place. Monteiro recounts a legend of the dire consequences of lapsing: th
tabanca could appease the angry saint only by dancing for him in the midst of a terrib
storm. Monteiro notes similarities in this legend between the figure of St John amd th
Yoruba god Xangô. This leads him into an interesting discussion of religio
syncretism. He notes similarities with *candomblé*, the Brazilian syncretic religion. Th
text is in Portuguese.

425 **Tradições orais do folclore infantil caboverdiano.** (Oral traditions from
the folklore of childhood.)
Luís Romano. *Arquipélago*, vol. 2, no. 8 (Dec. 1987), p. 30-6.
bibliog.
The stories, games and songs of childhood are a rich source of material from the or
tradition. Romano reproduces some examples from Cape Verde and gives notes o
context of 'performance' and thoughts on possible origins. He covers lullabies, th
extensive gallery of bogeymen of which the most common is the *gongon*, the popul

gures of Ti Lobo and Shibinho (Uncle Wolf and his nephew) and Tiganga (a giant
rd), and a variety of rhymes, games and riddles.

efesa do património sócio-cultural de Cabo Verde.
ee item no. 448.

Morna

26 **56 mornas de Cabo Verde.** (Fifty-six *mornas* from Cape Verde.)
    Collected by Jótamont, preface by Marmellande.   São Vicente, Cape
    Verde: Gráfica do Mindelo, [1988]. 123p.

he *morna* is a symbol of Cape Verdean cultural independence. Unique to the islands,
is a sentimental and sensuous Crioulo song set to the music of violins or guitar, which
in also be considered to be a poem in its own right. Dancing – usually a type of
xtrot – is an important part of the occasion of performance. Attempts have been
ade to find a direct kinship between the *morna* and the Portuguese *fado* or song-
rms from Martinique or even from Arabia, but it remains a symbol of Cape Verde's
nique cultural identity. Jótamont – the name is the one by which Jorge Fernandes
onteiro is usually known – has collected in this volume examples from various
urces, including traditional *mornas* from Brava and Boa Vista. Lyrics and music are
1 facing pages. Marmellande is Martinho de Mello Andrade's *nome de casa*.

27 **Da literatura colonial e da 'morna' de Cabo Verde. Conferência.**
    (On colonial literature and the *morna* of Cape Verde. A lecture.)
    Fausto Duarte.   Porto, Portugal: Edições da 1ª Exposição Colonial
    Portuguesa, 1934. 19p.

 sentimental, almost sexual, description of the performance of the *morna*, which is
mpared to Portuguese *fado* – a product of two homesick races, inspired by the 'sweet
ain of the Atlantic'. The article is very much a product of its colonial context.

28 **Mornas: cantigas crioulas.** (*Mornas*: creole songs.)
    Eugénio Tavares.   Lisbon: J. Rodrigues, 1932. 108p.

avares (1867-1930) is the most revered composer of both music and lyrics for the
orna. A native of Brava, he spent most of his life on that island, with short spells in
ie USA. The twenty-seven *mornas* in this volume present the classic themes of love,
paration and emigration and include the much-quoted 'Morna de despedida' (*Morna
f farewell): 'Hora de bai, / Hora de dor, / Ja'n q'ré / Pa el ca manchê!' (Hour of
aving, / Hour of sorrow, / Now I don't want / The sun to rise!). All are written in
rioulo using Tavares' own (sometimes inconsistent) etymological orthography. Osório
e Oliveira, who was instrumental in bringing this volume to publication, contributes a
ort essay. For an illuminating literary analysis of Tavares' poetry see Gabriel
ariano's essay *Amor e partida na poesia crioula de Eugénio Tavares* (Love and
arting in the Crioulo poetry of Eugénio Tavares) (Vila Viçosa, Portugal: Separata das
omunicações dos 1ᵒˢ encontros de Poesia, 1984. 20p.) in which Mariano looks at the
se and significance of these two fundamental themes in Tavares' poetry. Tavares was
so known for his campaigning journalism, and Félix Monteiro has gathered together
selection of his journalism, fiction and poetry in Portuguese in 'Paginas esquecidas de

Eugénio Tavares' (Forgotten pages of Eugénio Tavares) (*Raízes*, nos 17-20 [Jan.-Dec 1981], p. 121-73).

429 **Mornas e contra-tempos: coladeras de Cabo Verde.** (*Mornas* and counter-beats: *coladeras* of Cape Verde.)
Collected by Jótamont. São Vicente, Cape Verde: Gráfica do Mindelo, 1987. 37p.

This volume contains the music for eighteen *mornas* from various sources. Th introduction explains how a *morna* is transformed into the more frenetic *coladera* a the height of a dance by alteration of the tempo.

430 **Música caboverdeana: mornas de Francisco Xavier da Cruz (Bê Léza).** (Cape Verdean music: *mornas* of Francisco Xavier da Cruz [Bê Léza].) Transcribed by Jótamont. São Vicente, Cape Verde: Gráfica do Mindelo, 1987. 47p.

Bê Léza was indubitably one of the most talented and loved of Cape Verdea composers and performers. Twenty-one of his *mornas* are contained in this volume with music and lyrics on facing pages. Bê Léza (1905-85) is supposed to have acquire his name – which literally means 'beauty' – after playing with a group of friends. A little while later the group were playing without him, and were asked, 'But where ha your beauty gone?' Memories of Bê Léza and more information about his work can b found in *80° aniversário de B. Léza* (Eightieth anniversary of B. Léza) (in *Voz di Povc* a seven-page supplement to the 11 January 1986 edition). Contributions include thos of local musicians.

431 **Música caboverdeana: mornas de Jorge Fernandes Monteiro (Jótamont)** (Cape Verdean music: *mornas* of Jorge Fernandes Monteiro [Jótamont].)
Jorge Fernandes Monteiro, preface by G. Moacyr Rodrigues. São Vicente, Cape Verde: Gráfica do Mindelo, 1987. 63p.

Jótamont is a well-known musician in Cape Verde: he leads the Mindelo town banc and is passionately concerned to preserve Cape Verde's musical heritage. Twenty-si of his *mornas* are contained in this volume, with lyrics and music on facing pages Almost identical *mornas*, but with music scored for the piano, are contained in hi *Música caboverdeana: mornas para piano* (Cape Verdean music: *mornas* for th piano) (prefaces by Félix Monteiro, Martinho de Mello Andrade. São Vicente, Cap Verde: Gráfica do Mindelo, 1987. 71p.).

432 **Músicas de Cabo Verde: mornas de Eugénio Tavares.** (Cape Verdean melodies: *mornas* of Eugénio Tavares.)
Collected by Jótamont, preface by Félix Monteiro. São Vicente, Cape Verde: Gráfica do Mindelo, 1987. 55p.

Jótamont has become worried that, as a consequence of the popularity of Tavares *mornas*, both music and lyrics have become altered by constant use. To try to establis their original form, Jótamont has published eighteen examples with lyrics and music future volumes are planned.

433 **Subsídios para o estudo da morna.** (Contributions towards the study of the *morna*.)
José Alves dos Reis. *Raízes*, no. 21 (June 1984), p. 9-18.
A detailed analysis of the music of several *mornas* which leads dos Reis to remark that these musical characteristics are not easy to find in the folklore of other cultures.

434 **Três formas de influência portuguesa na música popular do ultramar: o samba, a morna e o mandó.** (Three forms of Portuguese influence on the popular music of the overseas territories: the *samba*, the *morna* and the *mandó*.)
Jean-Paul Sarrautte. *Gazeta Musical e de Todas as Artes*, 2nd series, vol. 10, nos 114-15 (Sept.-Oct. 1960), p. 132-4; vol. 10, nos 116-17 (Nov.-Dec. 1960), p. 146-7.
Sarrautte suggests that West African – possibly Balanta – musical culture may have influenced the syncopation of Cape Verdean *morna*. Similarities with Brazilian *samba* may be due to the presence of West African peoples in that country too. However, Portuguese six-eight time could also be an influence. The style of the lyrics is, he suggests, European in its verse form and in the sentimentality of subject matter.

Oral verse-forms

435 **Cantigas de Ana Procópio.** (The songs of Ana Procópio.)
Félix Monteiro. *Claridade*, no. 9 (Dec. 1960), p. 15-23.
Ana Procópio was an improvisatory singer of great renown. She was from Fogo, probably born in the 1870s, and died in 1956. Before her death Monteiro managed to record the lyrics to some of her songs. These he reproduces in this article with helpful notes on the context of performance, the singer's relationship with accompanying musicians, and the social context of Fogo. These snatches of verse are a vivid, witty and wicked commentary on sexual and social behaviour: 'Galho belho, sporom quebrado / Cantâ chumâ tê roquicê / Franga qui obi'l fra sim: coitado / Ja bu querê, ma bu ca podê' (Old cock, with broken spur / Crows and calls until he's hoarse / Chicken who hears him says: what a pity / You still want to, but you can't do it). Sabino Galvão Baptista has collected more examples of her work from people who remember hearing her performances. These are published in 'Cantar há muita gente que canta, mas cantadeira. . .era Ana Procópio' (Singing, there are many people who sing, but a singer. . .that was Ana Procópio) in *Magma*, vol. 1, no. 1 (April 1988), p. 33-7.

436 **Cantigas de trabalho.** (Work songs.)
Oswaldo Osório, foreword by Manuel Veiga. [Praia]: Comissão Nacional para as Commemorações do 5° Aniversário da Independência de Cabo Verde – Sub-Comissão para a Cultura, 1980. 83p. map.
(Tradições Orais de Cabo Verde).
This book is part of a recent effort to record the oral traditions of Cape Verde. The philosophy behind these various projects is that popular Crioulo literature and music is at the heart of the Cape Verdean identity, not on its folkloric fringe. The book contains nine transcripts, in Crioulo, of agricultural songs (four of which are recorded on the accompanying disc), and four sea-songs. Osório's text, translations of the songs

and annotations are in Portuguese. Osório places these songs in the context of their performance – routine agricultural activities such as bird-scaring or leading the animals which turn the sugar-presses. He also discusses the wider social context of their origins in the era of plantation slavery. Manuel Veiga's introduction is a concise explanation and defence of the orthography used for the Crioulo transcriptions. It is the orthography proposed by the 1979 conference on linguistics held in Mindelo, Cape Verde, and used in all the works in this series.

437 **Finasons di Ña Nasia Gomi.** (*Finasons* of Ña Nasia Gomi.)
Tomé Varela da Silva. Praia: Instituto Kauberdianu di Libru, 1985.
117p. (Tradisons Oral di Kauberdi).

T.V. da Silva has recorded, transcribed, annotated and introduced two *finasons* (improvised songs) from Santiago. The introduction gives some technical information on the performance of *finasons*. They generally follow a prescribed rythm, often marked by hand-clapping. Their lyrics may be incorporated into the music for the *batuku* (a traditional form of song, music and dance), although the *batuku* differs in using a chorus. This volume also contains a biography of the poet/performer, who was born Maria Inácia Gomes Correia in 1925 near Tarrafal, Santiago. The annotated texts of two of her *finasons* follow. They were recorded in 1981 and 1982. Thematically flexible, they contain social observations, advice, religious invocations, comments on the conditions of performance and autobiographical data. Verse style is characterized by repetition of sounds and syntax.

438 **O folclore poético da ilha de S. Tiago.** (The poetic folklore of Santiago Island.)
Baltasar Lopes. *Claridade*, no. 7 (Dec. 1949), p. 43-51.

Lopes looks at various aspects of some of the types of oral literature from Santiago. He discusses the origins and etymology of *batuque*, going on to explain the conditions of performance and give some examples of the more common of the lyrics and choruses. He also discusses the *finaçom*, quoting from parts of *finaçons* dedicated to a 'Doutor Honoré' which in content strongly resemble praise songs.

439 **Ña Bibiña Kabral: bida y óbra.** (Ña Bibiña Kabral: life and work.)
Edited by Tomé Varela da Silva. Praia: Instituto Caboverdiano do Livro, 1988. 285p. bibliog. (Tradições Orais de Cabo Verde).

Bibiña Kabral (1900-85) was an inspired performer and artist from Tarrafal, Santiago. With the help of Horácio Santos and Alexandre Semedo, T.V. da Silva recorded, on one day in 1984, her life-story and some examples of her work. Almost exclusively in Crioulo, this work is an invaluable record of the *finasons* and *sanbuna* (shorter verses, with voice quality more important than words). Bibiña Kabral's autobiography is remarkable. Marriage to an older man, an emigrant, repressed her performing life as she took care of his lands. As a widow she resumed her career as the living legend of Santiago *batuque*, but in the process her lands had to be mortgaged and eventually sacrificed to her art. The volume concludes with interviews with people who knew her.

Oral narratives

440 Folk-lore from the Cape Verde Islands.
Elsie Clews Parsons. Cambridge, Massachusetts: American Folk-Lore Society, 1923. 2 vols. (Memoirs of the American Folk-Lore Society, vol. 15).

In the summers of 1916 and 1917 the distinguished folklorist Elsie Clews Parsons visited the Cape Verdean immigrants in Massachusetts, Rhode Island and Connecticut. She collected 133 oral narratives as well as a substantial number of proverbs, sayings and riddles. The stories were nearly always told in Crioulo and an interpreter, Gregório Teixeira da Silva, made notes in an English translation. These were later written up in both English and in da Silva's Fogo Crioulo. Volume 1 (375p. bibliog.) contains the English version of the narratives. Parsons provides numerous footnotes. These give information on the speaker, noting the island of origin, and indicate comparable stories and motifs from around the world. Volume 2 (269p.) contains the Crioulo version of the narratives, together with the collection of riddles, proverbs and sayings (p. 194-267). Modern recording techniques far surpass those available to Parsons, and there exist undoubted problems in this respect. Not least of these is that all the Crioulo narratives are written in the Fogo variant regardless of the performer's own usage. Nevertheless, this is a fine and valuable collection. It is also interesting to observe this early attempt to use Crioulo as a written language.

441 Na bóka noti. (The night's voice.)
Edited by Tomé Varela da Silva. Praia: Instituto Caboverdiano do Livro, 1987. 399p. bibliog. (Tradições Orais de Cabo Verde).

Narratives are at the heart of Cape Verde's oral literature, and this is an exceptionally fine collection. Eighty-five stories, and some of their variants, were recorded between 1973 and 1985. Most come from Santiago, but there are some from Fogo, São Vicente and Santo Antão. Not surprisingly they are almost entirely narrated in Crioulo. T.V. da Silva has arranged them into four 'cycles': 'Ómi ku mujer' (Man and woman), 'Fetiséria' (Sorcery), 'Pedru ku Palu ku Manel' (Peter, Paul and Manuel) and 'Lobu ku Sibiñu' (Wolf and his nephew). At the back of the book there is biographical information on performers and collectors. Further volumes are planned, which is very good news.

Weaving

442 Panaria cabo-verdeano-guineense. (Cape Verdean and Guinean clothmaking.)
António Carreira, preface by Jorge Dias. [Praia]: Instituto Caboverdiano do Livro, 1983. 2nd ed. 226p. map. bibliog.

With his useful close reference to primary sources, Carreira has written what has come to be the standard work on the history of weaving in Cape Verde. Raw cotton was an important export in the first fifty years of the islands' settlement. By 1517 there is evidence that cloth (*panos*) was being woven there. For the next 300 years or more Cape Verde was to produce high-quality cloths, essential as currency in the slave trade of the Guinea coast. Carreira suggests that the cloth's characteristic geometric designs were Islamic in origin, being introduced via the Portuguese. These designs were then adapted by the Manjaco and Papel peoples of the mainland (Guinea-Bissau). Conversely, the techniques of weaving was brought to Cape Verde by the slave-weavers from the African mainland. Weaving and dyeing techniques are outlined for the classic Cape Verdean cloth. This was made of six indigo-and-white patterned strips, each of a palm's width, sewn together. Carreria helpfully explains the terminology used to describe the cloths and their different designs. One hundred and twenty-nine black-and-white photographs are appended to this volume. Some illustrate aspects of the production of cloths – weaving, dyeing and sewing – but the majority are of examples of cloths from Cape Verde and Guinea-Bissau.

443 **Weaving in Africa south of the Sahara.**
Karl-Ferdinand Schaedler, translated from the German by Leonid Prince Leiven, Judy Howell. Munich, Germany: Panterra-Verlag, 1987. 487p. 10 maps. bibliog.

A beautifully illustrated and well-researched volume, which covers Cape Verde and Guinea-Bissau on pages 104-13. The fundamentals of pattern and production techniques are described. The designs, of Moorish influence via Portugal, are said to be unusual for Africa south of the Sahara. A brief history is given of the introduction of weaving to the islands and their role as Portugal's 'currency workshop' for trade in Africa.

Food and drink

444 **Cozinha de Cabo Verde.** (Cape Verdean cookery.)
Maria de Lourdes Chantre, preface by António Aurélio Gonçalves. Lisbon: Presença, 1989. 2nd ed. 201p.

Every aspect of the Cape Verdean cuisine seems to have been included in this well-presented volume of recipes. Not only the classic fish dishes and *cachupa* – a heavy mixture of cornmeal, beans and, when available, pork – but all kinds of sweet and fruit dishes. Alcoholic refreshments are not omitted. *Grogues* (sugar-cane rums) and *ponches* (cocktails of rum, honey and lemon) have a chapter to themselves. Anyone detecting a similarity to the English words 'grog' and 'punch' would be quite right: these are some of the linguistic legacies of English-speaking sailors. Most chapters are headed by an apposite quotation from Cape Verdean literature, and a glossary of local culinary terms is provided, as is a list of the foods traditionally prepared for feast days. These touches are a reminder of the centrality of food to Cape Verde's cultural identity. For an account of the place of Cape Verdean cooking in an emigrant household in America, see *A Portuguese colonial in America. Belmira Nunes Lopes. The autobiography of a Cape Verdean-American*, p. 40-5.

445 **Cozinha e doçaria do Ultramar Português.** (Cookery and sweets in the Portuguese overseas territories.)
Edited by MAM. Lisbon: Agência-Geral do Ultramar, 1969. 84p. bibliog.

A book of recipes, each chapter devoted to a different colony. The thirteen recipes from Cape Verde can be found on pages 13-20, with footnotes explaining such things as nomenclature and regional variations. The advantage of this volume is that comparisons can be made with the other cuisines of West Africa.

Libraries, Archives
and Research

446 African studies.
Edited by Ilse Sternberg, Patricia M. Larby. London: British Library, 1986. 332p. (British Library Occasional Papers, no. 6).
This collection of papers presented at a colloquium at the British Library in 1985 is an interesting guide to African studies resources in Great Britain. See the paper by Gervaise Clarence-Smith, 'International library and archival cooperation: Portugal and Spain' (p. 179-82) for a description (with addresses) of the available archival and library material in Portugal.

447 Da Commissão de Cartographia (1883) ao Instituto de Investigação Científica Tropical (1983) 100 anos de história. (From the Commission for Cartography [1883] to the Institute for Tropical Scientific Investigation [1983] one hundred years of history.)
Lisbon: Instituto de Investigação Científica Tropical, 1983. 480p. 15 maps. bibliog.
A history of Portuguese research into their former overseas possessions, which, in its various manifestations, produced – and produces – many valuable social and scientific studies on Cape Verde. Perhaps the best known of these institutions was the Junta de Investigações do Ultramar (Board of Overseas Research).

448 Defesa do património sócio-cultural de Cabo Verde. (Defence of the socio-cultural heritage of Cape Verde.)
João Lopes Filho. Lisbon: Ulmeiro, 1985. 170p. (Biblioteca Ulmeiro, no. 18).
Lopes makes a convincing case for the preservation of the cultural heritage of newly independent countries in order that their cultural identity can be firmly established. He outlines a putative programme for this to take place in Cape Verde, taking into account the importance of the oral tradition and praising the work of the Direcção-Geral da Cultura in this field. He sees the need for Cape Verdean institutions responsible for anthropology and for museums and is critical of the under-exploitation

of the library and archive resources which are held in Lisbon. 'Culture' should be part of every citizen's life: Lopes proposes the mobilization of the population by educational programmes and the establishment of local cultural centres.

449 **A guide to resources in the United States libraries and archives for the study of Cape Verde, Guinea (Bissau), São Tomé-Príncipe, Angola and Mozambique.**
David S. Zubatsky. Durham, New Hampshire: International Conference Group on Modern Portugal, 1977. 29p. (Essays in Portuguese Studies, no. 1).

As well as giving a guide to the great collections of material relating to Africa which are maintained in the USA, Zubatsky indicates resources which are of particular potential for Cape Verdean research in the fields of whaling, the slave trade and Protestant missionary organizations.

450 **Materials for West African history in Portuguese archives.**
A.F.C. Ryder. London: Athlone Press, University of London, 1965. 92p.

The introduction gives a history of the archival material, much of which was lost in the 1755 Lisbon earthquake. The main body of the work gives details of the manuscript catalogues and indexes, and Ryder lists a number of individual works which refer to West Africa. Despite its age, this is a helpful guide to the Archivo Nacional da Torre do Tombo; Archivo Histórico Ultramarino; Archivo e Biblioteca do Ministério dos Negócios Estrangeiros; Biblioteca Nacional de Lisboa; Biblioteca da Ajuda; Biblioteca da Academia das Ciências de Lisboa; Biblioteca da Sociedade de Geografia de Lisboa (all in Lisbon): the Biblioteca da Universidade de Coimbra: Biblioteca Pública e Archivo Distrital de Évora: Biblioteca Pública Municipal do Porto. Sadly, Ryder's comments on the quantity of material not inventoried remain valid today.

451 **A note on the archives of the Republic of Cabo Verde.**
Christopher Fyfe. *History in Africa: A Journal of Method*, vol. 7 (1980), p. 347-8.

A brief but very informative note on the archives of Praia, Mindelo, São Nicolau and Boa Vista. The archives in Praia contain the official records of Portuguese rule up to 1975, although there may be nothing before the early 18th century. They were ransacked by celebrating crowds at independence and remain disorganized, unlabelled and sometimes damaged. Mindelo has records from Customs and also from an English firm called Miller and Corry. São Nicolau has municipal archives and church documents. Boa Vista has administrative, Treasury and Customs records.

452 **Notes on research facilities in Lisbon and the Cape Verde Islands.**
G.E. Brooks. *International Journal of African Historical Studies*, vol. 6, no. 2 (1973), p. 304-14.

Rather dated, but still of interest to researchers preparing to consult the Lisbon archives. There is also a brief description of the limited facilities of the Centro de Estudos do Cape Verde (the Study Centre of Cape Verde) in Praia, the Biblioteca da Cidade de Praia (Praia City Library) and the Mindelo public library. Brooks also notes his contacts with, among others, the Cape Verde scholars Avelino Teixeira da Mota, António Carriera and Deirdre Meintel.

Monografia-catálogo da exposição de Cabo Verde.
See item no. 15.

Periodicals and the Media

General

453   África. (Africa.)
Lisbon: Vozes da Tribo, Edições e Publicações, [1986]- . weekly.
Under the direction of Leston Bandeira, this newspaper publishes international news
focused on Portuguese-speaking Africa. It regularly contains news items and features
on Cape Verde.

454   Independência. (Independence.)
Ovídio Martins.   Praia: Instituto Caboverdiano do Livro, 1983. 116p.
A collection of news chronicles from July 1973 to October 1977, some of which were
broadcast on Radio Voz di Povo (the PAIGC radio station) before independence.
Unfortunately sources are not made clear, otherwise this would be a valuable
document of the press and broadcasting during a period of great change.

455   A informação na Guiné, em Cabo Verde e em São Tomé e Príncipe.
(Information in Guinea, Cape Verde and São Tomé and Príncipe.)
José Júlio Gonçalves.   In: *Cabo Verde, Guiné, São Tomé e Príncipe:
curso de extensão universitária, ano lectivo de 1965-1966.*   Lisbon:
Instituto Superior de Ciências Sociais e Política Ultramarina,
Universidade Técnica de Lisboa, 1966, p. 165-376.
An entertaining and informative study which is lavishly illustrated with facsimile
material. The section on Cape Verde can be found on pages 286-342. He gives a
history of publishing in Cape Verde, since the arrival of the first press for the *Boletim
Official* (Official Bulletin) in 1842. This is a particularly useful source for information
on 19th-century periodical publications, as well as for those of the 20th century. He
notes the publishing activities of the Church of the Nazarene, and gives brief reports
on cinema, radio, post and telecommunications. Library facilities are described. For
further information on 19th-century publications, see *Subsidios para a historia do
jornalismo nas provincias ultramarinos portuguezas* (Elements for a history of
journalism in the Portuguese overseas provinces) by P.W. de Brito Aranha (Lisbon:

Imprensa Nacional, 1885. 27p.). This lists newspapers published in the colonies and those published in Portugal which are relevant to the colonies. Six newspapers are listed as being published in Cape Verde.

456 **Periodicals from Africa: a bibliography and union list of periodicals published in Africa.**
Compiled by Carole Travis, Miriam Alman, edited by Carole Travis. Boston, Massachusetts: G.K. Hall, 1977. 619p.
Arranged geographically, with Cape Verde appearing on page 44. Twenty-two periodicals are listed, now somewhat dated.

457 **Revista Internacional de Estudos Africanos.** (International Journal of African Studies.)
Lisbon: Instituto de Investigação Científica Tropical, 1984- .
semi-annual.
Specializing in material on Portuguese-speaking Africa, this is a highly regarded academic journal of the social sciences. It is edited by Jill R. Dias of the Universidade Nova de Lisboa.

Liberation movements in Lusophone Africa: serials from the collection of Immanuel Wallerstein.
See item no. 154.

África: Literatura, Arte e Cultura.
See item no. 347.

Cape Verdean periodicals

458 **Almanach Luso-Africano.** (Luso-African almanac.)
Lisbon: Livraria de António Maria Pereria. 1894-99. irreg.
Edited and founded by Canon António Manuel da Costa Teixeira, a Cape Verdean teacher at the São Nicolau seminary, its stated aims were to disseminate practical information, to stimulate good taste in literature and to increase awareness of the riches of the Portuguese colonies. Three issues were published – in 1894, 1895 and 1899. The first part of the 1894 edition is full of information on such things as bureaucracy, taxes, postal services, ferry-boat fares, fees and licences, tides, religious festivals, and weights and measures: it is the sort of reference work which every Cape Verdean home should have had. The second part is devoted mainly to literature. The great Crioulo poet Eugénio Tavares was one of many contributors. Interspersed are descriptions of plants, children's games, a rescue at sea, court cases and the battle against locusts on Boa Vista. For some interesting comments see José Carlos Seabra Pereira's "'Lembro São Nicolau. . .'" – ou o limitado alcance do primeiro almanque africano de expressão portuguesa' ('I remember São Nicolau. . .' – or the limited range of the first Portuguese-language African almanac) in *Les littératures africaines de langue portuguese: à la recherche de l'identité individuelle et nationale* (q.v.), p. 283-9.

459 **Arquipélago.** (Archipelago.)
Dorchester, Massachusetts: *Arquipélago*, 1986- . quarterly.
Under the direction of Virgínio Melo, this is a journal of culture and informatio
principally directed towards the Cape Verdean emigrant community in the USA.

460 **Boletim Oficial de Cabo Verde.** (Official Bulletin of Cape Verde.)
Praia: Imprensa Nacional, 1955- . weekly.
This is a government publication recording official business, legislation, officia
appointments and so forth. After independence it was continued as *Boletim Oficial d
República de Cabo Verde* (Official Bulletin of the Republic of Cape Verde).

461 **Cabo Verde: Boletim de Propaganda e Informação.** (Cape Verde:
Bulletin of Propaganda and Information.)
Praia: Imprensa Nacional, 1949-64. monthly.
A rich source of short items on Cape Verdean society, culture, geography an
infrastructure. Agriculture probably forms its principal subject matter. Josep
McCarthy has indexed these items in his bibliography, *Guinea-Bissau and Cape Verd
Islands* (q.v.).

462 **Magma.** (Magma.)
[São Filipe, Cape Verde]: Secretariado Administrativo do Fogo, 1988-
irreg.
An immaculately presented review of literary, cultural, historical and contemporar
issues relating to Fogo. Each issue is beautifully illustrated by the work of local artists
The director is Arnaldo Silva.

463 **Notícias.** (News.)
Mindelo, Cape Verde: Editorial Notícias, 1988- . monthly.
Strongly reflecting its Mindelo base, this is an independent paper covering culture an
current affairs. Its director is Madalena Almeida.

464 **Raízes.** (Roots.)
Praia: Edições Raízes, 1977- . irreg.
Edited by Arnaldo França and with a policy of publishing mainly work by Cap
Verdeans, this is an authoritative journal of Cape Verdean history and culture. Eac
issue follows a similar tripartite format of essays, poetry and fiction, and documents. I
is reviewed by Gerald Moser in *Research in African Literatures* (vol. 13, no. 3 [Autum
1982], p. 440-3), where he points out the continuing spirit of *Claridade* (q.v.) in th
publication. Indeed, many of the contributors are the same.

465 **Tribuna.** (Tribune.)
Praia: PAICV, 1983- . fortnightly.
A publicly sold party newspaper, which while principally reporting on events relatin
to PAICV activities also covers international news and culture. It is not alway
uncritical of the government. Carlos Lopes Pereira is its director.

466 **Voz di Povo.** (Voice of the People.)
Praia: Direcção Nacional de Informação, 1975- . three issues a week.
An official national newspaper, which until 1989 was produced twice weekly. It is sold in all of the islands, and carries local and international news. Carvalho Santos is its director.

Mujer.
See item no. 216.

Unidade e Luta.
See item no. 245.

Colectânea de Jurisprudência.
See item no. 255.

Revista do Ministério da Justiça.
See item no. 262.

Notícias TACV.
See item no. 304.

Anuário Estatístico: Colónia de Cabo Verde.
See item no. 336.

Boletim Trimestral de Estátistica.
See item no. 337.

A Educação em Cabo Verde.
See item no. 343.

Claridade: Revista de Arte e Letras.
See item no. 350.

General Reference Sources

467 **Africa Contemporary Record.**
Edited by Colin Legum. New York; London: Africana Publishing Company. 1968-1969- . annual.
A reliable review of contemporary happenings in the continent of Africa. In three sections, the first of which contains essays on relevant topics; the second reports of individual countries; and the third documents and statistics on economic, social, regional, constitutional and international relations issues. The individual country reports summarize political events and the current economic and social situation. Cape Verde first appears in this section in vol. 4 (1971-72) as part of the entry on Guinea-Bissau. From vol. 7 (1974-75) onwards Cape Verde has its own entry.

468 **Africa South of the Sahara.**
London: Europa Publications, 1971- . annual.
A directory in three parts, the first of which is background essays, usually on historical themes; the second covers regional organizations; and the third is a country-by-country survey which includes Cape Verde. The latter contains brief notes on physical and human geography, recent history, economy, statistics, bibliography and a directory of practical information on ministries and businesses.

469 **Senegal, the Gambia, Guinea-Bissau, Cape Verde Country Report.**
London: Economist Intelligence Unit, 1986- . quarterly.
Summaries and reviews of news and economic trends are presented in a clear and accessible style. Recommended as a convenient way of keeping up to date on events.

Bibliographies

470 **Bibliografia caboverdeana: subsídios para uma ordenação sistemática.**
(Cape Verdean bibliograpy: contributions towards a systematic
ordering.)
Jaime de Figueiredo. *Cabo Verde: Boletim de Propaganda e
Informação*, vol. 5, no. 49 (Oct. 1953), p. 31-2; vol. 5, no. 50
(Nov. 1953), p. 31-2; vol. 5, no. 54 (March 1954), p. 31-2; vol. 5, no. 56
(May 1954), p. 37-40.
Figueiredo makes no claims that this study is an exhaustive work, but it still retains
value in certain specific areas. His first subject area is anthropology and ethnography
(in vol. 49): without doubt the bibliography to Manuel Ferrreira's *A aventura crioula*
(q.v.), supersedes this. Geology and general scientific research (vol. 50) contains only
one work later than 1932. Health and hygiene (vol. 54) is represented mainly by
reports, dating from 1845 to 1884 (several in English). These cover the outbreaks of
cholera, typhus and yellow fever. Agriculture and flora (vol. 56) are well represented,
with works from 1641 to 1920 covering the various waves of Portuguese, French,
British and German scientific interest. Cape Verde's role as a provisioning station for
ships meant that many of the great voyages of Western scientific discovery stopped off
here and carried out a little research at the same time.

471 **Bibliografia das publicações sobre a África de língua oficial portuguesa.**
(Bibliography of publications on Portuguese-speaking Africa.)
Jill R. Dias. *Revista Internacional de Estudos Africanos*, no. 2
(June-Dec. 1984), p. 201-27; no. 3 (Jan.-Dec. 1985), p. 241-61; nos 4-5
(Jan.-Dec. 1986), p. 355-74; nos 6-7 (Jan.-Dec. 1987), p. 307-31;
nos 8-9 (Jan.-Dec. 1988), p. 339-49.
A regular and extremely useful feature of this journal, the bibliographies are arranged
by country, with a section for general works. Until 1986 Guinea-Bissau and Cape
Verde are listed together. As well as monograph works, the bibliographies carry a
large number of journal articles from diverse publications. Their precursor is Dias'
Bibliografia das publicações sobre a África de língua oficial portuguesa entre Janeiro de

161

Bibliographies

1975 e Janeiro de 1983 (Bibliography of publications on Portuguese-speaking Africa between January 1975 and January 1983) (*Revista Internacional de Estudos Africanos*, no. 1 [Jan.-June. 1984], p. 243-303). This lists a total of 167 items for Guinea-Bissau and Cape Verde (p. 252-62).

472 **Bibliographies for African studies 1970-1986.**
Yvette Scheven.   London; Munich; New York; Paris: Hans Zell;
K.G. Saur, 1988. 615p.
An extremely useful bibliography of bibliographies, containing material up to August 1987. Items are arranged by subject and by country and there is a very helpful index. Cape Verde material is to be found on page 401: Portuguese-speaking countries are on pages 366-8: the Sahel is on pages 369-74.

473 **A bibliography of African ecology: a geographically and topically classified list of books and articles.**
Dilwyn J. Rogers.   Westport, Connecticut; London: Greenwood Press, 1979. 499p. 2 maps. (African Bibliographic Center Special Bibliographic Series. New Series, no. 6).
Without an index this volume is disappointingly inaccessible, but within the chapter on Western Africa it is possible to find works dealing with issues which affect the Sahel as a whole.

474 **Bibliography of documents and reports on the Sahelian countries (1977-1985).**
Club du Sahel, Sahel Antenna of the Development Centre.   Paris: OECD, 1989. 198p.
An inventory of 379 documents on the countries of the Sahel, assembled between 1977 and 1985. Mostly unpublished, they can be consulted at the Sahel Antenna of the OECD (Organization for Economic Cooperation and Development) Development Centre. Arranged within subject chapters, items are indexed by author, geographical location and by subject. As well as general works on the region, there are eight works specific to Cape Verde. These appear to be lengthy reports on such things as cooperation, agriculture, radio communications and health.

475 **Documentatieblad: The Abstracts Journal of the African Studies Centre, Leiden.**
Leiden, The Netherlands: Afrika-Studiecentrum, 1968- . quarterly.
Detailed abstracts in French, German or English of current works are arranged geographically, with author, geographical and subject indexes provided. This is a useful back-up resource.

476 **Documenting Portuguese Africa.**
Ronald H. Chilcote. *Africana Newsletter*, vol. 3 (Summer 1963),
p. 16-36.
Covers serial publications from Portugal and Portuguese Africa; archives, libraries and
institutes; a bibliographpy of general works on Portuguese Africa published since 1945;
and political groups in Portuguese Africa.

477 **Guinea-Bissau and Cape Verde Islands.**
Joseph M. McCarthy. New York; London: Garland, 1977. 196p.
(Garland Reference Library of Social Science, no. 27).
With a total of 2,547 entries and aiming to be comprehensive this is a very useful
starting-point for any research. Material is arranged alphabetically by author within
twenty different subject chapters. It is indexed by author. In the face of so much useful
bibliographical information it seems churlish to criticize, but the absence of any
distinction between material from Cape Verde and material from Guinea-Bissau can
be a little inconvenient.

478 **International African Bibliography.**
London: Mansell, 1971- . quarterly.
Edited by David Hall of the School of Oriental and African Studies (SOAS) Library,
University of London, it lists by geographical region current books, articles and papers
in African studies. Cape Verde has a separate section within the West African region.
A less sophisticated source for current material is *Current Contents Africa* (Munich:
K.G. Saur, 1976- . quarterly). Facsimiles of the Contents pages of current journals, but
without an index, make this only a small improvement over browsing through the
current periodicals section of an academic library.

479 **Portuguese Africa: a guide to official publications.**
Mary Jane Gibson. Washington DC: Library of Congress, General
Reference and Bibliography Division, 1967. 217p.
A useful guide to Library of Congress holdings for material published between 1850
and 1964. Items on Cape Verde appear on pages 39-43, and works published in
Portugal on pages 103-92. Items are indexed by author and subject. The Africa Section
of the Library of Congress, General Reference and Bibliography Division has also
produced *Sub-Saharan Africa: a guide to serials* (1970. 409p.) which, although
containing very little specific to Cape Verde, lists several serials relevant to Portuguese
Africa as a whole.

480 **Portuguese Africa: materials in English and translation.**
Robert D'A. Henderson. *African Research & Documentation*, no. 11
(1976), p. 20-4; no. 12 (1977), p. 15-19.
Although not attempting to be a comprehensive collection, this is a useful source for
information on the Portuguese involvement in Africa in the 20th century, particularly
for researchers using libraries in Great Britain.

481 **Portuguese-speaking Africa 1900-1979. A select bibliography.**
Volume 3: Portuguese Guinea/Guinea Bissau, Cape Verde, São Tomé e
Príncipe, Portuguese-speaking Africa as a whole.
Susan Jean Gowan. Braamfontein, South Africa: South African
Institute of International Affairs, 1983. 350p. 9 maps. (South African
Institute of International Affairs Bibliographical Series, no. 11).
A selective bibliography, with an emphasis on political and economic aspects. Material
on the three countries appears together, divided into pre- and post-independence, and
then further classed into four sections - a general section (including bibliographies);
politics and government (including liberation movements); foreign relations; and
economics and development. There are separate author and subject indexes. The
volume's main value is in the amount of material extracted from journals: over
400 journals have been consulted. Elna Schoeman's *Portuguese-speaking Africa 1900-*
1979. A select bibliography. Volume 4. United Nations documentation on Portuguese-
speaking Africa (44p.), also published by the South African Institute of International
Affairs, is bound together with *Volume 3*. It is intended as a guide to UN
documentation on the process of decolonization and attainment of independence. Nine
documents refer specifically to Cape Verde.

482 **Portuguese Studies Newsletter.**
Durham, New Hampshire: International Conference Group on Modern
Portugal, 1976- . semi-annual.
Each issue contains a small section of current bibliographical information on
Portuguese-speaking Africa. For a similar service see also *Portuguese Studies* (edited
by the Department of Portuguese and Brazilian Studies, King's College, London, and
published by Humanities Research Association, 1985- . annual).

483 **Preliminary checklist of 19th century Hispano-Lusaphone Africana.**
Compiled by the Hispanic Section, British Library. [London]: [British
Library], [n.d.]. [n.p.].
A photocopied list of the British Library's holdings, excluding imaginative literature
and literary criticism. Entries are arranged by country, and further divided by subject
for the larger countries. There are fifty-four general works, and six works specifically
on Cape Verde.

484 **The United States and sub-Saharan Africa: guide to US official**
documents and government-sponsored publications, 1976-1980.
Julian W. Witherell. Washington DC: Library of Congress, 1984.
721p.
Arranged geographically, entries on Cape Verde appear on pages 428-32 (entry nos
3518-51). The items listed include material on treaties between the USA and Cape
Verde, translations from Portuguese-language newspaper articles and microfiched
technical reports on agriculture and water resources. See also by the same author *The*
United States and Africa: guide to US official documents and government sponsored
publications on Africa, 1785-1975 (Washington DC: Library of Congress, 1978. 949p.)
for a small number of earlier items on Cape Verde.

Bibliografia geológica do ultramar português.
See item no. 46.

Géologie Africaine / African Geology.
See item no. 49.

Emerging nationalism in Portuguese Africa: a bibliography of documentary ephemera through 1965.
See item no. 153.

Amílcar Cabral: a bio-bibliography of his life and thought, 1925-1973.
See item no. 159.

Bibliografia Sobre a Economia Portuguesa.
See item no. 283.

Bibliografia das literaturas africanas de expressão portuguesa.
See item no. 349.

Elementos para uma bibliografia da literatura e cultura portuguesa ultramarina contemporânea: poesia, fição, memoralismo, ensaio.
See item no. 354.

Periodicals from Africa: a bibliography and union list of periodicals published in Africa.
See item no. 456.

Index

The index is a single alphabetical sequence of authors (personal and corporate), titles of publications and subjects. Index entries refer both to the main items and to other works mentioned in the note to each item. Title entries are in italics. Numbers refer to bibliographic entries.

A

Abdala Junior, B. 360
Abreu, A. Trigo 294, 311
Achebe, Chinua 371
Across the Atlantic 371
Adam, W. 83
Adolescence 221
  see also Youth
Advisory Committee on
  the Sahel 317
Afforestation 135, 314
  acacia trees 317
  role of army 247
  role of women 214
Africa
  bibliographies 49, 446,
    472-3, 478, 484
  directories 467-8
  ecology 473
  fishing 325
  geology 49
  liberation movements
    150
  libraries and archives
    446
  periodicals 456
  statistics 335, 339-40
  see also individual
    countries by name;
    individual
    organizations by
    name;
    Portuguese-speaking
    Africa; West Africa
Africa 453
*Africa Contemporary
  Record* 467
Africa Information Service
  163
*Africa: Literatura, Arte e
  Cultura* 347

Africa South of the Sahara
  468
African Development
  Bank 339
*African islands and
  enclaves* 294
African liberation reader
  150
*African socio-economic
  indicators 1986* 335
African studies 446
Afrika-Stuediecentrum 475
L'Afrique étranglée 296
*Afro-Asian dimension of
  Brazilian foreign
  policy, 1956-1972* 267
*Agreement on the accession
  of the Republic of
  Cape Verde to the
  Convention of Lomé*
  275
*A agricultura do
  arquipélago de Cabo
  Verde. Cartas
  agrícolas. Problemas
  agrários* 308
Agriculture 4, 12, 71, 278,
  281, 294, 308-24
  agricultural implements
    15
  agricultural reform 230,
    314, 316
  bibliographies 470, 474,
    484
  Fogo 11, 310
  legislation 314, 316
  periodicals 461
  Santiago 310-12
  Santo Antão 310
  São Nicolau 315
  see also Bananas;
    Coconuts; Coffee

cultivation;
  Cooperatives;
  Livestock; Maize;
  Soils
*Agroforestry in the West
  African Sahel* 317
Aid 9, 266, 268-9, 275-80,
  293-4, 296
  non-governmental aid
    225
  see also European
    Economic
    Community; Food aid;
    individual countries by
    name; Instituto
    Caboverdeano de
    Solidariedade;
    Instituto Nacional das
    Cooperativas; Lomé
    convention;
Aid in Africa 276
*Airports international
  directory* 304
Air transport 9, 90-1, 304,
  307
  see also Airports;
    Transatlantic crossing
Airports 9, 90
  Praia 394
  Sal 230, 266, 278, 304
Albuquerque, L. de 128,
  227
Alcântara, Osvaldo *see*
  Lopes, Baltasar
Alcohol *see* Rum
Alegre, M. 162
Alexander, Boyd 77
Alfama, J. Miranda 373
Algas e corais 393
Algeria 271
*Alma negra: depoimento
  sobre a questão dos*

167

168

export of horses to 123
Saharan dust 27
Barbosa, C. A. Lopes 413
Barbosa, E. 411
Barbosa, Jorge 94, 360-1,
365, 367, 371, 373,
375, 397, 400
Barbosa, Jorge Pedro 373
Barbosa, Káká see
Barbosa, C. A. Lopes
Barbosa, L. A. Grandvaux
18, 75, 77, 308
Barbosa, T. 305
Barcellos, C. J. de Senna
89, 137
Barriga, F. J. A. S. 62
Barros, A. de 344
Barros, L. Aires 56
Batuque 100, 420, 422,
437-9
Beaumont, J. de 79
Bebiano, J. Bacellar 8, 48,
285
Beeching, J. 136
Beiträge zur Flora der Cap
Verdischen Inseln 69
Bê Léza see Cruz, F. X. da
Bender, G. 173
Benincasa see History
Benot, Y. 162
Bernoulli, D. 66
Beyer, E. 79
Bibliografia das literaturas
africanas de expressão
portuguesa 349, 395
Bibliografia geológica do
ultramar português 46
Bibliografia Sobre a
Economia Portuguesa
283
Bibliographies 15, 19, 21,
46, 77, 79, 85, 90, 114,
129, 153, 159, 161,
279, 342, 349, 354,
414, 470-84
of bibliographies 472, 481
Bibliographies for African
studies 1970-1986 472
Bibliography of African
ecology: a
geographically and
topically classified list
of books and articles
473

Bibliography of documents
and reports on the
Sahelian countries
(1977-1985) 474
Big fish from salt water 82
Birds 76-7
bibliographies 77
economic potential 100
in popular culture 415
see also Flamingoes
Birth practices 121, 218,
418
Black and white make
brown 94
Black men of the sea 301
Blake, J. W. 140
Blockfreie Aussenpolitik
eines afrikanischen
Kleinstaates: das
Beispiel Kap Verde
266, 290
Boa Vista
general works 10
see also Crioulo;
Geology; History;
Morna; Shipping
guides; Soils; Yellow
fever
Boardman, R. 275
Boléo, J. de Oliveira 148
Boletim Official 455
Boletim Oficial da
República de Cabo
Verde 460
Boletim Oficial de Cabo
Verde 460
Boletim Trimestral de
Estatística 337
Boletim Trimestral do
Comércio Externo 337
Bolle, C. 77
Bond [Captain] see History
Bourderie, J. 7
Bourguet, L. 315
Bourne, W. R. P. 77
Boxer, C. R. 107
Bragança, A. de 150, 158
Um brasileiro em terras
portuguesas 211
Brásio, A. 201
Bratt, A. 304
Brava see Emigration;
Geology; Morna;
Nazarene Church;

Pereira, Aristides;
Society
Brava acolhe Presidente
Aristides Pereira 229
Brazil
comparison of society
210-12
cultural similarities 418,
422, 424
emigration to 174, 271
influence on literature
350, 365, 377
international exhibition
14
linguistic similarities 362,
422
music 417, 434
Pombaline monopoly
companies 117
relations with Cape
Verde 267, 271
slavery 114
Brazil and Africa 267
Bridges, H. 96
Britain
abolition of slave trade
143, 145
business and trade 13,
88, 98, 105, 123
libraries and archives
109, 480
scientific research 470
voyages of Francis
Drake 136
British Library 446, 483
British Museum 109
British Museum of Natural
History 52
Brito, A. de Paul 189
Brito, E. 169
Brito, J. 297
Brito, R. Soeiro de 4
Brooks, G. E. 141, 452
Brookshaw, D. 360
Browne, J. 101
Bulletin d'Informations 154
Burnay, L. Pisani 85
Burness, D. 353, 357, 360,
366, 371
Burri, C. 51
Business
private enterprise 249
Butterflies 77

169

Músicas de Cabo Verde: mornas de Eugénio Tavares 432

N

Na asa do vento: o livro 17
Ña Bibiña Kabral. Bida y óbra 439
Na bóka noti 441
Names *see* Personal names; Toponymy
Namorado, J. 392
Nascimento, L. Garcia do 360
Natal y kontus 410
National Development Fund *see* Fundo de Desenvolvimento Nacional
Nationality law 259
Naurois, René de 77
Les navigations médiévales sur les côtes sahariennes antérieures à la découverte portugaise (1434) 111
Nazarene Church
Brava 204
publications 455
Negreiros, A. de Almada 260
Negritude as a theme in the poetry of the Portuguese-speaking world 362
Negrume (Izimparín) 411
Netherlands
aid relationship 325, 331
emigration to 175
Neto, João B. Nunes Pereira 4
Neto, José Pereira 4
Neto, T. S. 327
Neve, M. 101
Neves, J. Alves das 360
New general collection of voyages and travels. Volume I 93, 98
New history of Portugal 103
New Testament 205

New voyage round the world 99
Newitt, M. 105
Newspapers 17, 466
Mindelo 463
PAICV 465
Portuguese-speaking Africa 453, 455
Newton, A. 91
Nieuhoff, J. 98
Niger
musical instruments 417
Nigeria 271
No fist is big enough to hide the sky: the liberation of Guinea-Bissau and Cape Verde 155
No reino de Caliban. 1° volume: Cabo Verde e Guiné-Bissau 373-4
Nogueira, R. de Sá
Noite de vento 388
Noli, António de *see* History
Noronha, A. R. 318, 324
Notas sobre o tráfico português de escravos 144
Notas sobre poesia e ficção cabo-verdianas 363
Notícia corográfica e cronológica do Bispado de Cabo Verde 203
Notícia sobre algumas aguas mineraes da ilha de Santo Antão (arquipélago de Cabo Verde) 63
Notícias 463
Notícias TACV 304
Nunes, A. 367, 373, 403
Nunes, Maria L. 181, 191
Nunes, Mateus 32, 34, 315
Nyström, V. 79
Nzongola-Ntalaja 162

O

OECD *see* Organization for Economic Co-operation and

Development
Oju d'agu 412
Oliveira, A. N. Ramires d 227
Oliveira, C. Fernandes Plácido de 264
Oliveira, H. de 175
Oliveira, J. Osório de 350 375, 428
Oliveira e Silva, C. 321
Olivry, J. C. 28
Oppenheimer, J. 277
Oral literature 350
bibliography 349
Fogo 435
preservation 448
Santiago 437-9
Santo Antão 419
see also Batuque; Finason; Music and song-forms; Oral narratives; Riddles and proverbs
Oral narratives 414, 419, 440-1
in English translation 440
Orchil 100, 124, 134, 299
L'organisation judicaire dans les colonies portugaises 260
Organização da Mulher de Cabo Verde 214-16
Organization for Economi Co-operation and Development 279
Organization of African Unity 268
Origin of species 101
Orimalade, A. 289
Osório, O. 367, 372-3, 394 398, 413, 436

P

Pacheco, M. C. 391
PAICV *see* Partido Africano da Independência de Cabo Verde
PAICV First Congress 239
PAIGC *see* Partido Africano da

Map of Cape Verde

This map shows the more important towns and other features.

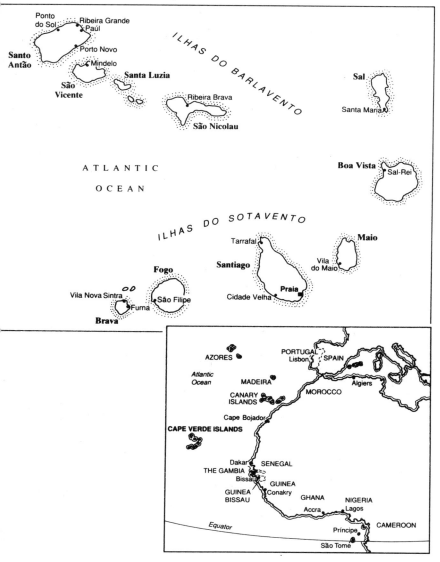